ADA LOUISE HUXTABLE

GARLAND BIBLIOGRAPHIES IN
ARCHITECTURE AND PLANNING
(General Editor: Arnold L. Markowitz)
Vol. 1

GARLAND REFERENCE LIBRARY
OF THE HUMANITIES
Vol. 242

For Yale & the Suino of architecture With warmest wishes—

ADA LOUISE HUXTABLE
An Annotated Bibliography

Ada Lousie Huxtable

Lawrence Wodehouse

July 2012

with a Foreword by
Ada Louise Huxtable

GARLAND PUBLISHING, INC. • NEW YORK & LONDON
1981

Library of Congress Cataloging in Publication Data

Wodehouse, Lawrence.
    Ada Louise Huxtable, an annotated bibliography.

    (Garland bibliographies in architecture and planning ;
v. 1) (Garland reference library of the humanities ;
v. 242)
    Includes indexes.
    1. Huxtable, Ada Louise—Bibliography.   I. Title.
II. Series.   III. Series: Garland reference library of
the humanities ; v. 242.
Z8430.53.W64   [NA2599.8.H87]   016.72′092′4   80-8510
ISBN 0-8240-9475-1   AACR2

Printed on acid-free, 250-year-life paper
Manufactured in the United States of America

PREFACE TO THE SERIES

It is most fitting that Lawrence Wodehouse's bibliography of Ada Louise Huxtable should be the first volume in *GARLAND BIBLIOGRAPHIES IN ARCHITECTURE AND PLANNING*. As a beginning to the series, Mrs. Huxtable's bibliography introduces every theme that will be the concern of future volumes. Annotated bibliographies and related research guides will focus on individual critics and historians, as well as individual practitioners of architecture, planning, and allied professions; on regional and local schools of architecture and planning, as well as periods of architecture and planning within broader geographic boundaries; on building types and building materials; on garden design, landscape, and land use; on the decorative arts and other arts ancillary to architecture; and on the preservation of the built and natural environment. It is my hope, as general editor of the series, that *GARLAND BIBLIOGRAPHIES IN ARCHITECTURE AND PLANNING* will provide a valuable scholarly resource for the study of those fields for which Mrs. Huxtable's writings, described in this present volume, provide brilliant critical perceptions and lucid insights.

Arnold L. Markowitz
Elmer Holmes Bobst Library
New York University

CONTENTS

FOREWORD

I have always thought of a bibliography as something devoted to the writings of a scholar, preferably deceased. It carries the connotation of an impressive list of profound works that serve to establish a reputation for posterity. This is not that kind of bibliography. First, I am still very much alive, and second, I make no claims to immortality. And the list of my writings is drawn largely from that most ephemeral of media, a newspaper.

If the New York Times is somewhat less ephemeral than most such journals, it is still not immune to the old definition of the daily newspaper as something in which to wrap yesterday's fish. What those pages contain, besides fish, can also be ephemeral—the causes and controversies that seemed enormously important and aroused intense passions at the time, which gave way to other causes and controversies of an equally transient nature. The unifying theme, or ultimate wrapup, for these articles is the concept of the built world as an act of design that I have tried to bring to the broadest possible audience, and the unchanging elements are those components of which that world is made, from art to politics. The issues may vary, but the concerns are constant—quality, responsibility and good sense.

If newspapers do not endure, the art of architecture does; civilization's most lasting monuments are those of its builders. My own small monument is this bibliography. I am extremely grateful to Professor Wodehouse for caring enough to carry out what was clearly an arduous and frustrating and often boring task. I am struck by the fact that this ephemeral work now covers almost a quarter of a century. And that there are more than 800 pieces from the Times, not counting editorials (more now, since the deadline process continues inexorably), a fact which will not impress the editors a bit. The journalistic definition of productivity is something like vitamins—one a day—spurred by the fact that all newspaper people live in mortal fear of the editorial nightmare of the empty page.

Looking back, I see that this is a chronicle of the esthetic and environmental wars fought in the urban jungle over places and policies, dealing in the quality of life and the most public of the arts. It is tempered—for relief and sanity, I suppose—by those things that give me the greatest personal pleasure—art and scholarship. I am not sure how I feel about the surprising amount of trivia in the listing, but for all the marginal and unimportant items, there are also those large projects that have a permanent impact. There are battles won and lost. The retroactive score might afford some satisfaction if one had time to pause for so-called victories, but there would be little point because this war for excellence, like all wars, is never won.

If the standards and commitments that have been responsible for the selection of all of these subjects are the same, what has changed significantly are public attitudes—far more aware and knowledgeable now—and my own attitudes, in which single-minded intensity has given way to more measured and informed consideration. Maturity involves everything from mastering the technical, legal and economic intricacies of building to seeing the full turn of the wheel in architectural style from modernism to antimodernism, with an accumulation of information and perspective that are the chief rewards of passing time. It involves living—the most valuable experience of all.

What this bibliography really means to me is a kind of affirmation of my existence. It gives my work a collective reality that it would not otherwise have had. Without it, there would be little to document these many years of architectural and urban criticism, which I am vain, or hopeful enough, to feel have been worth the considerable effort invested in meeting those deadlines. As a journalist and a historian, my ultimate respect is reserved for the record. To be on the record, and part of it, is the greatest satisfaction of all.

ADA LOUISE HUXTABLE

INTRODUCTION

Ada Louise Huxtable's fame rests upon her wide variety of achievements in the field of architectural criticism, her critiques of the associated arts, and work done in collaboration with her husband, Garth Huxtable, the industrial designer. Of all the honors bestowed upon her, however, there are two she considers of utmost importance. The first is that when *The New York Times*, in 1963, became the first newspaper in the United States to employ a full-time architecture critic, she was chosen for the position. The second is that seven years later, in 1970, when the Pulitzer Prize was first awarded for distinguished criticism, she was named the winner, for her architectural criticism, in competition with critics from all other fields.

It is her excellence in journalism and her "journalistic recognition of architecture as a public art and social responsibility" (item 939) which establishes her in the mainstream of American architectural criticism, in which the only other really outstanding name is that of Montgomery Schuyler, who lived at the turn of the century and whose criticism was related more directly to architecture than to the myriad of allied topics which also interest Mrs. Huxtable.

New York is where she was born, and where she grew up, loving all the great institutions of that city; where she was educated, has worked and married; and where she has resided all her life. Other awards have therefore been presented to her "for promoting the city's esthetic interests" (item 928) and for "her intention to provide a richer understanding of the texture and color of the city as it grows" (item 931). She is a "conservationist uninflicted with sentimentality . . . whose enthusiasm for the past is balanced by equal enthusiasm for the best of the present" (item 932), and it is toward this end that she sometimes "writes in a sort of controlled rage . . . against those who out of ignorance, timidity or greed lower the quality of the environment by profiteering . . . [or] . . . expediency" (item 996). She has made us all more conscious of our architectural heritage by her "'un-flagging watchfulness' over America's cultural treasures" (item 953), by "focusing the attention of an informed public on the environment" (item 945), and by "her consistently incisive and courageous defense of integrity in architectural design and urban planning" (item 941).

In May 1963 *The New York Times* appointed Mrs. Huxtable architecture critic and, just as the newspaper covers international events, so too do the articles of Mrs. Huxtable. But the newspaper, however cosmopolitan, emphasizes local events. Mrs. Huxtable likewise discusses design on a worldwide basis—architecture, city planning, preservation, restoration, renovation, and industrial and product design—but her concentration is upon Manhattan, and her attention is focused upon the borough's very life and existence. She is by no means the only writer concerned with the total environment of this particular rocky island, eighteen miles long and little more than a mile wide for most of its length. Sibyl Moholy-Nagy, concerned with the continuity of the city as an essential element of civilization, made her home in the Kips Bay section of Manhattan, and championed good design of the urban fabric in her *Matrix of Man*, 1968, which she dedicated to "Manhattan Island, my inspiration and my love." El exigente Moholy-Nagy, always ultracritical, was never a woman to squander her love. Likewise, Jane Jacobs, author of *The Death and Life of Great American Cities*, 1961, saw the old established neighborhoods of American cities as having "a sense of place," and fought for their preservation. She dedicated her book to "New York City, where I came to seek my fortune and found it . . ." and where she helped preserve Washington Square as an open green space not to be invaded by a highway. Greenwich Village was her home, and the quality of city life which exists there today, within the turmoil of the metropolitan area, is in no small part due to her advocacy.

It is the human domestic scale which has always appealed to these three women and which emerges in the hundreds of articles written by Mrs. Huxtable.

The tip of Manhattan is where urban development began, and pictorial views of the area below the Brooklyn Bridge at its

completion in 1886 illustrate a domestic-scaled, tightly knit collection of buildings, commercial, industrial, and residential,
dominated by the tower and spire of Richard Upjohn's Trinity
Church, 1846, on Broadway at the end of Wall Street; even Wall
Street, illustrated in photographs of the 1880s, had no building
taller than five stories along its length. Panoramic views of the
shore line show rows of tall masted ships with their prows over-
sailing the quays, as they are beginning to do again at the South
Street Seaport. This area of the seaport is the only part of Lower
Manhattan remaining intact, and its preservation has been as-
sured, but only after a lengthy fight dating back to 1966 when
the Landmarks Preservation Commission was asked to decide
between two areas, the other being the Fraunces Tavern block, because of the expense involved. The Rouse Company, which had
such a resounding success renovating the Faneuil Hall/Quincy
Market area of Boston, was willing in 1979 to spend $210 million
on the Seaport. The Fraunces Tavern block, including the 1907
tavern itself, was also to be preserved: "Because the block is a
historic unit, demolition of any part of it destroys the whole"
(item 621). Residential architecture south of the Brooklyn
Bridge was, until 1969, excluded from all developments of the
past hundred years; then a middle-income Mitchell-Lama housing project was designed almost adjacent to the Seaport area by
Gruzen and Partners. Situated between Gold, Frankfort, Water,
and Fulton Streets, Southbridge Towers is surrounded by a
perimeter of six-story walkup apartments which merge into the
scale of the area. The Tower blocks provide the high density
needed in such a project. This is an example of a scheme which
attempts to complement the existing scale, as opposed to the
twenty-two-story brick monolith at Number Four New York
Plaza, opposite the Fraunces Tavern block, built for Manufacturers Hanover Trust by Carson, Lundin and Shaw in 1968.
William Lescaze, who designed Number One New York Plaza,
contacted the architects of all adjacent sites being redeveloped in
the area with the hope of some type of coordination and cooper-
ation, possibly on the level of the Associated Architects of the
Rockefeller Center development of the 1930s. Carson, Lundin
and Shaw declined such a collaboration since they had "tried
honestly and sincerely to relate their building to that pseudo-

historic landmark site across Water Street, and to the Fraunces Tavern," according to a memorandum written by Lescaze on September 23, 1967. He felt that "you cannot today and you should not today try to imitate even a pleasant 'historic' thing nor can you adapt some of its characteristics" to a 1967 design, a philosophy which is close to that of Mrs. Huxtable, who wishes to preserve the past but also to build uncompromisingly modern structures for the present, especially if they both have the complementary common denominator of good design.

Lower Manhattan also contains some outstanding designs of the past hundred years. Cass Gilbert's United States Custom House (1907) at Bowling Green, a Beaux Arts building with its integrated sculptures of Asia, Africa, America, and Europe by Daniel Chester French, has a host of paintings around the oval-domed internal space of the monumental customs hall. The building illustrates the logic of Beaux Arts planning, a quality extolled in the exhibition "The Architecture of the Ecole des Beaux Arts," at New York's Museum of Modern Art, October 1975 to January 1976. Another grandiose space is in the Cunard Building (1921) at 25 Broadway, by Benjamin Wistar Morris, providing within a stone's throw two of a series of similar great spaces in New York City. (Others include Grand Central Station, the New York Public Library, and Scribner's bookshop at 597 Fifth Avenue). Cunard's vestibule measures 185×75 feet and has domes, pendentives, and vaults covered with frescoes.

Trinity Church, which once dominated Lower Manhattan, is now overpowered by twentieth-century skyscrapers, which in turn are towered over by the World Trade Center by Minoru Yamasaki; the twin towers were for a few months the tallest buildings in the world. Pedestrian plazas and walkways, some tree-lined, which weave east-west from the Center through spaces containing sculptures by Isamu Noguchi and Jean Dubuffet, are flanked by the Chase Manhattan Bank (1960) and 140 Broadway (1967), both by Skidmore, Owings and Merrill. Between these glass boxes and City Hall Park stands St. Paul's Chapel and churchyard (1766), by Thomas McBean, a pupil of James Gibbs, with its tower and steeple of 1796 in the style of St. Martin in the Fields. City Hall Park includes City Hall (1811), by Joseph Mangin and Henry McComb, and the New York City

Courthouse (1861–72), by John Kellum, now scheduled for demolition despite its cost of twelve million dollars, which helped to fill the pockets of Boss Tweed and his cohorts. The Park, the first tree-lined space along Broadway, contains numerous historic sculptures. Its perimeter includes Cass Gilbert's Woolworth Building (1913), and along the north side, on Chambers Street, Jonathan Snook's A.T. Stewart store (1845), the first department store anywhere. Terminating the eastern vista along Chambers Street is the Municipal Building (1914), by William Kendall of McKim, Mead & White. (This building had an influence on the wedding cake architecture of Moscow during the Stalinist era, after the suppression of modern architecture in Russia.) Outscaling the entire area between Worth and Duane Streets is the United States Federal Executive Office Building, two-thirds the size of the Pentagon, "the biggest checkerboard in the world" (item 217), by Eggers and Higgins with Kahn and Jacobs, begun in 1967. It is "the most monumentally mediocre Federal building in history" (item 284).

From Duane to Houston Streets, West Broadway to Broadway, is the Cast-Iron District, Hell's Hundred Acres as it was known because of its industrial accidents and numerous fires. It was originally a shopping center in the 1850s and 1860s, but today accommodates light industry, commercial warehousing, and manufacturing, although numerous lofts are being converted to studio and residential use (many illegally because of the risk of fire) with art galleries and such uses at ground level. When a group of Americans were admiring the refined cast-iron architecture of Glasgow under the guidance of Sir Nikolaus Pevsner, he commented upon the significance of the New York examples and, in so doing, stimulated interest in the district and instigated the formation of the Friends of Cast-Iron Architecture in New York City, led by Margot Gayle. "In downtown New York there is a veritable museum of cast-iron architecture, a greater concentration than anywhere else in the world," said Pevsner. Most noteworthy of this collection of Italianate facades along Broadway are: the Roosevelt Building (1874), at 478–82, by the dean of late nineteenth-century architects, Richard Morris Hunt; the Haughwout Building (1857), at 488–92, by J.P. Gaynor, which contained an early Otis hydraulic safe elevator and was built of iron produced by the (Daniel) Badger Iron Works; and the first Singer Building (1907), at 561, by Ernest Flagg, not to be confused with the architect's second, more famous, now demolished Singer skyscraper (1908), at 149.

Through this area of the Cast-Iron District it was at one time planned to build the Lower Manhattan Expressway to provide a quick route from Long Island to New Jersey. Mrs. Huxtable's articles explained that thousands of people would lose their homes, adjacent properties would be blighted, and historic structures would be lost (item 350). Congressman John V. Lindsay used the physical problems of urban design as an election issue in his 1965 bid for the mayoralty of New York City. As mayor he abandoned not only the Lower Manhattan Expressway but also the Cross Brooklyn Expressway; progressive planning does not take "white man's roads through black man's bedrooms" (item 375). Broadway turns for the first time at James Renwick, Jr.'s Gothic revival Grace Church, of 1846, across the street from which, on the northwest corner of East Eleventh Street, is the McCreery block. This fine cast-iron building was enlarged, and converted to residential use, in 1971: 144 apartments have unusually high ceilings and the cast-iron Corinthian columns appear randomly in the various internal arrangements. Greenwich Village is also the site of some outstanding renovations and conversions by Giorgio Cavaglieri. His conversion in 1967 of the Jefferson Market Courthouse into a branch of the New York Public Library has retained in the city one of the best extant examples in the United States of a structure in the Ruskinian Venetian Gothic style, by Vaux and Withers, of 1877. Cavaglieri was certainly aided by Mrs. Huxtable in his conversion of the Astor Library on Lafayette Street to the New York Shakespeare Festival Public Theater, 1967–76, with her article condemning the city for withdrawing public funds for its renovation on the grounds of poverty during the same year in which the city provided $200 million for Lincoln Center for the Performing Arts (item 461). The building could so easily have been lost, like so many other notable landmarks, due to flaws in the preservation law (item 199).

Broadway, which begins at Bowling Green and turns at Grace Church, acts as a "golden thread" and links all the major institutions of the city, whether federal or local government, shopping, hotels, commerce, industry, entertainment, museums, universities, colleges, residential developments, or open space. In some respects it is comparable to Regent Street in London. Classically inspired architecture lines the route of Regent Street, a picturesque streetscape, romantic in its planning for economic reasons, incorporating in its length existing developments. Broadway, New York, is unintentionally romantic in its planning in that it has evolved from the period of earliest European habitation, linking the settlements at the southern tip of Manhattan Island to those at its northern tip. As Manhattan expanded, Broadway was built and rebuilt along its length in whatever architectural style prevailed at a given period. Interesting vistas are created along its length, and in some cases major focal points of interest in the city are in close proximity.

At Fourteenth Street, for example, it traverses Union Square, from which one can see the Pan Am Building astride Park Avenue above Forty-second Street; the Pan Am can also be seen, side on, at Forty-third Street. Broadway also runs through Madison Square, and at Thirty-fourth Street, only a block from the Empire State Building, it is a focal shopping center where Macy's and Gimbels are situated, rival stores which cluster together, a mutual attraction for those on a spending spree. Little more than a block to the west is Madison Square Garden (no longer situated in Madison Square). Forty-second Street houses the "el cheepo" movies, the "porno shops," and the massage parlors, while only a block to the east is Bryant Park and the New York Public Library, a close friend of Mrs. Huxtable's (item 464).

Triangular or "flat iron" sites were created where Broadway traverses the grid of streets set up by the 1811 Commissioner's plan, and where the avenues join Broadway at an acute angle, notably at Twenty-second Street, where Daniel Burnham of Chicago designed the Fuller Building (1902). At Forty-third Street stood the old Times Tower, 1904, by (Leopold) Eidlitz and Mackenzie, "legitimately conceived for its day" but in the 1960s shockingly refaced beyond all recognition by Voorhees, Walker, Smith, Smith and Haines for the Allied Chemical Corporation (item 62).

North of this area is the theater district, synonymous worldwide with the name Broadway. Developers have continuously attempted to demolish the one-story legitimate and movie theaters, but city ordinances passed while Mayor John V. Lindsay was in office provide the realtor with additional height limits, and consequently more rentable office space, on condition that developers are willing to incorporate theaters at ground level.

Edward Durell Stone's Huntington Hartford Museum of 1965 (now the New York Cultural Center), the New York Coliseum, and the southwest tip of Central Park's 840 acres meet at Columbus Circle. Three blocks north is Lincoln Center for the Performing Arts, not a "dramatic contribution to the history of the art of building" (item 229). Max Abramovitz designed Philharmonic (now Avery Fisher) Hall (1962); Philip Johnson, the New York State Theater (1964), with its magnificent modern spaces, comparable to Beaux Arts interiors at the turn of the century; Eero Saarinen, the Vivian Beaumont Theater (1965), with a lake containing Henry Moore sculpture; Wallace K. Harrison, the Metropolitan Opera House (1966), "a sterile . . . throwback rather than creative twentieth century design" (item 228); and Pietro Belluschi, the Juilliard School of Music (1968), incorporating Alice Tully Hall, free from gold leaf, pretentiousness, and pomposity (item 389). Lincoln Center Towers, a gigantic 2000-unit residential development to the northwest, was the intended result of Lincoln Center, created as a focal point around which realtors would develop urban renewal projects by demolishing sound tenements in need of refurbishing but not of total demolition. The Towers are a soulless series of uninteresting slabs. For the next fifty blocks, housing, apartments, shops, hotels, and local amenities hold sway, many built in the rich Baroque revival styles of the Edwardian era. One example will suffice to illustrate the affluence of the period, and that, the Ansonia Hotel (1902), by E.D. Stokes, may not be there for long.

The next major grouping of buildings are collegiate, centered around Columbia University at 116th Street. Charles Follen McKim of McKim, Mead & White designed this campus dominated by its Pantheon-inspired Low Library (now an administration building), 1893–97. Columbia tried to expand with an Eggers and Higgins gymnasium to be located on two acres of

Morningside Park, with separate gym facilities for the Harlem community to the east of the park. Columbia was getting valuable parkland at a nominal sum and felt that in return it was giving neighborhood facilities to the community. But, without a necessary dialogue, the Columbia administration found the community and the students opposed to such an arrangement and was ultimately forced to build the gymnasium into the northwest corner of the campus. I.M. Pei became the campus planning consultant and made several worthwhile proposals for adding to the existing campus, including Alexander Kouzmanoff's 1977 underground expansion of the Avery Architectural Library, a home away from home for Mrs. Huxtable (item 748). Another addition to the northeast corner, on top of an existing podium, is Mitchell and Giurgola's Sherman Fairchild Center for the Life Sciences. Barnard College faces the Columbia campus across Broadway. Union Theological Seminary is located to the north of Barnard, across 120th Street, and Teachers College borders Columbia to the north. Completing this academic grouping on Morningside Heights is the Jewish Theological Seminary of America, to the north of Teachers College.

Further along Broadway are the Museum of the American Indian, the American Geographical Society, the Hispanic Society of America, the Numismatic Society, and the National Institute of Arts and Letters. Opposite the Columbia-Presbyterian Medical Center is the San Juan entertainment center and movie theater and at West 175th Street is Loew's Theater (1930), by Thomas Lamb, in all its Moorish splendor. At the Manhattan end of O.H. Ammann's George Washington Bridge, of 1931, with a clear suspension span of 3500 feet, is Pier Luigi Nervi's Port of New York Authority bus station (1963). It straddles Broadway and has direct access to the bridge, while the expressway passes below it (as well as below the four apartment slabs to the west, built in 1964).

Along Broadway's northern limit is Fort Tryon Park, in which is located The Cloisters, built 1934–38 with money given by John D. Rockefeller, Jr., incorporating capitals from the cloisters of St. Michel de Cuxa, France. This museum now houses the Medieval collection of the Metropolitan Museum of Art.

There is no grand climax to Broadway. Rather, it just dies out at the point where the subway, above ground again for several blocks, crosses the Harlem River bridge just north of 220th Street and proceeds through The Bronx, originally a part of Westchester County.

Regent Street in London is a continuous vista of delight. Broadway, a meandering cow path, is not a vista of delight by intent, but by pure chance, providing focal links throughout Manhattan. Today, more by chance than intent, Broadway has become the golden thread which unites all the qualities of New York, a city of diverse interests. Admittedly, Fifth and Madison Avenues on the Upper East Side cater to museums, art galleries, boutiques, and high-class shopping. But, then, Bond Street and Picadilly complement Regent Street in a similar adjacent manner. Regent Street incorporates shopping, professional offices and institutions, and clubs and hotels, with parks at either end.

Another priority in New York City is open space, most notably Central Park, designated a scenic landmark in 1965, and thereby protected from the well-wishers who want to clutter it up for the public good. Playgrounds, tennis courts, skating rinks, an open-air theater for summer performances, and a children's zoo began the encroachments: "pastoral sabotage, or parkicide" (item 254). If all suggestions for new entertainments to be located in Central Park were implemented, there would not be a single tree or blade of grass left. Mrs. Huxtable has always held that nothing should take place in the park which can be located outside of it, and outside of it is where theaters and like structures belong. "Public good . . . what crimes against the park have been committed in thy name!" (item 254). To a certain extent she justifies the extensive police facility in the park, because it was intended from the beginning. Calvert Vaux, who with Frederick Law Olmsted won the design competition for the park in 1857, designed the Twenty-second Precinct House for the New York Police Department in 1871. The Metropolitan Museum of Art does cover fourteen acres, and for the record Mrs. Huxtable wants it to be clearly understood "that the museum is superlatively and dangerously wrong" in its expansion program (item 451). Even in the new Lehman Wing "the Met has done the wrong thing impeccably" (item 654). What she wanted from the Parks Department was a little more attention to the park itself, "Just a Little Love, a Little Care" (item 595), notably after $21,000, plus labor, had been expended to refurbish the 9 × 15 feet ladies pavilion and $327,000 was projected for the repair of a bridge spanning ninety feet. Continuous and careful maintenance would obviate this type of expense.

Around the park, notably along Fifth Avenue, range the robber barons' residences, many of which are fast disappearing. Carrere and Hastings's Henry Clay Frick Residence, of 1914, at Seventieth Street has been retained for the Frick Collection, but the Dodge House at Sixty-first Street was replaced in 1978 by a tall apartment house by Ulrich Franzen. The block between Seventy-eighth and Seventy-ninth Streets containing Horace Trumbauer's Duke House, of 1912, now New York University's Institute of Fine Arts, the Whitney House, of 1906, by McKim, Mead & White, now housing the French Embassy's Cultural Services, and the Stuyvesant House, 1899, by C.P.H. Gilbert, now the Ukrainian Institute of America, provides a continuous row of residences typical of the original scale of buildings along the east side of the park. Just across Seventy-ninth Street, however, the Brokaw Mansion was demolished and then replaced by visual pollution which encroaches upon those who utilize the park for recreation. The unified urban quality of the avenue was thus lost, and the only people who benefited were those real estate brokers who profiteer by destructive urban developments (item 294).

Speculative highrise commercial developments have always eaten away portions of all avenues throughout Manhattan, notably Third Avenue, where sixteen block-busters were erected in ten years, 1956–66, between Thirty-ninth and Eightieth Streets. They invariably replaced five-story walkups which incorporated interesting commercial developments at their street level. The glass tower replacements, some five hundred feet tall, have dull entrance halls and banks, insurance companies, and similar offices at street level providing a non-streetscape for those who had previously promenaded the avenues. Rockefeller Center Management Corporation expanded along Sixth Avenue in the Fifties, with the same disastrous results. The fountains, pools, and uninteresting sculptures do nothing to relieve the monotony, and because these elements are repeated so often they become as wearisome and tedious to see as the taxicabs which line the same sidewalks. Compare the humdrum expanse of water with its cluster of water spouts outside the Exxon Building to the much more dynamic Isamu Noguchi cube outside the Marine Midland Bank, 140 Broadway, by Skidmore, Owings and Merrill or the Dubuffet trees at the Chase Manhattan Plaza nearby.

Now that profits have been realized along the avenues, greedy realtors are turning their attention to the sabotage of crosstown side streets, the soul of the city (item 331). The spoilers have already diverted their avaricious attentions to Sixty-second Street (item 798), and once a major precedent is set, it will lead to the destruction of the human scale of the side streets throughout Manhattan.

One major achievement in preservation, on Madison Avenue between Fiftieth and Fifty-first Streets, is the palazzo-like group known as the Villard Houses, designed 1882–85 by Stanford White and his capable assistant, Joseph Wells. In 1968 some of the occupants, including Random House, moved out and the Roman Catholic Archdiocese of New York, part owner, was in desperate need of money (item 328). Harry Helmsley acquired the prime Madison Avenue property and employed Emery Roth and Sons to design a new fifty-two-story hotel, the Palace. It was proposed to demolish all the interiors and retain only the outer shell of the Villard Houses. At that time preservation law could demand retention only of street facades, but Mrs. Huxtable wanted the magnificent interiors retained, and justifiably so, as a backdrop for such events as the society weddings which are so much a part of the hotelier business in major New York hotels. Ultimately Mr. Helmsley was persuaded, and Mrs. Huxtable suggested that "we raise a glass" to him (item 663). McKim, Mead & White's Villard Mansion has thus to a certain extent been saved, but their Penn Station, a great Caracallaean monument, was lost in the 1960s, although Warren and Wetmore's Grand Central Station has been preserved, including its superb internal concourse. The United States Supreme Court upheld its landmark designation against stiff opposition, including three projects by Marcel Breuer, 221 feet south of the Pan Am Building and 150 feet higher (items 785 and 314).

There are, of course, many notable modern structures in New York, especially those by Gordon Bunshaft of Skidmore, Owings and Merrill, including Lever House (1952), the first of the elegant glass skyscrapers, whose precedent was to be found in unexecuted projects by Mies van der Rohe, whose Seagram Building, diagonally across Park Avenue, was built in 1958. Bunshaft's Manufacturers Hanover Trust Company, on Fifth Avenue at Forty-third Street, expressed the wealth of a bank which could afford to build essentially a three-story structure on such an expensive site. Pepsi Cola (later the Olivetti Building and now investor owned) is perhaps the best glass box in Manhattan, for its scale and the overall proportions of its elevations. Skidmore, Owings and Merrill have contributed some horrors, too, including the Grace Building, on Forty-second Street, and its sister on Fifty-eighth Street. North and south elevations of these two gargantuan buildings sweep down to the street, curving out in so doing, like roots of a tree entering the ground. Streetscape is thereby altered and the blending of the new into an existing pattern of buildings is unresolved, even though such a structural design saves on steel.

Other buildings on crosstown streets have attempted to create north-south links through the long sides of the city blocks, to cater to pedestrians. The Ford Foundation, 1967, by Roche and Dinkeloo, was the first to inadvertently achieve this linking of streets, with its 120-feet-high crystal palace courtyard full of luscious foliage. Encouraged by later zoning, David Specter and Philip Birnbaum's Galleria (1975), on Fifty-seventh Street, mimics both the Ford Foundation and the Galleria in Milan, and the 1970 remodelling of the 1912 building at 33 West Forty-second Street, next to the Grace Building and now occupied by the City University Graduate Center, provides a similar link. So will Philip Johnson's A.T.&T. Building, now under construction on the west side of Madison Avenue between Fifty-fifth and Fifty-sixth Streets.

The only major disagreement the compiler has with Mrs. Huxtable concerns her assessment of Hugh Stubbins's Citicorp Building on Lexington Avenue: "It seems to be very strong on urban design and very weak on architecture ... quite simply awful" (item 598), and even upon completion she was not too happy about it (item 728). Yet this compiler considers that its interior spaces are second only to the Ford Foundation, for that type of building, and that its elegant aluminum facades on tall piloti straddling the new St. Peter's Church (with sculpture interiors by Louise Nevelson) make it, in all respects, a major contributor to that part of town.

Jane Holtz Kay in reviewing *Kicked a Building Lately?* asked why Mrs. Huxtable dwells upon monumental public buildings at the expense of those of social amenity (item 1015), not realizing, perhaps, that architecture is, as Philip Johnson would have it, primarily an art and very little of anything else. But Mrs. Huxtable does concern herself with residential and non-monumental architecture. She praised Co-op City as a "singularly New York product" with good planning, architecture, and "low-budget success" (item 342) for 15,372 families. Battery Park City, on landfill along the Manhattan side of the Hudson from the island's tip to Forty-second Street, was to accommodate a large population which would also have worked in New York City, with office buildings and the new West Side Highway to subsidize the amenities. Unfortunately, commercial office buildings were no longer required in a saturated market and the project, having passed through ten schemes, is now drastically modified.

The firm of residential architects most successfully combining low- and highrise apartments to complement the existing cityscape is Davis, Brody and Associates. Their East Midtown Plaza, on East Twenty-third Street (a major crosstown street) between First and Second Avenues, accommodates lowrise apartments above ground-level stores and intersperses tower blocks within the same development. Concerning this and numerous other high-density projects in New York City by Davis, Brody and Associates, Mrs. Huxtable has stated, that since, despite all the bureaucratic red tape of the metropolis, this firm can achieve such a high caliber of design for the environment, "There should be penalties for architects who do less" (item 602).

Mrs. Huxtable has also championed the latest movements in architectural design and theory, interpreting and explaining the new attitudes, whether the new banality of Robert Venturi, the neo-Corbu aesthetics of the New York Five, Post-Modernism, or

"The Austere World of [Aldo] Rossi" (item 837). In the Introduction to *Kicked a Building Lately?*, Mrs. Huxtable suggests that "If some of these [more recent] essays seem mellower, if the tone seems a little less desperate . . . it is not because there are any fewer battles to be fought" but because the campaigns now have public backing to prod political leadership. Her impact has been tremendous, her criticism and analysis of a situation dynamic and logical. "Johnson's Latest—Clever Tricks or True Art?" (item 773) is not only a clear exposition of the architectural intent, but also defines the role of the proposed A.T. & T. Building in New York's cityscape and considers the impact it will have. Equally excellent is her castigation of architect and developer in their proposed Sixty-second Street sabotage, in "As East 62d Street Goes, So Goes New York" (item 798). The proposed skyscraper on Sixty-second Street is out of scale with the crosstown streets, and no words are minced concerning the "bad preservation, bad urbanism and bad architecture." Mrs. Huxtable is, according to William Thompson, "part evangelist, part judge, part historian, part educator, part satirist, part advocate, and part prophet" (item 1003), and it is because of this that an annotated bibliography of writings by and about Ada Louise Huxtable is totally justifiable.

Over a period of more than twenty years, through the end of 1979, 849 articles signed by Mrs. Huxtable have appeared in *The New York Times* in addition to her editorial comments. Since her editorials are unsigned and represent the voice of *The Times* and not specifically of Mrs. Huxtable, they have, at her request, been omitted here. Other magazines and periodicals have carried an additional sixty-eight articles.

Since *The New York Times Index* lists its material only by subject and not by author, it is sometimes difficult to trace an article. A large proportion will be found under "ARCHITECTURE," "CITY PLANNING," or "NYC–City Planning" or "NYC–Historic Buildings and Sites," but who would imagine that an article on President Johnson's Conference on Natural Beauty as discussed in "Drive for Natural Beauty" (item 172) would be found under the subject heading "US–General"? Even more irritating, some articles cannot be located at all. For example, when Riis Plaza, New York, was landscaped and described in "At

Last, a Winner" (item 214), the article was listed under "PARKS–NYC." But "Grass at Riis Houses Giving Way to a Plaza" (item 181), reporting the proposal of this mall, was not to be found under any of the subheadings of "PARKS," "NYC," or "HOUSING."

In preparing a listing of writings by Mrs. Huxtable, one could search through every issue of *The New York Times* over a twenty-two-year period, but because some articles are tucked away in obscure parts of the newspapers they could easily be overlooked. On Sunday, for example, her pieces may appear in the main portion of the newspaper (Section 1), Arts and Leisure (Section 2), Business and Finance (Section 3), The Week in Review (Section 4), Magazine (Section 6), Book Review (Section 7), or Travel (Section 10). Fearing omissions in compiling this bibliography, it was decided to use Mrs. Huxtable's scrapbooks at *The New York Times* office as a ready source of available material. Articles are clipped from the newspaper and sent to her secretary who pastes them in the books. Unfortunately, the date of the newspaper is not always appended, though a date is stamped on the newsprint, and unless the article is in the appropriate top corner of the page, the page number is also missing. Thus it was necessary to use the *Index* to locate the date, section of the newspaper, and pagination. In searching through the *Index* the compiler came across many articles by Mrs. Huxtable which had been omitted from her scrapbooks, and it became apparent that there is no foolproof method of locating *all* of her articles. Even *The New York Times Index* makes errors. Under "HUXTABLE" in the 1975 *Index*, it inaccurately lists "The New School Center for New York City Affairs Honors Mrs. Huxtable," as May 28, p. 55. There are also a series of wrong dates given for articles in *Kicked a Building Lately?* "Pow! It's Good-by History, Hello Hamburger" was dated March 31, 1971, not March 21, 1971. "Covent Garden Plan: It Just Isn't Loverly" should have been June 4, 1971, not June 14, 1971. But oddest of all, "How Great Buildings Shape a City's Soul" of October 19, 1975, was given as November 6, 1975. Of the sixty-eight articles in *Will They Ever Finish Bruckner Boulevard?*, forty are not to be found in the scrapbooks.

The date, newspaper section, and page numbers of all *New York Times* articles were cross-checked on microfilm for accuracy.

Other articles were verified in the appropriate magazine or periodical. Even so, despite every effort to be complete and accurate, there will undoubtedly be some errors and omissions, for which apologies are offered.

The listing of Mrs. Huxtable's articles in *The New York Times* is followed by a listing of her articles in other periodicals, and then her books. Then follows a listing of fifty-one articles about Mrs. Huxtable in *The New York Times* and sixty-one articles about her in other publications. Each listing is arranged chronologically. The articles about Mrs. Huxtable in publications other than *The New York Times* were traced through the *Art Index*, *Avery Index*, *Reader's Guide to Periodical Literature*, and *Access: The Supplementary Index to Periodicals*. *Access* tends to index publications devoted to a locality, such as *Houston Home* or *Texas Monthly*, and lesser-known magazines which do not have wide distribution and are thus not easily located, such as *Keeping Up* and *Viva*; three of the aforementioned magazines reviewed *Kicked a Building Lately?* *Book Review Index* and *Book Review Digest* were also used in locating reviews of Mrs. Huxtable's publications.

Thanks must be given to J. Lee Glenn, my graduate assistant during 1980 at the University of Tennessee, for checking the whole manuscript for errors, and to Danielle Bafkas, Mrs. Huxtable's secretary in 1974, when this project was begun. It was then shelved for several years, but was taken up again when Garland Publishing, Inc., became interested. Mrs. Huxtable's present secretary, Sandy Ratkowsky, has also been more than helpful. And finally Mrs. Huxtable must be thanked, for without her pen and permission such a publication would have been impossible.

Part I

Articles by Ada Louise Huxtable
in *The New York Times*

1. "Dissenting View. Correspondent Questions Venezuelan
   Architectural Achievements." September 8, 1957,
   Section 2, p. 10.

   Progress in the form of ugly brutal buildings, is the
   description given by Mrs. Huxtable in a letter to the
   editor, in reply to an Art Page article concerning the
   architecture of Caracas. Some buildings are fine, but
   others are merely photogenic. Many have replaced rural
   slums which at least formed sociological neighborhoods.

2. "Park Avenue School of Architecture. Business and Its New
   Sleek and Shiny Temples Have Transformed a Famous Residential Street." December 15, 1957, Magazine Section,
   pp. 30-31, 54-56.

   Commercial interests and new glass boxes are replacing
   apartment buildings which had a sense of historic style.
   The new architecture is modular, made of standard compon-
   ent parts, and the result is uniformity--economic and
   mediocre. Some of the new buildings are well designed,
   but others hardly merit being called architecture.

1958

3. "Capitol Remodelling Arouses Criticism." February 16,
   1958, Section 2, p. 14.

   Additional space for restaurant and other facilities,
   at a cost of $200 per square foot, is no excuse to demolish
   the only remaining visible portion of the U.S. Capitol--the
   east front, that is. If the front is to be saved, action
   by concerned groups must be sounded; several resolutions
   have been made.

4. "The Art We Cannot Afford to Ignore (But Do)." May 4,
   1958, Magazine Section, pp. 14-15, 86.

   Architecture is a forgotten art, but it has the greatest

effect upon us, since it shapes the environment. Describes
examples of humanistic architecture.

5. "Heritage in Peril. Defense of Architectural Landmarks Is
    Purpose of Museum Display." October 5, 1958, Section 2,
    p. 11.

    Reviews an exhibition, "Architecture Worth Saving," at
the Museum of Modern Art, consisting of notable examples
countrywide. Why not preserve America's heritage rather
than destroy it to re-erect pastiches of the past.

1959

6. "Four Model Buildings under Museum Review. Experimental
    Styles in Architecture at the Museum of Modern Art."
    February 15, 1959, Section 2, p. 17.

    Reviews an exhibition entitled "Architecture and Imagery,"
comprised of provocative works showing new directions in
modern design which rely to a great extent on engineering
dexterity. This engineering freedom could be disastrous
in the hands of designers, since anything can be built;
the forms used in the city strips could become the forms of
tomorrow's architecture.

7. "Buildings That Are Symbols Too." April 5, 1959, Magazine
    Section, pp. 18-19, 103.

    Symbolism in building "has been, and continues to be, a
spiritual and emotional necessity." Discusses several
worldwide examples.

8. "Ten Buildings That Say Today." May 24, 1959, pp. 32,
    34-35 (correction June 7, 1959, Magazine Section, p. 34).

    Ten buildings from Europe, Asia, and America are illus-
trated and described as "architecture's latest frontiers."
(See item 924.)

9. "Art with Architecture: New Terms of an Old Alliance."
    September 13, 1959, Section 2, p. 20.

    Sculpture and art works as a complement to modern archi-
tecture.

10. "Future Previewed. Innovations of Buckminster Fuller Could
     Transform Architecture." September 27, 1959, Section 2,
     p. 21.

     Buckminster Fuller's work was on exhibition at the Museum

of Modern Art. His engineering products and imaginative
vocabulary are explained.

11. "That Museum: Wright or Wrong." October 25, 1959, Maga-
     zine Section, cover and pp. 16-17, 91.

     Wright claimed that the Guggenheim Museum would be "an
     unusual container for an unusual collection.... Here for
     the first time you will see twentieth-century arts and
     architecture in their true relation.... This is the liber-
     ation of painting by architecture."

12. "Triple Legacy of Mr. Wright." November 15, 1959, Maga-
     zine Section, pp. 18-19.

     "The extraordinary public response to the new Guggen-
     heim Museum again puts the limelight on the lifetime of
     accomplishment of its creator." A brief statement ac-
     companies this two-page spread which illustrates several
     of Wright's projects.

13. "Three Buildings, Three Ages." November 29, 1959, Maga-
     zine Section, p. 82.

     In the background of the Gothic Church of St. Thomas,
     Fifth Avenue and Fifty-third Street, New York, rises a
     Buckminster Fuller dome on exhibit in the garden of the
     Museum of Modern Art.

1960

14. "Olympian Designer." January 17, 1960, Magazine Section,
     pp. 30-31.

     Pier Luigi Nervi, the sixty-nine-year-old Italian
     engineer, is the "Olympian Designer." Some of his most
     recent works are illustrated.

15. "Marvel or Monster. Grand Central City Is Mass Architec-
     ture." January 24, 1960, Section 2, p. 13.

     "What is good design and planning in New York," an
     exhibition at the New School, first brought to public
     attention the size and scale of Grand Central City (the
     $100 million, 830-foot-high Pan Am Building). Emery
     Roth, in coordinating the design, sought "a balance
     between esthetics and economics."

16. "Architecture Prizes and a Prize Architect." February 28,
     1960, Section 2, p. 13.

     The New York Architectural League awarded Mies its archi-
     tectural gold medal for his Seagram Building. Other awards
     by the League are mentioned.

17. "Opportunity Muffed. On Television, Architecture Is Again
     the Stepchild of Criticism." March 13, 1960, Section 2,
     p. 13.

     "The Shape of Things," an NBC program, was a comic-book
     production, ignoring the great and substituting the gim-
     micky and the atrocious. The pathway to hell is paved
     with good NBC intentions.

18. "Architecture on TV. 'Greatest Non-building Architect
     of Our Time' Expounds His Ideas." March 27, 1960,
     Section 2, p. 13.

     "Camera Three," on CBS, was the second television
     program on architecture, following one on NBC (see item
     17). The subject was architect Frederick Kiesler, whose
     practice seems to contradict his theories of architecture.
     He squeezes his client's requirements into sculpturesque
     designs, but does not seem to have developed structural
     techniques for his kind of architecture.

19. "City for People. San Francisco Offers Its Inhabitants
     Much That New York Is Losing." May 8, 1960, Section
     2, p. 11.

     Mrs. Huxtable went to the conference of the American
     Institute of Architects in San Francisco but found the
     streets of San Francisco more interesting. As in New York
     City, however, some of the qualities are being eaten away
     by development.

20. "What Should a Museum Be?" May 8, 1960, Magazine Section,
     pp. 42-48 (correction May 22, 1960, Magazine Section,
     p. 92).

     Numerous architects of international repute are design-
     ing museums of architectural significance throughout the
     world. The historic role of the museum has changed; thus
     the design concepts have evolved. "Each designer offers
     his own idea of the best way to house the museum's updated
     functions." Attitudes of museum administrators are quoted.
     "Ideally, the museum should be a fusion of art and archi-
     tecture."

21. $24,000,000 Shrine Is Proposed for Capital. Critique
     of Project Questions Its Style." June 3, 1960, pp. 1,
     25.

     Eric Gugler, a New York architect, has designed a $24
     million Freedom Shrine for Washington, D.C., proposed by
     President Eisenhower. The legislators on the commission
     for the monument, although respected, do not necessarily
     have good ideas concerning architectural design. The
     history of the project is provided, including the fact
     that Gugler was consultant to the commission and then its
     architect.

22. "Acoustical Hall." June 5, 1960, Magazine Section, p. 18.

     The acoustics of Carnegie Hall, New York, are due as
     much to Adler and Sullivan as to its architect, William
     Burnet Tuthill, says Mrs. Huxtable in a letter to the
     editor.

23. "Towering Question: The Skyscraper." June 12, 1960, Maga-
     zine Section, pp. 16-17, 69-71.

     The drama of the skyscraper has reached the financial
     proportions of consuming much of the $7.7 billion spent
     on building in New York City each year. But is it not
     helping to destroy the city? Invariably the skyscraper
     is ugly, massive, characterless, monumental, and mediocre,
     and produces overcrowded and inhuman conditions. Zoning
     laws and lack of coordinated planning, along with the
     shape and massing, aid the skyscraper in the destruction
     of the city's vitality. ·

24. "Sharp Debate: What Should an Embassy Be? It Should Look
     American, Yet Suit Its Foreign Setting, Which Poses a
     Delicate Problem." September 18, 1960, Magazine Section,
     pp. 36-46.

     American-flavored embassies are not always accepted by
     the people of the countries in which they are built, or
     by government officials at home. Climate, site, and
     local conditions are considered. Several examples are
     illustrated and described.

25. "Worlds They Never Made." September 25, 1960, Magazine
     Section, pp. 30-31.

     Visionary megastructure projects are a "professional
     escape hatch." An exhibition entitled "Visionary Archi-
     tecture," illustrating these ideas, was staged at the
     Museum of Modern Art.

26. "The Architect as a Prophet." October 2, 1960, Section 2,
     p. 21.

     "Visionary Architecture," an exhibition at the Museum
     of Modern Art, presented the work of the "most respected
     architectural theorists and philosophers of the twentieth
     century."

27. "The Significance of Our New Skyscrapers." October 30,
     1960, Section 2, p. 13.

     Impressive skyscrapers are rising all over the city and
     ingenious engineering solutions are being devised to over-
     come difficulties, notably below ground level. Some
     are esthetically pleasing as works of art, incorporating
     sculptures, planting, and water.

28. "Designers with Dash." November 6, 1960, Magazine Section,
     pp. 77-78.

     Charles Eames was the winner of the Kaufmann International
     Design Award.

29. "Some New Skyscrapers and How They Grew." November 6,
     1960, Section 2, p. 12.

     Following on from the October 30 article, considers
     examples of skyscraper construction in greater detail.
     Are not skyscrapers a fitting expression of our day and
     age and the way in which we operate?

30. "The City on TV. Our Major Architectural Problem Is In-
     telligently Aired at Last." November 20, 1960, Section
     2, p. 25.

     "Big City--1980," a CBS-TV program, presented the city
     as one continuous piece of urban development, and the group
     of planners as people with "an uncontrollable urge for
     wide open spaces and the crashing roar of bulldozers clear-
     ing away the past."

1961

31. "New Look of the Campus." January 15, 1961, Magazine
     Section, pp. 34-35.

     A pictorial survey of some of the more interesting
     "experimental one-of-a-kind designs" on the American
     college campus.

32. "For a Living Image of FDR."   January 22, 1961, Magazine
       Section, pp. 12-13.

       Illustrates and comments on four of the 574 entries in
       the FDR Memorial competition.

33. "Architects Examine New Directions at Summit Meeting."
       May 21, 1961, Section 2, p. 11.

       Ten seminars at Columbia University were soul-searching
       discussions for architects. The sessions analyzed the
       four great makers of modern architecture, Wright, Corbu,
       Mies, and Gropius, the latter three of whom received
       honorary doctoral degrees from Columbia in 1961. Lists
       the gala array of speakers.

34. "What Is Your Favorite Building?" May 21, 1961, Magazine
       Section, pp. 34-35.

       "The *Times* asked six leading architects, designers of
       noteworthy new structures, to name their favorite buildings.
       ... All turned to examples of the past.... All emphasized
       quality of spirit, serenity and timelessness ... enclosure
       of space and the emotional experience."

35. "In Philadelphia, an Architect." June 11, 1961, Section
       2, p. 14.

       Presents the ideals of Louis Kahn along with the strength
       and function (with its shortcomings) of his Richards Medical
       Research Building in Philadelphia.

36. "Eero Saarinen 1910-1961." September 10, 1961, Section 2,
       p. 26.

       An obituary of Saarinen, whose death at the age of fifty-
       one ended a distinguished career of daring architectural
       productions.

37. "To Keep the Best of New York." September 10, 1961, Maga-
       zine Section, pp. 44-52.

       Casualties of the bulldozer abound in the city. Result:
       the best of the past is lost and the replacements are
       larger and less distinguished. It seems that public opinion
       is on the side of "progress" and all that is "new."

38. "Sculpture of Fantasy." September 24, 1961, Magazine
       Section, pp. 76-77.

       Three floors of the Whitney Museum were devoted to the

work of the Austrian-born sculptor Bernhard Reder. His
productions range from sculptures of human form to buildings of geometric shapes.

39. "Shape of the Future Fairs." October 15, 1961, Magazine
     Section, pp. 44-45.

     A pictorial essay, with annotations, on outstanding
     fairs from London, 1851, to Seattle, 1962.

40. "Must Urban Renewal Be Urban Devastation?" December 24,
     1961, Section 2, p. 14.

     Some developers had their eyes on the Cast-Iron District
     of New York, which they described as having "rundown,
     bad buildings." This area was, in 1961, a dozen or more
     years away from protection. The battle cry for preserva-
     tion was sounded in this article. Buildings have values
     other than the economic.

                                1962

41. "Art: Wright Mythology. 'Twentieth Century' on CBS-TV
     Aims at Perpetuating Legend of Architect." February 19,
     1962, p. 24.

     The myth, but not the facts, of Wright's career and
     Wright's greatness was presented in the television program
     here reviewed.

42. "Drawings and Dreams of FLW." March 11, 1962, Magazine
     Section, pp. 24-25.

     A brief comment with illustrations of Wright's drawings,
     1895-1959, from an exhibition at the Museum of Modern Art.

43. "The Facts of Wright's Greatness." March 18, 1962, Section
     2, p. 21.

     The reality, as opposed to the legend, of Wright, as
     seen in his projects, is exemplified in his drawings,
     250 of which, out of the Wright Foundation's collection
     of 8,000, were on view at the Museum of Modern Art.

44. "Jet Age Triumph. Saarinen's New Airport for Washington
     Is a Superb Monument to Our Time." April 8, 1962,
     Section 1, p. 21.

     This innovative modern structure is praised for its
     architect's rethinking old problems and emerging with
     new solutions. Moreover, the building is a creative
     work of architecture with structural daring.

45. "Remembrance of Buildings Past." April 15, 1962, Maga-
    zine Section, p. 92.

    The Anonymous Arts Recovery Society is interested in
    preserving ornaments from demolished buildings. Some of
    the buildings are illustrated.

46. "Controversy Widens on Design of Development in Washington.
    Fine Arts Commission Battling to Prevent Approval of the
    Watergate Project—Session Here Fails to End Dispute."
    April 29, 1962, Section 1, p. 62.

    This $50 million luxury development for residences, a
    hotel, and offices could destroy the scale and character
    of Washington.

47. "Our New Buildings: Hit and Misses." April 29, 1962,
    Magazine Section, pp. 16-17, 105-106.

    New York's skyline is continually changing and growing
    but is it improving? There are a few good buildings, but
    the many bad are only poor imitations. The successes and
    the failures are reviewed.

48. "Kennedy Adopts Building Plan to Give Capital a Modern
    Look." June 1, 1962, pp. 1, 12.

    President J.F. Kennedy instigated a policy of good de-
    sign for government buildings, notably along Pennsylvania
    Avenue in Washington, D.C. The Congress will have to
    concur.

49. "Memorial Design Faces House Unit. Abstract Monument
    Would Honor F.D. Roosevelt." June 3, 1962, Section 1,
    p. 72.

    A memorial of eight concrete slabs, a winning competi-
    tion entry by Pedersen and Tilney, has come under attack.

50. "Nervi in—and on—New York." June 3, 1962, Section 2,
    p. 10.

    Nervi was in New York on an inspection tour of the new
    bus terminal at the George Washington Bridge. It is tech-
    nologically a part of the twentieth century. Nervi's
    attitude toward the architecture of New York is described.

51. "Capital Program. Architectural Light in Washington."
    June 10, 1962, Section 2, p. 10.

    The federal government is attempting to improve quality
    in the design of its buildings by employing good designers.
    But how does who define what is good architecture?

52. "Soaring Pattern--The Air Force Chapel." July 22, 1962,
     Magazine Section, pp. 22-23.

     Brief statement and photographs of this building at
     Colorado Springs by Skidmore, Owings and Merrill, with
     comparative examples of other modern religious buildings.

53. "New (Architectural) Frontier in Washington." August 19,
     1962, Magazine Section, pp. 18-19, 68, 70.

     Private and public developments are creating a building
     boom in Washington, D.C. Each sector is spending a half
     billion dollars or more. Style has developed from early
     nineteenth-century classicism to "contemporary bandwagon."
     In the early phase, the government pioneered the way, but
     architecture of the last ten years, private and public,
     is totally undistinguished. It could be otherwise if the
     government employed architects of distinction.

54. "Concertgoers Give Building Life. Architect Uses Men and
     Materials to Create Motion." September 24, 1962, p. 35.

     Philharmonic Hall, New York, is pleasant enough as a
     piece of architecture, but if it fails functionally and
     acoustically, it can be considered unworkable. Circulation
     is spectacular. Harrison and Abramovitz, architects.

55. "Balancing Up. A Highbrow Ideal, Lincoln Center Is a
     Likely Middlebrow Monument." October 28, 1962, Section
     2, p. 15.

     Entry, access, stairs, and the usual associated accommoda-
     tions at the entrance level of Philharmonic Hall seem tight
     and mean. Future structures at Lincoln Center do not fore-
     cast any great breakthroughs in architectural design.

56. "Federal Pavilion for New York World's Fair Is Nearing a
     Decision." November 11, 1962, Section 1, p. 79.

     Congress appropriated $17 million for the pavilion, and
     architect Charles Luckman produced a design prior to the
     announcement of the appointed commission by the General
     Services Administration. The design was never published,
     but description of it stimulated objections.

57. "Idlewild: Distressing Monument to Air Age." November 25,
     1962, Section 2, p. 25.

     The Beaux Arts circular plan of Idlewild Airport was
     beginning to take shape in 1962, with the construction
     of individual pavilions as additions to the central main
     arrivals building. Each building is briefly reviewed.

58. "Pools, Domes, Yamasaki--Debate." November 25, 1962,
    Magazine Section, pp. 36-37, 150-58.

    Is Yamasaki "the best or the worst thing to hit the
    profession since the skyscraper"? Yamasaki says, "we
    should have no reluctance to interpret the richness of
    the past through logical modern means." Those who feel
    that he has a positive contribution to make, and those
    who feel negatively about his architecture, are quoted.
    His background and his struggle for success are discussed,
    along with his philosophical attitudes and examples of
    his work.

                              1963

59. "A Fair US Pavilion. Controversy over Exhibit Building
    Ends with Selection of Happy Design." January 26,
    1963, p. 7.

    An analysis of the evolving design by Charles Luckman
    for the Federal Pavilion at the New York World's Fair.

60. "Echoes of the Age of Victoria." April 7, 1963, Magazine
    Section, p. 46.

    A picture essay on British Victorian architecture.

61. "Architecture Stumbles On." April 14, 1963, Section 2,
    p. 23. Reprinted as "Pan Am: The Big, the Expedient
    and the Deathlessly Ordinary." *Will They Ever Finish
    Bruckner Boulevard?* pp. 81-82.

    The "physical and sociological implications: the effect
    of 17,000 new tenants and 250,000 daily transients on
    the already crowded Grand Central area and its services"
    were the main criticisms levelled at this project.

62. "Architecture: How to Kill a City." May 5, 1963, Section
    2, p. 15. Reprinted as "The Impoverished City." *Will
    They Ever Finish Bruckner Boulevard?* pp. 44-46.

    Pennsylvania Station "is a monument to the lost art of
    magnificent construction, other values aside," and Times
    Tower "was legitimately conceived for its day." The
    former, by McKim, Mead & White, was demolished and the
    latter, by Cyrus L.W. Eidlitz and Alexander Mackenzie,
    has been altered beyond all recognition by Voorhees,
    Walker, Smith, Smith and Haines. This is a general article
    on preservation.

63.   "Architectural Dynamite. City Club Criticism of Municipal
      Design Underscores Need for Drastic Reform." May 14,
      1963, p. 28.

      The City Club of New York, which annually sponsors the
      Bard Awards for good architectural design, claimed that
      no municipal buildings worthy of an award had been built
      since 1958.

64.   "Another Chapter in 'How to Kill a City.'" May 26, 1963,
      Section 2, p. 11. Reprinted as "Legislating Against
      Quality." *Will They Ever Finish Bruckner Boulevard?*
      pp. 46-50.

      Increase property taxes for a prestige building seems
      to be the attitude of the City of New York, specifically
      with relation to the Seagram Building. The scheme dis-
      criminates against good design, since the tax will be
      based upon construction costs. A speculative building is
      built cheaply for a reasonable return in profits. If a
      company builds a prestigious structure for itself at
      higher than usual costs, it will be penalized in additional
      taxes. Thus mediocrity will reign.

65.   "Bold Harvard Structure. Le Corbusier's Carpenter Visual
      Arts Center Collides with Colonial Charm." May 28, 1963,
      p. 34.

      Controversial from many viewpoints, this, the only struc-
      ture by Le Corbusier in the United States, makes surrounding
      buildings, ivy-clad, look stale. Covers details of con-
      struction, esthetics, and other aspects.

66.   "Stone to Design Civic Center. Reidy Says Mayor Approves
      Plan for Architects to Coordinate Project. 2d Firm Will
      Aid Work. Eggers and Higgins to Draft Design on the
      Municipal and Archives Building." May 30, 1963, p. 19.

      Edward D. Stone was to have designed the new Federal
      Building at Civic Center Mall, New York, in collaboration
      with Eggers and Higgins.

67.   "Architects Back Criticism of City." June 19, 1963, p. 39.

      Some members of the local chapter of the American Institute
      of Architects objected to the decision of the City Club
      concerning the Bard Awards (see item 63). Other members
      of the profession agreed with the City Club and signed a
      statement to that effect.

68. "Litho City: Hit or Flop?   Union Housing Plan Meets Snags
    in Bid for 'Greatness.'"   June 21, 1963, p. 16.

    The Amalgamated Lithographers of America proposed to
    build the greatest of housing projects between West End
    Avenue and the West Side Highway, from West Fifty-ninth
    to West Seventieth Streets.

69. "Parley on Design Views US Image.   Arts Studied as a Cold
    War Link to Backward Lands."   June 24, 1963, p. 24.

    Report on the International Design Conference with an
    emphasis on "Design and the American Image Abroad."   Lists
    speakers and topics.

70. "The New York Hilton's Two Faces."   June 30, 1963, Section
    2, p. 13.   Reprinted as "Schizophrenia at the New York
    Hilton."   *Will They Ever Finish Bruckner Boulevard?*
    pp. 102-105.

    "It is a package, since the functions are neatly wrapped
    in curtain wall components, figured according to cost-
    accounting procedures to produce an international hotel
    formula."   William B. Tabler, architect.

71. "Study Will Weigh Law Use in Design.   Seattle Architect
    Awarded $5,000 Brunner Grant."   July 17, 1963, p. 28.

    The Brunner Award, given by the New York Chapter of the
    American Institute of Architects, will be used by this
    year's recipient to study planning laws and their impact
    on urban architecture in Europe.

72. "End Papers."   July 18, 1963, p. 25.

    Nikolaus Pevsner's *An Outline of European Architecture*,
    first published in 1943, with 160 pages and 60 illustra-
    tions, is reviewed in its latest edition, which contains
    500 pages and 295 illustrations.

73. "Fine Arts Panel Falls to New Frontier."   July 25, 1963,
    p. 23.

    Comments on new members of Washington's Commission of
    Fine Arts.

74. "Building's Case History.   Award of Capital Contract to
    Breuer Calls to Mind Hunter College Edifice."   August 9,
    1963, p. 51.

    Marcel Breuer has been awarded the commission for a
    Washington headquarters for the Housing and Home Finance

Agency (now HUD), but his administration building for
Hunter College at its Bronx campus receives most attention
in the article.

75. "Chicago Saves Its Past. New Law for Preserving Landmarks
     P. 30 [New Bank for Q Huxtable (sic. Printer's directions
     which inadvertently became part of title)]." August 14,
     1963, p. 30.

     Assesses the value of Chicago's landmarks law. The law
     became necessary as more historic structures of architec-
     tural importance were razed, and concerned people world-
     wide demanded action.

76. "Plan for Rebuilding Pennsylvania Ave. Is Near Completion."
     August 20, 1963, pp. 1, 30.

     Comments on plans for Washington, D.C., with reference
     to the most recent plan for Pennsylvania Avenue. Gives
     detailed information.

77. "Design for Progress. Novel Concept for East Harlem
     Project Is a Break from Tired Boxes of Past." August
     23, 1963, p. 22.

     Good design usually results from architectural competi-
     tions, and this East Harlem housing scheme should be no
     exception.

78. "New Pattern for City Housing." August 25, 1963, Magazine
     Section, pp. 12-13.

     A follow-up to the August 23 article (item 77) on housing
     competitions for New York City. Several award-winning
     schemes are illustrated.

79. "Wright House at Bear Run, Pa., Will Be Given Away to Save
     It." September 7, 1963, p. 21.

     Edgar J. Kaufmann, Jr. studied with Wright in the 1930s
     and induced his father to commission Wright to design
     "Fallingwater," the summer retreat for the family, which
     was given to the Western Pennsylvania Conservancy. An
     endowment fund, grants, and 500 acres accompany the gift
     of the house.

80. "Experts on Preservation End 4-Day Meeting at Williams-
     burg. International Group Attempts to Develop a New
     Set of Working Principles for the Saving of Landmarks."
     September 12, 1963, p. 37.

     Concerned preservationists met to set up guidelines to
     save America's architectural heritage.

81. "Yale to Dedicate New Laboratory. Johnson Building Un-
     veiling Scheduled for Today." September 27, 1963, p.
     26.

     Geology, geophysics, and geochemistry are to be housed
     in the new Kline Laboratories at Yale, in a $3.5 million
     complex of a $10 million science center. Philip Johnson,
     architect.

82. "Architecture: Designs for American Synagogues. Recent
     Building Models at Jewish Museum. Recent Project by
     Louis Kahn Is Shown." October 5, 1963, p. 22.

     "Recent American Synagogue Architecture," an exhibition
     at New York's Jewish Museum, presented the work of seven-
     teen architects.

83. "State Will Revamp College Campus Designs. Billion Dollar
     Plans Stress Architecture for 22 Schools." October 8,
     1963, pp. 1, 39.

     Governor Nelson Rockefeller stated, "we have devised a
     scheme for tapping the best talent in the country." New
     facilities are needed for the 150,000 students expected in
     1970, double the number in 1963.

84. "Upheaval at Battery. Stock Exchange Urban-Renewal Plan
     Posing Touchy Architectural Issues." October 10, 1963,
     p. 53.

     Battery Park Development is an attempt to house and
     retain the New York Stock Exchange in the city.

85. "Planner Defends Cars in Midtown. New Chief of Commission,
     Sworn by Mayor, Backs Municipal Garage." October 16,
     1963, p. 47.

     "The better and fuller life includes the free use of
     the automobile," according to the new chairman of the
     New York City Planning Commission, William F.R. Ballard.
     He stated his likes and dislikes on many issues.

86. "Architecture: Virtues of Planned City. Model of New Town
     in Finland Displayed." October 24, 1963, p. 38.

     "Tapiola," Finland, is the title of a new town exhibi-
     tion at the Architectural League of New York. There is
     a great deal that the United States can learn from this
     European new town. "To American viewers of the exhibition
     it is an example and a rebuke."

87. "Complex in Boston Is Radically Designed. State Center
     Project Is Striking Departure in Urban Planning."
     November 7, 1963, p. 25.

     This $29 million project for the State of Massachusetts
     Health, Education, and Welfare Building is to be built
     in "the most conservative city in the United States."
     Paul Rudolph, architect.

88. "Winner at Yale. The New Art and Architecture Building
     Lives Up to Great Expectations." November 10, 1963,
     Section 2, p. 19.

     Announces the opening of the new Art and Architecture
     Building for Yale. It leaks. Paul Rudolph, architect.

89. "Natural House of Frank Lloyd Wright." November 17, 1963,
     Magazine Section, pp. 78-79.

     Between 1893 and 1959 Wright designed 262 houses, one
     of which was destroyed by fire and demolished, but in
     1963, the remainder still stood. Edgar Kaufmann, Jr.
     donated "Fallingwater" to the Western Pennsylvania Con-
     servancy. Photographs of this house were exhibited at
     the Museum of Modern Art in November 1963. (See letter
     by Henry Hope Reed, Jr., December 8, 1963, item 927.)

90. "Renewal Project Splits Cleveland. Opponents Continue
     Battle as Construction Nears." November 24, 1963, Sec-
     tion 1, p. 24.

     Concerned citizens of Cleveland want to preserve the
     natural beauty of University Circle, where thirty insti-
     tutions are building on 488 acres. Many of the new
     structures are described by irate citizens as ugly.

91. "End Papers." November 26, 1963, p. 35.

     Merrill Folsom's book *Great American Mansions* records
     the good, the bad, and the ugly.

92. "Pre-Columbian Art Exhibition Opens New Museum in Capital."
     December 10, 1963, p. 50.

     Dumbarton Oaks, Georgetown, D.C., is displaying the
     Robert Woods Bliss collection of pre-Columbian art in
     its new extension designed by Philip Johnson.

93. "Architecture in Capital. National Geographic Society's
     Building Sets a Standard for Washington." December 11,
     1963, p. 57.

     "A straightforward, first-class piece of contemporary

architectural design without the harem overtones that
have been so disturbing to admirers of his [Edward D.
Stone's] work."

94. "Whitney Museum Reveals Design. Plans Indicate Building
     Will Have Very Few Windows." December 12, 1963, p. 41.

     A new addition to an old brownstone neighborhood, which
     is changing into a popular commercial and residential
     area of the city. Internal environment will be controlled,
     as perhaps it should be in a museum building. Marcel
     Breuer, architect.

95. "Something Awry. Three New Buildings Pose Big Problems."
     December 22, 1963, Section 2, p. 15.

     Criticism has poured in concerning Breuer's design for
     the Whitney Museum, but two blockbusters, forty- and forty-
     two-stories high respectively, for the federal government
     are accepted as inevitable progress. "The greatest
     private economic good [produces] ... the lowest esthetic
     result."

96. "2 Contracts Let for Air Museum. Preliminary Work to
     Begin on Smithsonian Branch." December 28, 1963, p. 20.

     The new National Air and Space Museum, part of the Smith-
     sonian Institution, Washington, D.C., will document the
     history of air and space movement and exploration.

                              1964

97. "America the Beautiful, Defaced, Mutilated." January 12,
     1964, *The New York Times Book Review*, p. 7.

     A review of Peter Blake's *God's Own Junkyard*, a muck-
     raking book which emphasizes the mess of urban and rural
     America. Free enterprise equals esthetic bankruptcy.
     Illustrations are paired in contrasting values, pleasant
     and disastrous.

98. "Architecture: Toward the New World in Building. Two
     Federation Shows with Similar Bases." January 14,
     1964, p. 29.

     A review of "Churches and Temples," an exhibition at the
     Architectural League of New York. This building type is
     constructed in a variety of materials--concrete, brick,
     and stone--but Mrs. Huxtable admires some examples in
     wood.

99. "Federal States of Flux: Switch from Culture to Welfare
    in Washington Brings Architectural Change and Challenge."
    January 19, 1964, Section 2, p. 22.

    Human condition rather than esthetic condition is the
    mood of Washington in 1964, as opposed to the period of
    the Kennedy years, and this applies to architectural
    building types.

100. "A New Era Heralded. Architectural Virtue of Trade
    Center Expected to Enhance City's Skyline." January
    19, 1964, Section 1, p. 78.

    The proposed World Trade Center could be a breakthrough
    and a new trend in a second period of skyscraper concepts
    and construction. Two towers have exterior loadbearing
    walls. They have cityscape scale, and the whole project
    relates to the pedestrian. Yamasaki, architect.

101. "Architecture: Blending the Classical and Modern: The
    Museum of History and Technology of Smithsonian Opens
    Doors Today." January 23, 1964, p. 28.

    This huge $37 million monster was designed by McKim,
    Mead & White, or, rather, by the partnership that it has
    become: Steinmetz, Cain and White. The structure is monu-
    mental externally but is a warehouse for the exhibition
    of machines--"it is a monstrous and meaningless misalli-
    ance.... For an easy answer, see Lincoln Center ... an
    architectural approach that may be a bit stodgy for New
    York, but would be brilliantly suitable for Washington's
    problem of classical continuity."

102. "Biggest Buildings Herald New Era." January 26, 1964,
    Section 8, pp. 1, 4.

    "Nothing ever done before in a high building was right,"
    according to Yamasaki. Thus, new technology comes into
    its own in the two towers of the World Trade Center.
    External loadbearing walls should be considered as sides
    of a tube with holes punched through. "If we do not
    improve the art of building through this project, we
    are not fulfilling our task" (Yamasaki).

103. "Clusters Instead of Slurbs." February 9, 1964, Magazine
    Section, pp. 31, 36, 37, 40, 42, 44.

    Subtitled "Along with new towns, they are an innovation
    in residential developments that may help to rescue the
    suburban dream from the nightmare of mass produced hous-
    ing." Twenty-three billion dollars worth of suburban

housing will be constructed in 1964 by speculators. The
problem does not lie solely with the builders but equally
with government red tape. Improvements have been suggested
by various organizations. Some good alternate examples
of housing developments are given.

104. "First Light of New Town Era Is on Horizon. Housing Bill
     Would Spur Program of Planned Growth." February 17,
     1964, p. 28.

     Since America is at the beginning of a new town boom,
     such developments are analyzed and are compared to the
     usual sprawling suburbs. Numerous examples, American
     and British, are cited. They are praised, not only for
     the inclusion of cluster developments, but also for con-
     siderations of open space. Costs are high and financing
     hazardous, but the environment is enhanced and thus the
     human aspect is improved.

105. "Architecture: Huntington Hartford's Palatial Midtown
     Museum. Columbus Circle Gallery Will Open in Mid-
     March." February 25, 1964, p. 33.

     "It begs for a canal or garden setting rather than the
     dusty disorder of a New York traffic circle," which was
     until recently "a sordid and dismembered open space."
     Galleries circumambulate around the elevators at half
     levels, with the major galleries on the circus side of
     the structure. Edward D. Stone, architect.

106. "Low Bid Gets Park Ave. Home on Promise Not to Rip It
     Down." February 28, 1964, p. 31.

     Pyne-Davison Row on Park Avenue, between Sixty-eighth
     and Sixty-ninth Streets, built between 1909 and 1926,
     is to be purchased. The Institute of Public Administra-
     tion is selling the properties at a slight loss to Peter
     Grimm, who agreed not to demolish them. Higher bidders
     wanted to purchase the row, demolish it, and erect apart-
     ments.

107. "Fairs and Architecture. Metropolitan Museum Show Recalls
     Expositions since the First in 1851." March 13, 1964,
     p. 21.

     "World Fairs--The Architecture of Fantasy" was the title
     of an exhibition at the Metropolitan Museum of Art. High-
     lights of the fairs are recounted.

108. "State Arts Unit Cites Landmarks. Report Finds 64 Build-
     ings Worthy in Syracuse Area." March 14, 1964, p. 25.

     Architecture Worth Saving in Onondaga County suggests

that sixty-four landmarks in the area of Syracuse, New
York, are worth saving.

109. "Syracuse: Ugly Cities and How They Grow." March 15,
      1964, Section 2, p. 24. Reprinted as "Syracuse, N.Y.:
      Ugly Cities and How They Grow." *Will They Ever Finish
      Bruckner Boulevard?* pp. 115-17.

      Like so many American cities with a strong architectural
      heritage, some of which remains, Syracuse is laying much
      to waste and producing mediocre acreages of dull, uninter-
      esting buildings. Several historic structures are noted.

110. "Civic Club Honors Private Building. Pepsi-Cola Struc-
      ture Cited--City's Architectural Hit." March 17, 1964,
      p. 32.

      The Bard Awards, given by the City Club of New York
      for city-sponsored buildings, were not awarded in 1963,
      due to the lack of examples of good design. In 1964,
      privately-sponsored buildings were included for considera-
      tion. The winner was Skidmore, Owings and Merrill's
      Pepsi-Cola headquarters on Park Avenue at Fifty-ninth
      Street.

111. "Architecture: That Midtown Tower Standing Naked in the
      Wind. Skyscraper Buffs See Antique Skeleton." March
      20, 1964, p. 30.

      The Times Tower of 1904, by Cyrus Eidlitz, was, at 375
      feet, the tallest building in New York. In 1964 it was
      refaced by Allied Chemical Corporation. In the process,
      the structure of the building was exposed to view and
      presented to architectural buffs what "a Bugatti Royale
      is to automobile fans."

112. "Promenade Will Be One of State Theater's Bright Stars.
      Glass Fronted Room Glinting with Gold Lends Regal Air."
      March 23, 1964, p. 26.

      Philip Johnson has not expressed the structure of the
      New York State Theater at Lincoln Center, but has provided
      a glorious internal promenade--60x200 feet and fifty feet
      high. In the auditorium "every detail is classic theater
      in its function, and freshly devised in its design."

113. "The Block." March 30, 1964, p. 59.

      "The Block" was an educational television program con-
      cerning the area of Manhattan between Second and Third

Avenues, from Twenty-ninth to Thirtieth Streets. It
concerned people and small businesses within an area
of large-scale construction.

114. "Architecture: Maritime Union Builds Dream House. Former
      Wright Student Designs a Battleship for Hiring Halls."
      March 31, 1964, p. 31.

      Albert C. Ledner of New Orleans designed this New
York structure which is described in relation to Wright's
Guggenheim Museum. Ledner was a pupil of the master.

115. "New York Area Homes Scored in Report. Conservation
      Group Proposes Clusters for Development." April 3,
      1964, p. 30.

      The American Conservation Association condemned New
York City for lagging behind new housing trends. Cluster
groupings are praised because they increase densities
and thereby reduce sprawl. Reasons are given for New
York's backwardness.

116. "Love, Not Logic, Sets Design." April 5, 1964, Section
      13, pp. 1, 19.

      Gentlemen prefer automobiles to blondes?

117. "Architecture: A View of Giants of Our Town, 1970. 22
      Models and Photos Go on Display Today." April 6, 1964,
      p. 63.

      Reviews "Our Town, 1970," an exhibition by the Munici-
pal Art Society of twenty-two major building schemes for
New York City's future. Comments on some of the projects.

118. "Penn Station Giving Way to New Sports Arena. Model for
      Madison Square Garden Is Put on Display." April 7,
      1964, p. 37.

      The projected new Madison Square Garden was displayed
in model form at the exhibition "Our Town, 1970" (see
item 117). Circular in shape, it will seat 22,000 under
a cable-hung roof, which will cost $44 million (of a total
cost for the whole project of $66 million).

119. "Renewal in Boston: Good and Bad." April 19, 1964, Sec-
      tion 2, p. 24.

      Boston built its expressway, but having made one mis-
take the city is not continuing to make them. It is

reappraising and questioning its urban renewal program.
Praises preservation programs and the work of I.M. Pei
and Kallmann, McKinnell and Knowles.

120.   "54 Story Building Planned for Civic Center. New Pro-
          posal Urges Single Skyscraper with Plazas." April 21,
          1964, p. 39.

   This proposal for the New York Civic Center called for
a fifty-four-story skyscraper by Edward D. Stone at the
north end of a "plaza-park," with City Hall at the southern termination. Much would have to be demolished in
the process.

121.   "Architecture: Chaos of Good, Bad and Joyful. Grotesque
          Contrasts, Wholly Unplanned Give Fair Charm." April 22,
          1964, p. 25.

   Reviews the 1964 World's Fair, an exhibition of expensive individual designs of technological dexterity,
placed apparently randomly next to each other without
any organized plan.

122.   "World's Fair International Scope." May 10, 1964, Sec-
          tion 2, p. 19.

   The New York World's Fair is the fair of the big sell,
that is, to private companies, if national governments
will not participate. The outstanding and the dreary
designs are discussed.

123.   "NYU Seeks Master Plan for 10 Years of Building." May
          25, 1964, p. 1.

   Announces that Philip Johnson will coordinate the planning of New York University's Washington Square Campus
and will also design several of the buildings, in a planned
ten-year development. Details are provided, as is a history of the campus from 1831, and background on the di-
vision of the university into two separate campuses.

124.   "Architectural Forum Dropped; House and Home Magazine
          Sold." May 28, 1964, p. 31.

   The 64,000 readers of *Architectural Forum* will cease
to have the magazine as of August 1964. Henry Luce
bought the magazine in 1932; it ceased publication just
five weeks after he stepped down as editor-in-chief.

125.   "... And It's Big and Beautiful. Redesigned Museum Is
          Good Architecture, Fine Cityscape." May 31, 1964,
          Section 2, p. 15.

At thirty-five, the Museum of Modern Art has been
enlarged by Philip Johnson at a cost of $5.5 million.
Garden and galleries are described.

126. "A Grand Boulevard for Washington." May 31, 1964, Maga-
      zine Section, pp. 8-9.

Appalled at the run-down appearance of Pennsylvania
Avenue, which he saw while driving to his inauguration,
President Kennedy established a commission for the im-
provement of this axial boulevard. Proposal sketches
are illustrated.

127. "Pennsylvania Avenue Plan Calls for Vast Renovation."
      May 31, 1964, Section 1, pp. 1, 64.

Expansive grandeur on the scale of Paris and Rome is
planned for Washington, D.C.; old structures will be
razed to provide open space and $500 million worth of
redevelopment.

128. "Groundbreaking Today for Bay State School. New South-
      eastern Institute Will Be Finished in 1975." June 14,
      1964, Section 1, p. 82.

The Southern Massachusetts Technological Institute at
North Dartmouth was set up in 1960 on 700 acres of land.
Gives details of proposed early developments.

129. "Architecture: Fitting Site. American Institute of
      Architects Meets in St. Louis, a Changing City."
      June 18, 1964, p. 32.

Reviews what's happening, architecturally speaking, in
St. Louis, Missouri, site of the 1964 convention of the
American Institute of Architects.

130. "Architects Back Plan for Capital. Institute Supports
      Proposal to Reshape Washington." June 19, 1964, p. 28.

A report on actions and resolutions concerning Washington, D.C., and St. Louis passed at the St. Louis convention
of the American Institute of Architects.

131. "Monumental Troubles. Rejection of Design Is Latest
      Storm in History of Roosevelt Memorial." June 26,
      1964, pp. 31, 33.

Pedersen, Tilney, Hoberman, Wasserman and Beer won the
FDR Memorial competition and modified the design to satisfy the Washington Fine Arts Commission. Now the Roosevelt family finds it inappropriate.

132.   "St. Louis and the Crisis of American Cities."   June 28,
          1964, Section 2, p. 13.

       The waterfront and most of the Victorian downtown area
       of St. Louis are gone. The downtown sports stadium has
       created a central automobile parking area. "St. Louis
       has been acting with a singular lack of vision."

133.   "Modern Museum Assays Engineering."   June 30, 1964, p. 35.

       Reviews "Twentieth Century Engineering," a show at the
       Museum of Modern Art. A selection of the 195 examples
       are described and illustrated.

134.   "Dams, Domes and the Battle of Styles."   July 5, 1964,
          Section 2, p. 15.

       "Twentieth Century Engineering" is again reviewed (see
       item 133) emphasizing twentieth-century examples. There
       are those architects who are sympathetic to engineering
       and are called "structural purists," and there are others
       who dissent.

135.   "Call for a Master Plan. Architect's Report on State of
          the City Focusses Attention on Serious Problems."
          July 13, 1964, p. 24.

       New York City architects, realizing the plight of their
       environment, have demanded a master plan for reordering
       priorities and the use of resources.

136.   "Architecture: Rumania's Ambitious Building Plan. Show
          of Photos and Models at Columbia."   July 21, 1964, p. 28.

       Rumania's architecture is the subject of an exhibition
       at Columbia University. Rumania is divided into sixteen
       building regions which control architectural and planning
       development. Results are compared to the non-planning
       attitudes of the United States. Some of the buildings
       are criticized as being monotonous.

137.   "Cities: Great Plains [sic. Typographical error. Should
          be "Plans"] or Cut-Rate Cures."   August 2, 1964, Section
          2, p. 15.

       The Museum of Modern Art exhibited a model and drawings
       of Pennsylvania Avenue, Washington, D.C., as it is to be
       refurbished using "20th-century art to serve an 18th-
       century ideal." Discussion of proposals, and high praise
       for this non-official plan.

138.   "Romantic Science Hall. Harrison's Building at World's
          Fair Reminds One of 13th Century Cathedral."   September
          10, 1964, p. 27.

Wallace K. Harrison's Hall of Science for the 1963 New York World's Fair is exotic in a soaring Medieval Gothic sort of way. "The fact that so many of today's architects are diligently searching for new ways to do something as basic as enclosing space against the elements is making architecture an extremely lively art and producing some highly provocative results."

139. "Despair of Demolition. Plans to Raze 79th Street Mansions in Line with City's Destructive Trend." September 17, 1964, p. 39.

Three more houses, at Seventy-ninth Street and Fifth Avenue, are being lost to highrise apartment construction. The land on which the houses stand is valuable, and adaptive reuse of the buildings cannot readily be found. A history of the houses is given.

140. "Design of Garden City Plant Stirs Extreme Reactions. But the Endo Center Stands Triumphant Amid Controversy." September 20, 1964, Section 8, pp. 1, 14.

Paul Rudolph's Endo Laboratories, in Garden City, Long Island, "is one of the best buildings in the New York area," even though the Long Island State Park Commission planted trees to hide the structure named "Concrete Building of the Year."

141. "The Salvage of the Old Jeff. Determination of 'Villagers' to Save Historic Courthouse Proves Effective." September 23, 1964, p. 38.

The Jefferson Market Courthouse in Manhattan's Greenwich Village is to be converted by Giorgio Cavaglieri into a library. Named one of the ten most beautiful buildings in the United States in 1876, it has remained a noteworthy landmark in the hearts of most villagers ever since.

142. "Bold Plan for Building Unveiled." September 29, 1964, p. 45.

Plans by Roche and Dinkeloo for the Ford Foundation's new headquarters were announced. A photograph of the model complements the description.

143. "600 Acres of Trouble. Morningside, City Top Renewal Area, Is a Crucible of Crime and Creativity." September 30, 1964, p. 34.

Many college campuses, including that of Columbia University, are situated in the Morningside General Neighborhood Renewal Area. Decay, overcrowding, crime, lack of social concern, and suspicion of Columbia's expansion plans have created an exceedingly sensitive situation.

144. "Pop Architecture: Here to Stay. Mass Taste Creates a
      Mass Art That Reveals the Face of America in Sixties."
      October 4, 1964, Section 2, p. 23. Reprinted in *Will
      They Ever Finish Bruckner Boulevard?* pp. 172-74.

      "Pop Architecture is the true democratization of the
      art of architecture in that it represents not just mass
      consumption but mass taste," and it is catching on every-
      where. "Where Pop Art shocks the layman, Pop Architecture
      does not--perhaps the most terrifying comment of all."

145. "Arts Group Saves Bits of Landmark." October 6, 1964,
      p. 41.

      Sullivan's only New York building, The Bayard at 65
      Bleeker Street, has had its facade mutilated and changed.
      Some pieces of the decoration are being saved.

146. "Civil Center Inches On. Balancing Act Is Required of
      the City with Architectural Gain Its Objective."
      October 9, 1964, p. 42.

      The Civic Center plan is here restated. Opposition
      is coming from businessmen and preservationists.

147. "HHFA--Design at the Top." October 25, 1964, Section 2,
      p. 15.

      Winners of the Housing and Home Finance Agency's 1964
      awards for planning and design are discussed.

148. "Test Case in Park Plans. Proposal for Washington Square
      Marks Triumph in Designing for Local Needs." October
      28, 1964, p. 48.

      The formality in the design of New York parks seems to
      differ from the needs of the neighborhoods in which they
      are located. Funds and salaries for designers are, how-
      ever, low.

149. "Anonymous Architecture." November 8, 1964, Magazine
      Section, pp. 92-93.

      Reviews Bernard Rudofsky's exhibition "Architecture
      Without Architects," at the Museum of Modern Art.

150. "Some New Faces on Fifth Avenue." November 8, 1964,
      Section 2, p. 20.

      A very general article on new and renovated buildings
      on Fifth Avenue between Forty-seventh and Fifty-seventh
      Streets.

151. "Unusual House Designs Win Architectural Accolades. New
      and Remodelled Homes Are Cited in Competition." Novem-

ber 8, 1964, Section 8, pp. 1, 8.

Fourth annual house design awards, sponsored by the
New York Chapter of the American Institute of Architects,
announcement. Projects for new houses and conversions,
from several states, won awards. They are listed and
described.

152. "Architectless Architecture--Sermons in Stone." November
      15, 1964, Section 2, p. 23.

      "Architecture Without Architects" at the Museum of
Modern Art, organized by Bernard Rudofsky, is reviewed
as "the sermon of a prophet in today's architectural
wilderness."

153. "Visual Pollution in US Bemoaned. Parley on Quality of
      Homes Ends in Washington." November 21, 1964, p. 24.

      Report of a conference which brought together artists,
scientists, and philosophers who are concerned with the
total environment, including the visual scene, especially
in the field of housing.

154. "Two Design Takeoffs for the Air Age." November 22, 1964,
      Section 2, p. 18.

      Hellmuth, Obata and Kassabaum are to design the National
Air and Space Museum, Washington, D.C., and Roche and
Dinkeloo the Air Force Museum at Dayton, Ohio. Both de-
signs are "unequivocally twentieth-century solutions."
Both are illustrated.

155. "Architecture: Alvar Aalto, Finnish Master Represented
      Here." November 30, 1964, p. 38. Reprinted as "The
      Seductive Virtues of Alvar Aalto." *Will They Ever
      Finish Bruckner Boulevard?* pp. 201-204.

      Aalto designed the interior of part of the twelfth-
floor conference facilities at the Institute of International Education, New York, in 1963. The result is
subtle but sophisticated in form, color, texture, and
materials (notably the natural woods).

156. "Kennedy Family Announces the Selection of Pei to Design
      Library." December 14, 1964, p. 1.

      Pei feels that he can capture the spirit of adventure
of politics, in creating the Harvard University Kennedy
Memorial Library and Institute for Advanced Political
Studies.

157.   "Nothing Inviolate Here.   Plan for Tower on Savoy Plaza
       Site Raises Some Questions of Esthetics."   December
       16, 1964, p. 31.

       The Savoy Plaza Hotel in New York is to razed for the
       new General Motors Headquarters by Edward D. Stone, a
       quality building within tight financial limitations--a
       showroom with rentable space above.

                                1965

158.   "A Glimpse of Tomorrow Provided by Architectural Award
       Winners.   Designs of Future Almost Victorian.   Boldly
       Sculptured Masses Dominate Citations."   January 10,
       1965, Section 8, pp. 1, 5.

       The magazine *Progressive Architecture* announces award-
       winning projects in its annual January issue.   It is an
       "uncanny forecast of trends."

159.   "A Plan of Taste.   Design for Wing at Gracie Mansion,
       Overcomes Some Awkward Problems."   January 12, 1965,
       p. 24.

       Gracie Mansion, New York City, a small Georgian house,
       needs to expand to cater to the entertaining requirements
       of the mayor.   In this case, an imitation eighteenth-
       century addition seems justifiable.

160.   "A Creative Truce: City College Turns from Gothic of '03
       to Significant New 'Platform Concept.'"   January 29,
       1965, p. 34.

       Skidmore, Owings and Merrill is to organize a three-
       stage, $40 million development of City College of New
       York.   Details are provided in this article and in
       another on pp. 1 and 34.

161.   "Seasoning the Witches' Brew."   January 31, 1965, Section
       2, p. 18.

       Brown, Lawford and Forbes have designed a modern glass
       library link between the 1880 and 1905 additions to the
       Metropolitan Museum of Art.

162.   "New York's Architectural Follies."   February 14, 1965,
       Section 2, p. 19.   Reprinted as "The Architectural
       Follies."   *Will They Ever Finish Bruckner Boulevard?*
       pp. 40-43.

       Architectural jokes in the form of Colonial buildings

acting as skyscrapers, or is it skyscrapers masquerading
as Colonial structures, are still being built, sometimes
at the expense of demolishing an inherently urban structure of some note. The Brokaw Mansion by Rose and Stone,
1887, which stood at Fifth Avenue at Seventy-ninth Street,
is another historic structure which has been razed. It
has been replaced by Horace Ginstern's residential highrise.

163. "1832 Village Landmark Faces Demolition." February 18,
      1965, p. 35.

      The old Merchant's House, 29 East Fourth Street, was
occupied by the Seabury Tredwell family from 1835 to
1933, when Tredwell's last daughter died at ninety-two.
Thereafter, her nephew purchased the contents of the
house for conversion to a museum. The house is in jeopardy.

164. "US, State and City Aid Asked to Save Landmark on
      East Side." February 19, 1965, p. 18.

      A follow-up to the February 18 article (item 163) on
the old Merchant's House, in need of financial support.

165. "More on How to Kill a City." March 21, 1965, Section
      2, p. 17. Reprinted as "Abortive Cafes and Redundant
      Plazas." *Will They Ever Finish Bruckner Boulevard?*
      pp. 50-53.

      Zoning is a tool for profit; thus, the squared-off
General Motors Building by Edward D. Stone, between
Fifth and Madison Avenues and Fifty-eighth and Fifty-
ninth Streets, will have a redundant plaza within
Grand Army Plaza, off the great open space of Central
Park. "Not only does it provide extra space at the one
spot in New York where it is not needed, but it breaks
the building line where enclosure is desirable."

166. "Planning for the Nation's Cities." March 22, 1965, p.
      32.

      Is it possible to do anything about "the mess that is
man-made America"? A great deal of help is needed from
the executive and legislative branches of the federal
government.

167. "Complaints Grow on New House Office Building." March
      30, 1965, p. 32. Reprinted as "The Rayburn Building:
      A National Disaster." *Will They Ever Finish Bruckner*

Boulevard? pp. 156-59.

"Architecturally, the Rayburn Building is a national disaster"; financially, too, costing between $86 and $122 million. Only fifteen percent of the building will be used for offices and committee rooms. From many aspects, the building is questionable.

168. "Lively Original vs. [sic. Typographical error. Should be "U.S."] Dead Copy." May 9, 1965, Section 2, p. 19. Reprinted in *Will They Ever Finish Bruckner Boulevard?* pp. 210-12.

Bernard Maybeck's Palace of Fine Arts, San Francisco, 1916, is to be razed so that it can be rebuilt. This is the theme of an article on preservation, restoration, and reconstruction.

169. "Architecture: Trend-Setting Departures and Pinnacles of Excellence in US. The Modern Displays Changes since '00." May 18, 1965, p. 43.

Evaluates the seventy-one designs by thirty-eight architects, 1900-1965, in "Modern Architecture USA," an exhibition at the Museum of Modern Art.

170. "Victory by Default." May 23, 1965, Section 2, p. 18.

The fourth survey of modern architecture at the Museum of Modern Art is called "Modern Architecture, U.S.A." The earlier ones were in 1932, 1944, and 1953. This one surveys 1900 to 1965 at a period when modern design is no longer a crusade but an accepted idea.

171. "Planning for Beauty: White House Parley to Flex Muscles Over the Total American Environment." May 24, 1965, p. 28.

An array of notable delegates met at the White House Conference on Natural Beauty, concerned with the wrong uses of open space (scrap yards, mining, and other causes of blight).

172. "Drive for Natural Beauty. Johnson Begins to Implement Plans of a Scholarly White House Parley." May 27, 1965, p. 23.

President Johnson gave stimulus to his Conference on Natural Beauty by submitting four bills to the Congress on junkyards, billboards, and highway beautification. There is a summation of attitudes of the conferees.

173. "Fraunces Tavern Controversy." June 6, 1965, Section 2,
      p. 15.

      Richard Irwin Johannesen objected to Mrs. Huxtable's
      article "Lively Original vs. [sic. Typographical error.
      Should be "U.S."] Dead Copy" (item 168) concerning the
      "Fraunces Tavern Controversy" (item 933). Mrs. Huxtable
      replies, providing her side of the case, based on the
      fact that it is a twentieth-century fabrication.

174. "Architect Named for Ellis Island. Philip Johnson Is
      Chosen to Design 27.5 Acre Park." June 8, 1965, p.
      24.

      Philip Johnson has 27.5 acres of Ellis Island on which
      to design a National Immigration Museum and Park. All
      existing buildings except the main structure will be
      demolished.

175. "Architecture: Why Planners Get Gray." June 13, 1965,
      Section 2, p. 24.

      Zoning is meant to preserve a part of Murray Hill which
      includes the J.P. Morgan house, in a block between Thirty-
      seventh and Thirty-eighth Streets east of Madison Avenue.
      The house is surrounded by commercial developments, and
      application has been made for change of zoning which will
      lead to its destruction and the loss of its special urban
      character.

176. "New Departures in Design Are Honored by Architects.
      Top Honors Taken by Housing Ideas. Site Plans Scored
      in Larger Nonresidential Buildings." June 13, 1965,
      Section 8, p. 1.

      Creative and innovative designs won awards presented
      by the American Institute of Architects. The geographic
      span included housing in California, Texas, and Massa-
      chusetts. Some housing was constructed of factory-
      made modular components, while others were integrated
      into the landscape.

177. "Architects Challenged. They Seem Unwilling at Conven-
      tion, to Face Their Task in an Urban World." June 19,
      1965, p. 27.

      A report of the conference of the American Institute
      of Architects on the theme "Cities of the New World."

178. "Architecture: The Federal Image." June 27, 1965, Section
      2, p. 22.

      The Johnson Administration is "embracing progressive
      architectural standards and ideals." President Johnson
      backs his attitudes with speeches and action, as new
      buildings in Washington testify.

179. "Cities Are Target at Design Parley. Seminars Consider
      Problem of Urban Design." July 4, 1965, Section 1, p.
      36.

      The American Institute of Architects organized a con-
      ference on "Design and the City" at Harriman, New York.
      This report on the content of most speeches concludes
      that "the lesson hammered home by the architects and
      investors was the same in every case: good design pays
      off."

180. "A Code for 20th Century. Revised Building Rules Could
      Bring Beauty to New York--or New Abuses." July 9, 1965,
      p. 12.

      The new building code for New York City, although in-
      troduced with good intent, could end innovative design
      as seen since World War II. "Good buildings cannot be
      legislated."

181. "Grass at Riis Houses Giving Way to a Plaza. Open Space
      to Be Developed for Use by Tenants." July 14, 1965,
      p. 39.

      Landscaping and a mall are to replace the grass planted
      eighteen years ago at Riis housing, Avenue D to East River
      Drive, Sixth to Eighth Streets. Rather than keep people
      off the grass, people will be encouraged into the mall
      area.

182. "Noted Buildings in Path of Road. Cast Iron Structures
      on Broome St. Seem Slated for Expressway." July 22,
      1965, pp. 33, 62.

      Major New York cast-iron structures would be lost in
      the path of the proposed Lower Manhattan Expressway.

183. "Lindsay Surveys City from Copter. Views Problems in
      Company with Two Architects." July 24, 1965, p. 8.

      United States Representative John V. Lindsay's election
      campaign for mayor of New York City was based on the
      physical problems of urban design. He opposed such
      negative projects as the Lower Manhattan Expressway (see
      item 182).

184. "Staten Island's Beauty Losing to Builders." August 9,
     1965, pp. 1, 28.

     This article won the award of the Newspaper Women's
     Club of New York (see item 934). Speculative realtors
     moved in on Staten Island and made a killing once the
     Verrazano-Narrows Bridge was begun. There is no control,
     no master plan, but instead continuous sprawl.

185. "From a Candy Box, a Tardy and Unpleasant Surprise."
     August 22, 1965, Section 2, p. 17.

     Sixty days before construction is due to begin, the
     Pennsylvania Avenue Commission is questioning the "ap-
     palling" design of the $46.4 million Kennedy Center,
     Washington, D.C., "a glorified candy box by Edward Durell
     Stone."

186. "Architectural Giant. Le Corbusier's Plans Shaped Cities
     and He Was Always Ahead of Field." August 28, 1965,
     p. 18.

     Le Corbusier's obituary emphasizes the limited number
     of commissions which he received during his lifetime,
     relative to his widespread influence. His importance in
     relation to other notable figures of the modern movement
     is evaluated.

187. "Urban Renewal Threatens Historic Buildings in Salem,
     Mass. Foes Fear Plans Will Mar Old New England Heri-
     tage." October 13, 1965, pp. 49, 51.

     Salem's Redevelopment Authority is attempting to re-
     tain the tax base of its shopping area, but opponents
     say it will destroy Salem's historic heritage.

188. "For Those Who Are Growing Weary of Suburbia's Split-
     Level Vistas, Castellaras, France, Is Definitely 'In.'
     Art Houses Glow at $160,000. Each." October 30,
     1965, p. 37.

     Five free-form houses at Castellaras, France, are for
     sale. There will ultimately be fifty limited editions
     of this art form by architect Jacques Couelle.

189. "Old Town Blues." November 14, 1965, Section 2, p. 25.
     Reprinted in *Will They Ever Finish Bruckner Boulevard?*
     pp. 256-60.

     St. Paul de Vence, France, has no amenities, even
     though it is an historic monument. It should have some

physical activities to make it jell and bring in the
tourists. Such sarcasm! But the people do come because
"the hills around are full of big-name artists like Cha-
gall and Picasso."

190. "Restoration of St. Paul's Area Near Finish. Project
      in London Is Viewed as Failure to 'Think Big.'" Novem-
      ber 15, 1965, p. 3.

      New, dull, uninteresting architectural expression has
grown out of the war-damaged ruins of the St. Paul's area
in London. "The English reason and write with style and
grace even if they build less well."

191. "Western Europe Is Found to Lead U.S. in Community Plan-
      ning. Major Builders Are Impressed after a Tour."
      November 22, 1965, p. 39.

      Some of America's homebuilders went on a tour of Eng-
land, Germany, and Scandinavia. "The response was a
stunned mixture of admiration and skepticism." America
has attempted similar experiments, but they have not been
as successful in most respects as those across the Atlantic,
where new towns are either self-sufficient or satellites.
Each country's policies are explained.

192. "Scottish New Town: Pattern for Growth. Cumbernauld Has
      Its Mud and Blues But It Delights the Eye." November
      24, 1965, p. 18.

      Cumbernauld new town fits into the Scottish landscape
and is a culmination of twenty years of British town
planning. The town is pedestrian-oriented, well planned,
and well designed.

193. "Sweden Avoids US Suburban Sprawl by Close Control of
      Housing. Result Is High Rate of Building--and New Way
      of Life." November 28, 1965, Section 1, p. 148.

      Stockholm's satellite new towns are well planned and
well disposed in the landscape. Each town is a total
entity.

194. "Architecture: Tall Housing Rises in Europe. Skyscraper
      Complex Is Revolutionizing Way People Live." December
      2, 1965, p. 44.

      Emphasizes that the skyscraper is an American phenomenon
in invention and development, and that Europe, now getting
into the highrise syndrome, can learn about highrise building from the United States. Some European designers are

skillful but the results are usually gargantuan. An
article a few days later (item 196) says that America
can learn from Europe with regard to housing.

195.   "Fully Planned Town Opens in Virginia." December 5,
       1965, Section 1, pp. 1, 85.

       A totally planned community was being built, European
style, on 6,800 acres and at a cost of $30 million. The
first village center of Reston, the new town, has cluster
housing, shopping facilities, highrise buildings, and a
lake with a fountain. Gives details on housing costs
and the difficulties of overall financing, and on some
of the architects involved in the design.

196.   "America: Land of the Disposable Environment." December
       6, 1965, p. 36.

       Government action in Europe with relation to housing
and other allied problems is twenty years ahead of the
United States; thus, much can be learned from this information bank, which has gained experience from practical
application. Government know-how must work hand in hand
with the building industry.

197.   "Dutch Planning: Cities in a Box." December 12, 1965,
       Section 2, p. 20. Reprinted in *Will They Ever Finish
       Bruckner Boulevard?* pp. 137-40.

       Holland has built 1.3 million new dwellings since 1945,
but the housing shortage in 1965 was as great as in 1945.
Housing design is good, but the planning is regimented.
There is, however, some good planning.

198.   "Critics Attack Design of Antipollution Plant to Be Built
       in the Hudson Here." December 13, 1965, p. 50.

       This proposed pollution control plant was to have been
seven blocks long and project 500 feet into the Hudson
River. Some people feel that this development is against
the policy of riverfront planning and that the top of the
plant should at least be covered over by a park. Public
Works officials claim that other facilities, such as
those provided for recreational uses, involving people,
could interfere with the workings of the plant.

199. "A Landmark Is Saved. Historic Building Scheduled for
      Razing Is Rescued with Aid of City's New Law." Janu-
      ary 6, 1966, pp. 29, 53.

      Astor Library on Lafayette Street, New York, is to be
      purchased by the New York Shakespeare Festival. It could
      so easily have been demolished and lost (the fate of so
      many other notable landmarks), due to flaws in the pres-
      ervation law.

200. "The Environment and Economics." January 17, 1966, pp.
      65, 90.

      Emphasizes careful coordination of all aspects of plan-
      ning. For example, pollution affects good water supply,
      and deforestation curbs recreational areas. Europe,
      Britain, and America are compared in their handling of
      planning matters. Most developers would like to be left
      alone, but without government control, amenities and good
      planning are not provided.

201. "Landmarks at Work. Exhibit Suggests New Uses for Old
      Buildings Making Preservation Pay." January 17, 1966,
      p. 44.

      The Architectural League of New York mounted an exhibi-
      tion of New York landmarks. Some are discussed.

202. "Architecture: Sullivan's Powerful Inspired Legacy. 54
      Drawings Shown in Low Library." January 27, 1966, p.
      66.

      Columbia University exhibited 54 fragile drawings from
      a total of 122 given by Sullivan to Wright in 1924.
      Avery Library purchased them from Mrs. Wright.

203. "Building a Third-Class City." January 30, 1966, Section
      2, p. 24.

      "Budget-Banal to Modern Miscarriage" is the way in
      which Mrs. Huxtable describes the Chelsea area of New
      York City. President Kennedy and Governor Rockefeller
      achieved better architecture by directive, and this is
      what Mayor Lindsay must do.

204. "Program to Save Historic Sites Urged in Report to White
      House." January 30, 1966, Section 1, pp. 1, 68.

      Federal legislation, in addition to backup financial
      aid, was proposed for historic landmarks. Public opinion

helped, but many problems still remain, including the
clarification needed with relation to tax laws, etc.

205. "Experiment in Parks. Vest-Pocket Concept to Get First
      Test on Prime Land." February 2, 1966, pp. 37, 42.

      Vest pocket parks are new. Although expensive, they
      are a needed addition to the New York environment.

206. "Mies: Lessons from the Master." February 6, 1966, Sec-
      tion 2, pp. 24, 25. Reprinted in *Will They Ever Finish
      Bruckner Boulevard?* pp. 204-209.

      A general appreciation of the Master's works, with a
      list of some of his more recent designs, plus architec-
      ture by others who followed in his footsteps.

207. "New Era for Parks. Hoving and Young Appointees Hope to
      Scrap the Traditional and Try the New." February 10,
      1966, p. 50.

      Youthful reformers of Central Park are committed "to
      criticize but seldom serve." Now they are being em-
      ployed to serve by New York City Parks Commissioner
      Thomas P.F. Hoving. Innovative projects will result,
      and old ones will be evaluated.

208. "A House That Belongs to History." February 13, 1966,
      Magazine Section, pp. 64-65, 67, 69.

      Eliel Saarinen's house, Hvitträsk, near Helsinki, Fin-
      land, 1900-1901, an example of "national romanticism,"
      was sold after the Saarinens left for the United States
      in 1923, and the furniture was dispersed. It has now
      all been brought together again under a foundation of
      joint private and government auspices.

209. "Revamping of Architectural Education Being Pressed in
      Nation." February 20, 1966, p. 77.

      The need for drastic developments in architectural
      education is known, but exactly how it is to be done is
      not. Harvard's new program is described. Others are
      mentioned.

210. "Toward Excellence in Urban Redesign." February 21,
      1966, p. 38.

      Sophistication and control are the keys to solving the
      problem of making urban planning really work.

211. "The Uses of the Past. Design for Park Shrine on Ellis
      Island Utilizes Ruins to Evoke U.S. History." Febru-
      ary 25, 1966, p. 28.

      Nostalgia and monumentality are Philip Johnson's themes
      for the Ellis Island National Landmark Shrine.

212. "The Art of Architecture: The End of the Line?" Febru-
      ary 27, 1966, Section 2, p. 22. Reprinted as "The End
      of the Line." *Will They Ever Finish Bruckner Boulevard?*
      pp. 175-77.

      "Given the choice between hot modern and cold Colonial,
      one hardly blames Franklin National Bank for settling
      for ersatz nostalgia." By Eggers and Higgins at Howard
      Street and Broadway, this is one of many horrors mentioned.

213. "Eero Saarinen's Somber Skyscraper." March 13, 1966,
      Section 2, pp. 27, 28. Reprinted as "CBS: Eero Saar-
      inen's Somber Skyscraper." *Will They Ever Finish Bruck-
      ner Boulevard?* pp. 98-102.

      It is "classic ... a complete design in which technology,
      function and esthetics are conceived and executed integral-
      ly for its purpose ... the first of the city's landmarks
      to be executed in reinforced concrete and one of the first
      to use an exterior bearing wall.... No frills, no non-
      sense, no tricks ... one architectonic piece," but with
      standard corporate interiors by another designer.

214. "At Last, a Winner. Riis Plaza Is Breakthrough in the
      Use of Space, Certain to Have Wide Impact." May 24,
      1966, p. 50.

      Riis Plaza is a success. Grass has been replaced by
      sculpture, seating, water, planting, and diverse facil-
      ities, including a theater. Children are encouraged
      to walk through flower beds on stepping stones and to
      climb over walls--a new attitude in environmental design.

215. "Who's Afraid of the Big Bad Bldgs?" May 29, 1966, Sec-
      tion 2, pp. 13-14. Reprinted as "World Trade Center:
      Who's Afraid of the Big Bad Buildings?" *Will They
      Ever Finish Bruckner Boulevard?* pp. 27-32.

      There are good as well as bad points about the fifteen-
      acre site for the two twin, 110-story, 200-feet-square
      structures of Yamasaki's World Trade Center. They are
      not "muscling into an overcrowded neighborhood," but
      rather have "the planning logic of the location." Re-
      vitalization of the economic base of the area will be

improved, but at the cost of its numerous small businesses.
Esthetically, the gigantic scale incorporates "the world's
daintiest architecture for the world's biggest building."

216. "Breuer to Shape Roosevelt Shrine. Selection by Memorial
      Unit Ends 5 Years of Debate." June 9, 1966, p. 39.

Fifty-five architects were recommended by the American
Institute of Architects after the controversial compe-
tition-winning memorial was finally rejected. A commission chose Breuer, who actually liked the design of the
competition winner, but did not know exactly how he would
tackle the problem.

217. "Architecture: Fun and Games." June 19, 1966, Section
      2, p. 21.

New York is an urban loser, especially with Edward D.
Stone's new General Motors Building, Fifty-eighth to
Fifty-ninth Streets, Fifth to Madison Avenues. Ditto
for Kahn and Jacobs' Federal Office Building, Foley
Square, "the biggest checkerboard in the world." Other
examples are provided.

218. "City of Hope, Despair." June 26, 1966, Section 2, p.
      22.

Coordination in planning is the new theme for Lower
Manhattan in a plan developed by planners, architects,
and landscape designers. The World Trade Center, plus
new housing, in addition to pedestrian walk-ways and
other amenities, have been carefully considered.

219. "Capitol Project Stirs Architects. Parley Debates Resolu-
      tion on West Front Repair." June 28, 1966, p. 18.

Architects at the American Institute of Architects
convention in Denver argued against the desecration of
the west front of the United States Capitol. Other
convention activities are noted.

220. "Remodelling of National Capitol Divides Institute of
      Architects." July 1, 1966, p. 19.

The American Institute of Architects convention in
Denver resolved that a commission should be set up (consisting of architects, landscape architects, preserva-
tionists, sculptors, and laymen) to advise Congress
prior to any construction or alterations to buildings
of the national government. Arguments against the

resolution were based upon architectural etiquette of
non-interference with the work of one architect (or firm)
by another.

221. "A Vision of Rome Dies. Shorn of Its Proud Eagles, Last
      Facade of Penn Station Yielding to Modernity." July
      14, 1966, p. 37. Reprinted in *Will They Ever Finish
      Bruckner Boulevard?* pp. 212-16.

      "The passing of Penn Station was more than the end of
      a landmark. It made priority of real estate values over
      preservation conclusively clear." Comments on the his-
      tory, evolution, and destruction of Penn Station and on
      the men who perpetrated the acts of destruction.

222. "Credit to Originators. Successors Are Outshone by
      Olmsted and Vaux, Who Designed Central Park." July
      20, 1966, p. 43.

      It's hard to improve upon the original designs for
      Central Park, especially with a "dollshouse modern"
      kiosk.

223. "Functionalism Triumphs. Solid Granite Courthouse Van-
      ishing in Trend to Businesslike Buildings." July 22,
      1966, p. 33. Reprinted as "Hudson County Courthouse:
      Whatever Happened to the Majesty of the Law?" *Will
      They Ever Finish Bruckner Boulevard?* pp. 148-53.

      A move from an old building with all the luxurious
      materials of a bygone era to a new building lined with
      imitation materials is typical of the march of "prog-
      ress." The old and the new Hudson County Courthouse
      in New Jersey provide a case in point. (See supporting
      letter, item 940.)

224. "A Cultural Fable for Our Time." July 24, 1966, Section
      2, p. 18.

      "Villa Savoye: Destruction by Neglect" is the self-
      descriptive title of an exhibition at the Museum of Mod-
      ern Art. After damage to the building by Germans and
      Americans, the bankrupt Mme. Savoye farmed the land and
      used the house as a barn. It was proposed to replace
      it with a school but now it has been declared a *Monu-
      ment Historique.*

225. "Capitol Architect Under New Attack." July 27, 1966, p.
      1.

      J. George Stewart, Architect of the Capitol, is not an

architect but an engineer. He was responsible for the
east front extensions to the United States Capitol, the
proposed extension to the Library of Congress, and the
new building for the James Madison Memorial Library. The
story of Stewart vs. the American Institute of Architects
is told.

226. "Extending the Debate over Extending." August 1, 1966,
      p. 26.

      Capitol Hill is an entity unto itself, yet Congress-
men tend not to have the background for aesthetic de-
cision-making, and the engineer who is Architect of the
Capitol consults himself. "His love of the Capitol is
genuine, but misguided, and his talents are largely
political."

227. "Harsh and Handsome. The New Whitney Is Superbly Suited
      for an Art That Thrives On Isolation." September 8,
      1966, pp. 49, 57.

      Mrs. Huxtable's first impression of Breuer's design on
this tight site is that it is sculptured architecture
which incorporates a brutal dignity.

228. "Met as Architecture. New House, Although Technically
      Fine Muddles a Dramatic Design Concept." September
      17, 1966, p. 18. Reprinted as "The Met's Design
      Muddle." *Will They Ever Finish Bruckner Boulevard?*
      pp. 96-98.

      A design and a dream that evolved over forty years had
to be drastically changed because of expense. The clients
got good acoustics, a good plan, and glitter from Wallace
K. Harrison, but also "a sterile ... throwback rather than
creative twentieth century design."

229. "Adding Up the Score." September 25, 1966, Section 2,
      p. 29. Reprinted as "Lincoln Center: Adding Up the
      Score." *Will They Ever Finish Bruckner Boulevard?*
      pp. 24-27.

      Lincoln Center is agreeable, lush, and conservative,
but not a "dramatic contribution to the history of the
art of building," except perhaps the Juilliard School
and the Vivian Beaumont Theater. But is Lincoln Center
successful urban renewal? Or did it destroy too many
social and physical qualities of a neighborhood, replacing it with culture--for whom?

230. "A Worthwhile Addition. The Reception Wing of Gracie
      Mansion Viewed as Object Lesson in Excellence." Sep-
      tember 28, 1966, p. 49.

      How else would one add to an historic eighteenth-
      century residence, except with taste (plus antiques and
      good reproductions) at a cost of $800,000 of private
      donations?

231. "5 Top Architects Vie on Park Plan: To Compete on $5.7
      Million Police Station and Stable." October 1, 1966,
      Section 2, pp. 1, 27.

      The competition (though not the first project by any
      means) was for a Central Park police station, stables,
      and riding facilities, to cost $5.7 million.

232. "Art: The Whitney Museum Shows What It Can Do ... in the
      Right Building." October 2, 1966, Section 2, p. 23,
      25.

      "At the moment, the most disliked building in New York
      is undoubtedly the Whitney Museum" by Marcel Breuer; it
      is considered "brashly unconventional." It is a thought-
      ful, sensitive landmark.

233. "SOS to Washington: Save Our City!" October 3, 1966,
      p. 46.

      New York's renewal funds will be spent in the three
      worst ghettos of the city. It is "funds not rhetoric"
      that New York slums need from Congress.

234. "A New Leaf in the Parks." October 9, 1966, Section 2,
      pp. 27-28.

      "The Parks Department has not abandoned its policy of
      keeping buildings out of Central Park." The police sta-
      tion has always been there and five outstanding archi-
      tectural firms will compete, to ensure that the new
      police facility will not intrude. Past intrusions are
      discussed.

235. "Work Is Starting on Brooklyn Bridge Southwest, a Total
      Renewal. Project, Planned 10 Years, Has Been Called
      Unsound." October 21, 1966, pp. 43, 81.

      Bulldoze and build was the city's solution to planning
      in the mid-1950s, and the Brooklyn Bridge area is just real-
      izing the fruits of that policy--destruction of New York's
      architectural heritage. Lists details of the demolished

structures and the new housing and college facilities which replace them.

236. "Outdoor Living with Underground Art." October 30, 1966, Section 2, pp. 27, 29.

    After briefly mentioning Philip Johnson's earlier structures at his New Canaan spread, discusses his underground art gallery and the paintings stored there.

237. "Expansion at Columbia. A Restricted Vision and Bureaucracy Seen as Obstacle to Its Development." November 5, 1966, pp. 33-34.

    Columbia University is expanding to the extent of fourteen new buildings at a cost of $200 million but development into the Morningside neighborhood is a dangerous policy. Town and gown relationships are explained.

238. "New Bedford Waterfront a Model Renewal Project. U.S. Invests $83,050 in Trial Plan for Old Whaling City." November 21, 1966, pp. 47, 50.

    About two percent of a total federal fund of $4.5 billion will be spent at New Bedford, Massachusetts, for redevelopment, historic renewal, and economic improvement.

239. "Of Symbolism and Flying Saucers." December 4, 1966, Section 2, pp. 37, 40. Reprinted in *Will They Ever Finish Bruckner Boulevard?* pp. 195-98.

    St. John the Divine was designed as a medieval cathedral in 1891, when the skyscraper age was being ushered in. The style was changed from Romanesque to Gothic, but the New York building still remains incomplete. "What all this leads up to is the simple fact that it doesn't really matter how the cathedral is finished now." (Since the article was written, it was first decided not to complete the cathedral, as other needs in the community were more pressing. Now the latest decision is to complete it as originally planned, training neighborhood youths in the necessary crafts.)

240. "Landmark Plans Stir Wall St. Controversy. City Requested to Aid One of Projects." December 17, 1966, pp. 35, 66.

    Preservation is so expensive that the Landmarks Preservation Commission is having to choose between two historic areas of Lower Manhattan--South Street and the Fraunces

Tavern block. The former involves preservation of existing structures while the latter involves demolition of
existing buildings and infill of old buildings moved from
other sites.

241. "A Planning Happening." December 18, 1966, Section 2,
     pp. 35, 37.

     A planned mall between Lincoln Center and Central Park
     is a poor idea from any standpoint.

242. "Creative Plan for River. An Architect and a Builder
     Find Key: Gain Sponsorship at the Top for Project."
     December 21, 1966, p. 28.

     Proposals have been introduced by Davis, Brody and
     Associates for Waterside, a highrise housing develop-
     ment, with recreational facilities, on the East River.
     This is not the usual sterile housing project with
     added gimmicks, but a well-designed and integrated
     piece of comprehensive development with cooperation
     between architect and builder.

                                1967

243. "If at First You Don't Succeed." January 1, 1967, Sec-
     tion 2, p. 19.

     After the revision and the rejection of the F.D.R.
     Memorial competition entry, Breuer has come up with a $4
     million design. It is described and illustrated. "The
     Roosevelt Commission can either build this one or forget
     it, for it is unlikely that a more appropriate version
     will come along."

244. "The Esthetic Mystique. For the Businessmen, Instant
     Status: And Art, of Course, Is Beside the Point."
     January 14, 1967, pp. 35, 39.

     Subtitles provide suggestions of what the article is
     about: "For the businessman, instant status; and art,
     of course, is beside the point. Continues as "Art and
     business: an examination."

245. "A Man for All Styles." January 22, 1967, Section 2,
     pp. 25-26.

     The Metropolitan Museum of Art exhibited drawings by
     A.J. Davis (1803-92). Some of his architecture survives.
     General discussion.

246. "Planning the New City. Modern Museum Exhibits Projects
     That Link Esthetics and Sociology." January 24, 1967,
     pp. 39, 45.

     "The New City: Architecture and Urban Renewal," an
     exhibition at the Museum of Modern Art, consists of four
     projects by university students. They suggest new ways
     for the city and include costs.

247. "City Is Building 12 Movable Playgrounds." Designs Allow
     for Freedom in Shaping." January 28, 1967, p. 29.

     Federal funds amounting to more than $400,000 are being
     spent on prototypes for design developments in playgrounds.
     These play-area facilities are demountable for re-use
     elsewhere.

248. "How Success Spoiled SMTI." February 12, 1967, Section
     2, pp. 17, 19.

     Southern Massachusetts Technological Institute, at
     North Dartmouth, was established in 1960 with a budget
     of $65 million for ten buildings. With Paul Rudolph as
     consultant to Desmond and Lord, the plan evolved as
     "strikingly logical, coherent and expandable," but it
     was expensive and Rudolph was dismissed.

249. "Home Design Drab in US, Study Says. A Federal Report
     Deplores Mediocrity in Planning." February 13, 1967,
     pp. 1, 40.

     A 223-page report, *Design of the Housing Site, a Cri-
     tique of American Practice*, published by the Department
     of Housing and Urban Development, reiterates the low
     calibre of housing design in the United States. The
     report does not dwell upon what's wrong, but makes spe-
     cific suggestions of ways to improve design.

250. "Horses Anyone." February 19, 1967, Section 2, pp. 21,
     23.

     Kelly and Gruzen are to design a police station and
     stables in Central Park. "The park must be preserved
     and at the same time it must be made to function in to-
     day's public terms." But twenty-two acres for a police
     station?

251. "Latin Victorian." February 19, 1967, *The New York Times
     Book Review*, p. 6.

     Review of Carroll L.V. Meeks, *Italian Architecture,*

1750-1914 (New Haven: Yale University Press, 1967). What
the enlightened think of as Renaissance Italy is, in some
cases, nineteenth-century revival architecture, and this
heavy volume is a scholarly analysis of that era's architectural contribution.

252. "*Iconography of Manhattan*, Being Reissued Soon." March
      3, 1967, p. 37.

      I.N. Phelps Stokes' 5,000-page, six-volume iconography,
      covering 1498 through 1909, originally published from
      1915 to 1928, is being reissued at $795. Facsimile
      publishing, as a whole, is briefly touched upon and so
      too is the life of Stokes. See also item 263.

253. "How to Build a City, If You Can." March 12, 1967,
      Section 2, p. 31.

      "The American city has been reviled and rejected by
      American intellectuals." The linear city as an idea
      goes back to 1910 and has practical application. This
      article concerns the air rights over the Cross Brooklyn
      Expressway, and a proposal by McMillan, Griffis and
      Mileto.

254. "Up in Central Park." March 19, 1967, Section 2, pp.
      27, 29. Reprinted in *Will They Ever Finish Bruckner
      Boulevard?* pp. 53-56.

      "Public good-- ... what crimes against the park have
      been committed in thy name!" Fourteen acres of Metro-
      politan Museum, plus the formalism around the obelisk,
      an outdoor theater, etc. etc. provide "pastoral sabotage,
      or parkicide."

255. "Monumental Questions." March 26, 1967, Section 2, pp.
      23-24. Reprinted in *Will They Ever Finish Bruckner
      Boulevard?* pp. 188-91.

      "Monuments, Tombstones and Trophies," an exhibition
      held at the Museum of Contemporary Arts, New York, did
      not give any reassurance that monumental architecture
      is any better than the blandness of other architectural
      attitudes.

256. "Downtown New York Begins to Undergo Radical Transforma-
      tion. Battery to Get Superblocks and Towers." March
      27, 1967, pp. 35, 37.

      Nine skyscrapers on five blocks will change the physical

appearance of the Battery area of Lower Manhattan before 1969. It is successful economically, but a disaster to those who support preservationist attitudes toward the environment. Each new structure is described and its architects listed.

257. "It's Only a Paper World." April 9, 1967, Section 2, pp. 25, 27.

"Festival Designs by Inigo Jones" is the title of an exhibition at the National Gallery, Washington, D.C. The drawings date from 1604 to 1640 and include all aspects of the theater.

258. "Down Town Blues." April 16, 1967, Section 2, pp. 29–30. Reprinted as *Will They Ever Finish Bruckner Boulevard?* pp. 56–60.

"New York is the only major city in the country that has been planned exclusively for profit and built to that pattern by its businessmen with the city easing the way." Numerous examples of "official urban mutilation" are given.

259. "A Fair with Flair. Expo 67 Shows How to Provide Variety Within a Controlled Plan." April 28, 1967, p. 18.

Coordinated planning for Expo '67 at Montreal does not mean uniformity. Far from it. Pavilions vary in scale and form, some good and others not so good.

260. "Habitat: Exciting Concept, Flawed Execution. Landmark at Expo Breaks All Rules of Construction." April 30, 1967, Section 1, p. 46.

Moshe Safdie's expensive, controversial Habitat at Montreal is as varied as a north Italian hill town, although of prefabricated box modules. It is costly, even though the excuse for standardization is that economy will result from repetition of the parts. It has problems.

261. "The Expressway Debate: Progress or Destruction? Projects in Baltimore and New Orleans Stir Controversy." May 1, 1967, p. 40.

Whether Colonial or futuristic in design, the scale of expressways, bridges, and other elements in highway construction are evoking considerable public criticism. Baltimore and New Orleans are major battlegrounds in the controversy.

262. "Fair, Fairer, Fairest." May 7, 1967, Section 2, pp.
      25, 27.

      At the Montreal Expo '67, where the United States
      Pavilion consists of a geodesic dome, "everything goes
      with it," since many exhibits are experimental. Many
      pavilions are mentioned.

263. "The New York That Was." May 14, 1967, *The New York
      Times Book Review*, pp. 7, 40.

      Another review (see item 252) of I.N. Phelps Stokes'
      Iconography of Manhattan Island, emphasizing its value
      as a research source.

264. "Soviet Architectural Gem. Resort Being Built on Black
      Sea Hailed as Revelation of New Design Standards."
      June 17, 1967, p. 12.

      Pitsunda, on the Black Sea, is a showplace of archi-
      tecture in the U.S.S.R. Built and controlled by trade
      unions, it is a people's resort. The architecture is
      of a refreshing design compared to Stalinist wedding
      cake projects. Industrial standardization is typical
      of Soviet construction today.

265. "118-Year-Old Holly Bush Takes It All Like a Proper
      Victorian." June 26, 1967, p. 18.

      Alexander Jackson Davis and Andrew Jackson Downing
      designed Holly Bush, New Jersey, 1849, as a Tuscan
      villa. "In the 118 years ... from stylish new status
      symbol of a prosperous glass manufacturer to sedate
      home for a college president."

266. "When Life Is Stranger Than Art." July 30, 1967, Section
      2, pp. 25-26.

      Architects are divided between the visionaries and the
      pragmatists. "Architectural Fantasies," a show at the
      Museum of Modern Art, illustrates the abstractions.

267. "Flushing Meadows Park Plan Delayed by Auditing." August
      12, 1967, pp. 27, 53.

      The New York City Auditing Department objected to the
      employment of designers from out of state and to profes-
      sionals practicing outside their fields of expertise.
      Landscape schemes were being projected by architects who
      were commissioned without the necessary permission from

the Controller's Office. This caused delays—and not
only in the payment of fees. The calibre of world-famous
designers was ignored because protocol was flouted.

268. "Full Speed Backward." September 24, 1967, Section 2,
      p. 21. Reprinted as "The Madison Memorial Library:
      Full Speed Backwards." *Will They Ever Finish Bruckner
      Boulevard?* pp. 160-64.

      "The new, $75 million Madison Memorial Library for
      Capitol Hill in Washington is to be another mammoth
      mock-classical cookie." Approval for the scheme was
      granted by committees of politicians and not by profes-
      sionals in the design field. Unfortunately, the Archi-
      tect of the Capitol, who supervises all buildings on
      Capitol Hill, was in 1967 (and still is) a political
      appointee, who in turn chooses his own men.

269. "A Crucial Test for American Town Planning." September
      25, 1967, p. 44.

      Reston, Virginia, "changed from one man's dream to a
      corporate subsidiary" overnight, when Gulf Oil came to
      the rescue of Robert E. Simon. Success or failure will
      depend upon how much Gulf's Director of Development inter-
      feres with Simon's initial, highly original concept.
      (We now know how negative and destructive Gulf's intent
      was.)

270. "Metropolitan Museum to Expand in Park and Revamp Col-
      lections." September 29, 1967, pp. 1, 23.

      Gives details of the Roche and Dinkeloo development.

271. "Architecture: Full Speed Forward." October 1, 1967,
      Section 2, p. 19. Reprinted as "Washington Tax Court:
      Full Speed Forward." *Will They Ever Finish Bruckner
      Boulevard?* pp. 164-67.

      Compared to other recent buildings for Washington, this
      design by Victor Lundy was "a progressive, sensitive,
      contemporary solution ... in an obvious and extremely
      handsome organization of the building's working parts."

272. "Faith, Hope and Muscle. City Proposes to Save Theater
      District from Perils of Commercial Blandness." October
      2, 1967, p. 37.

      The New York City Planning Commission provided advan-
      tageous zoning and building regulations to encourage

realtors to incorporate theaters in new structures,
replacing those demolished in the name of progress.
Other permits, variances, adjustments, usually given
for little in return, are now being used advantageously.

273. "Cities Getting Full Hearing in Capital." October 3,
      1967, p. 30.

      A Washington, D.C., conference of 2,400 city planners
      had as its theme "the future environment and democracy."
      Their program is described.

274. "Hope for the Poor Urged by Rustin. He Tells Planners
      the Nation Has Encouraged Riots." October 6, 1967, p.
      35.

      At a conference of the nation's planners, Bayard Rustin
      urged advocacy planning. The underclassed must have hope,
      and minorities must have a voice. Equal opportunity must
      exist for all Americans.

275. "Freeman Asks Alternative to Big City." October 7, 1967,
      p. 23.

      Orville Freeman advocates "the town-country community"
      which is being tried in twenty-six states. He says,
      "There must be a viable alternative to the big city."

276. "Planning for Cities in Chaos." October 16, 1967, p. 44.

      "To put it bluntly, the traditional practice of plan-
      ning has failed" and the profession is going through a
      reappraisal. Advocacy planning in an interdisciplinary
      path is the new attitude toward more positive results.
      The Architects Renewal Council of Harlem is part of the
      effort of advocacy planners, even though black planners,
      who can surely forward such ideals, are in short supply.

277. "Soviet Architecture Assumes a New Look." October 19,
      1967, pp. 1, 26.

      The visitor in Moscow during the Spring of the fiftieth
      anniversary of the Russian Revolution seems to have been
      elated by climate and nature, and by consumer products!
      Preservation is being forwarded, new housing is being
      mass produced at minimum cost and labor and is not of the
      wedding cake variety of a few years back. But materials,
      mechanical services, and city planning are generally poor.
      Housing has always been in short supply but attempts to
      alleviate the problem are good, at least as supported by
      statistics.

278.   "Soviet Has Mastered the Industrialized Technology of
       Low Cost Mass Building." October 20, 1967, p. 26.

       A continuation of the previous day's article. The
       emphasis is on the mastering and adapting of twentieth-
       century technology to Russia's building needs. Space
       is still in short supply, especially in residential
       apartment buildings, but costs are low and the quality
       of external finishes is improving. New developments in
       Moscow and elsewhere are less monotonous and more adventur-
       ous, due in part to improvements in the architectural
       profession.

279.   "New World, Old Dreams." October 29, 1967, Section 2,
       pp. 33, 35.

       Konstantin Melnikov, a revolutionary architect in the
       post-Revolutionary U.S.S.R., built several structures in
       Moscow. He is still alive at eighty years old. Mrs.
       Huxtable visits him in a Moscow hospital.

280.   "The Theater: 'Hair,' a Love-Rock Musical, Inaugurates
       Shakespeare Festival's Anspacher Playhouse--Structure
       Is the First Saved as Landmark." October 30, 1967, p.
       55. Reprinted as "Anatomy of a Success" in *Will They
       Ever Finish Bruckner Boulevard?* pp. 237-40.

       Scheduled for demolition in 1965, the old Astor Library
       on Lafayette Street was purchased in 1966 by the New York
       Shakespeare Festival, and preserved and renovated for
       them by the architect Giorgio Cavaglieri. A success story.

281.   "Ford Flies High." November 26, 1967, Section 2, pp. 23,
       25. Reprinted as "The Ford Foundation Flies High" in
       Will They Ever Finish Bruckner Boulevard? pp. 86-91.

       This huge greenhouse and office building by Roche and
       Dinkeloo was constructed on a lot measuring 200 feet
       square. "It is a horticultural spectacular and probably
       one of the most romantic environments ever devised....
       It is also an architectural spectacular." As opposed to
       the usual trend of providing a plaza with a building, this
       design situates the plaza within the building, but links
       it visually to an adjoining small park. It is "one of
       the foundation's more valid contributions to the arts."

282.   "Architecture: Felt Forum. New House Is Sensible and
       Quietly Attractive." November 27, 1967, p. 62.

       The Felt Forum at New York's $125 million Madison Square

Garden can accommodate a maximum of 5,200 spectators,
viewing "popular pleasures.... The question is whether
high art really belongs with mass art," as in the case
of "48 continuously automated bowling lanes."

283. "Old Jeff's Conversion. Preservation of 'Village' Court-
      house Marks Triumph of Will over Reality." November
      28, 1967, pp. 49, 94.

New York's Ruskinian fourteenth-century-revival Venetian palazzo, as seen in the 1876 Jefferson Market Courthouse, has been converted into a branch library. The
impetus came from professionals and local lay-people.
Architect Giorgio Cavaglieri has sympathetically added
lighting and other such elements. This is preservation
at its best, since it suitably adapts an old structure
to a new use.

284. "King of Checkerboards. Towering New Blockbuster Is
      Impossible to Miss in Matter-of-fact Sort of Way."
      December 9, 1967, pp. 49, 64. Reprinted as "The Fed-
      eral Government Lays a Colossal Architectural Egg" in
      Will They Ever Finish Bruckner Boulevard? pp. 105-107.

The Civic Center Area, New York, has been destroyed by
a soulless new federal building--"the biggest checkerboard in the world.... It is a suspended structure, or
is it? ... the Federal government has laid a colossal
egg ... the most monumentally mediocre Federal building
in history." At present, a forty-one-story concrete
wall faces Broadway, at least until this huge building
doubles in size and provides the checkerboard effect on
all sides. Eggers and Higgins, architects.

285. "The Imperial: Going, Going, Gone." December 10, 1967,
      Section 2, p. 40.

"The world has deemed the Imperial Hotel," Tokyo, by
Frank Lloyd Wright, "a disposable treasure." The hotel
is discussed especially with reference to the 1923 earth-
quake, which failed to destroy it.

286. "Housing: The Death Wish City." December 31, 1967,
      Section 2, p. 18. Reprinted as "The Dilemma of Housing"
      in *Will They Ever Finish Bruckner Boulevard?* pp. 72-73.

Waterside, a superior plan for the East River, Twenty-
fifth to Thirtieth Streets, is to be built by Davis, Brody
and Associates, but it is all a very slow process.

1968

287. "Chamber Finally Admits Public to Its Great Hall." January 6, 1968, p. 31.

 James Barnes Barker was architect of the New York Chamber of Commerce at 65 Liberty Street. Its great hall, 90x60 feet and three stories in height, has its walls covered by paintings of famous New York businessmen by well-known American painters. The Beaux Arts building has been listed as a New York landmark.

288. "World of the Absurd." January 14, 1968, Section 2, p. 25. Reprinted as "The World of the Absurd." *Will They Ever Finish Bruckner Boulevard?* pp. 7-11.

 At a period when the United States was reaching to the moon, cities were in upheaval with ghetto districts, the growing scale of the metropolis, loss of a sense of place, and numerous published studies on how to solve the problem. "We are obviously in the world of the absurd.... The failure of the environment is our theme."

289. "Pentagon: A Cosy Fortress." January 16, 1968, p. 41.

 This thirty-four-acre office complex, the largest in the world, seems to function well in 1968, although it was highly criticized when built in 1943 at a cost of $83 million. The article includes many statistics.

290. "Architecture: Elegance Returns at a Bargain Price." January 26, 1968, p. 26.

 Powell Hall, St. Louis, built by Rapp and Rapp during the "silver screen era" of 1925, has been converted into a concert hall for the St. Louis Symphony. The purchase price was $338,475 and the conversion cost $2 million, approximately twenty-five percent the cost of a new hall. It is an excellent example of the re-use of an old building. Pittsburgh take note.

291. "A Matter of Urban Delight." January 28, 1968, Section 2, pp. 31, 33.

 The good news and the bad news of recent achievements and demolitions in New York City.

292. "St. Louis: Success." February 4, 1968, Section 2, pp. 33, 35. Reprinted as "St. Louis, Mo.: Success and Blues." *Will They Ever Finish Bruckner Boulevard?* pp.

117-21.

St. Louis is discussed in general terms, from the demolition of its cast-iron waterfront area to the raising of the Jefferson Memorial Arch and the Busch Stadium in the downtown area. Acres of downtown parking and open space produce a negative effect on the city.

293. "Hard Questions for Harlem." February 11, 1968, Section
      2, p. 24.

Governor Nelson Rockefeller announced plans in early February for a State Office Building at 125th Street in Harlem. This and other buildings in Harlem "are meant to be anchors for a revitalized community. But too many anchors can sink a ship."

294. "New York City's Growing Architectural Poverty." February 12, 1968, p. 38. Reprinted as "Death by Development" in *Will They Ever Finish Bruckner Boulevard?* pp. 12-14.

Highrise developments in place of town houses can be the death knell to the inherent qualities of the city. The Brokaw Mansion on Fifth Avenue at Seventy-ninth Street was, for example, a part of an urban unified streetscape that has now been destroyed by highrise developments. Developers are not urbanists. New York is learning a little too late that a city can be killed by profitable real estate developments. Groups of small residential buildings are being replaced by huge skyscrapers.

295. "Slab City Marches On." March 3, 1968, Section 2, p.
      22.

"Chaos solidified" is how Mrs. Huxtable describes the second Regional Plan for the Central Business District of Manhattan, exhibited at the Architectural League. It is discussed with reference to specific buildings.

296. "Saratoga: Losing Race." March 10, 1968, Section 2, p.
      10. Reprinted as "Saratoga, N.Y.: Losing Race." *Will
      They Ever Finish Bruckner Boulevard?* pp. 121-24.

Saratoga, a resort spa of historic architectural importance, is slowly being lost. Rather than accept an old hotel within the confines of the Saratoga park, Holiday Inns, with its atrocious signs, has built outside of the park. The discussion then leads on to the theme of good and bad graphics (with examples).

297. "Anatomy of a Failure." March 17, 1968, Section 2, p.
     35. Reprinted in *Will They Ever Finish Bruckner Boule-*
     vard? pp. 232-36.

     Satirically observes that art has value, but architec-
ture has not: The only value is in the land on which
the architecture stands. This is demonstrated by Wright's
Imperial Hotel, Tokyo, where not a single element was saved
for posterity. (A small part of it was subsequently re-
erected in a park-museum of nineteenth- and twentieth-
century architecture in Japan.)

298. "How Not to Build a Symbol." March 24, 1968, Section 2,
     p. 23. Reprinted as "Columbia Gym: How Not to Build a
     Symbol." *Will They Ever Finish Bruckner Boulevard?*
     pp. 32-36.

     Two acres of Morningside Park, adjacent to Columbia
University, were to have been the site of a Columbia
gymnasium, designed by Eggers and Higgins, with separate
facilities for the neighboring community. Was the university getting valuable parkland at a nominal sum? Was
it offering good and costly facilities to Harlem? The
projected design would have been massive. Columbia's
intentions were good, but its understanding of neighborly
relationships was almost nonexistent.

299. "Will Slab City Take Over Times Square?" March 25, 1968,
     p. 40.

     However brash Times Square is, it has a "sense of place"
which is slowly being lost due to overdevelopment; the
old is being replaced by the new standardization.

300. "Sometimes We Do It Right." March 31, 1968, Section 2,
     p. 33. Reprinted in *Will They Ever Finish Bruckner*
     Boulevard? pp. 14-18.

     There is a lot wrong with New York City, but also a
great deal that is good, including Isamu Noguchi's cube
sculpture at 130 Broadway, the surrounding buildings, and
the spaces created by the juxtaposition of old and new
structures--many of the latter by Skidmore, Owings and
Merrill. Their skyscraper walls are "reduced to gossamer
minimums of shining, thin material hung on a frame of
extraordinary strength through superb contemporary technology."

301. "Hemisfair, Opening Tomorrow, Isn't Texas-Size, But It's
     Fun." April 5, 1968, pp. 49-50.

     "This is the first World's Fair held in the Southwest

[at San Antonio], the first to be located in the heart
of a city ... and the first to save and incorporate a
group of landmark buildings for use in the fair." All
aspects of the fair are reviewed.

302. "Where Ghosts Can Be at Home." April 7, 1968, Section
      2, p. 25. Reprinted in *Will They Ever Finish Bruckner
      Boulevard?* pp. 216-21.

      A Landmarks Preservation Commission was established in
      New York City in 1965. Much has been lost in the city,
      but much remains that must be preserved.

303. "Remember the Alamo." April 14, 1968, Section 2, p. 31.

      After condemning the "colored skies" of Braniff Air-
      lines, Mrs. Huxtable discusses the "pretty colorful"
      HemisFair at San Antonio, Texas, a convention center
      with a Southwestern flavor for international parties.
      Facts, figures, and descriptions are provided.

304. "Model Cities Construction to Start Here by Fall." April
      19, 1968, p. 49.

      Bedford-Stuyvesant, an area in Brooklyn, is to have
      "2,300 units of public housing on 54 vest-pocket sites."

305. "Buildings That Stretch the Mind." April 21, 1968, Sec-
      tion 2, p. 32. Reprinted as "Romantic Classicism:
      Buildings That Stretch the Mind." *Will They Ever
      Finish Bruckner Boulevard?* pp. 252-56.

      "Visionary Architects" was an exhibition of 148 draw-
      ings and prints of late-eighteenth-century French Roman-
      tic Classicists, circulated under the auspices of the
      Art Department of the University of St. Thomas in Houston,
      Texas. The projects of these visionaries were huge,
      simple, "orchestrating nature," totalitarian, sublime,
      eerie, funerary, and defying economics.

306. "The Miesian Lesson." April 28, 1968, Section 2, p. 34.
      Reprinted in *Will They Ever Finish Bruckner Boulevard?*
      pp. 204-209.

      The Art Institute of Chicago exhibited the work of Mies
      van der Rohe, but Chicago in itself is also an exhibition
      of the works of Mies and his followers.

307. "Architecture: Tribute to a Landmark's Survival." May
      4, 1968, pp. 41, 44. Reprinted as "Coming of Architec-
      tural Age." *Will They Ever Finish Bruckner Boulevard?*

pp. 240-44.

The Patent Office, Washington, D.C., begun by Robert Mills in 1836 and continued by others, was threatened with demolition. It has been preserved as the Smithsonian Institution National Collection of Fine Arts and the National Portrait Gallery. It is a good conversion and a part of America's "coming of age."

308. "In This Corner, New York City." May 5, 1968, Section 2, p. 32.

Avenue of the Americas from Forty-seventh to Fiftieth Streets is due for three glass boxes, fifty stories high, a $160 million extension to Rockefeller Center. There are alternatives to this banality. An alternative solution has been proposed by the Urban Design Group of the Department of City Planning.

309. "Nobody Here But Us New Yorkers." May 19, 1968, Section 2, p. 34.

Lawrence Halprin has prepared a report called "New York, New York" for the Housing and Development Administration. He has analyzed six major projects which are in the works, and has come to the conclusion that "there is a sense of disorientation in these projects."

310. "Albany's Threat to New York's Planning." May 20, 1968, p. 46.

"The Governor's Urban Development Corporation for the rebuilding of city slums" has unlimited potential. "But that potential is overshadowed by the dread of an authoritarian state paternalism with arrogant powers and no guarantee of the requisite sensitivity to local needs." Some results are positive, but the governor likes "the kind of impersonal, grand scale, formal concepts popular forty years ago."

311. "Strike at Columbia Architecture School Traced to Anger over Exclusion from Planning." May 20, 1968, p. 70.

Columbia planned to build a gymnasium in adjoining Morningside Park. This proposal, plus the University's arbitrary attitude toward its expansion and development, sparked off a strike by mature (mainly graduate-level) students of architecture.

312. "The Architecture of Destruction." May 26, 1968, Section
      2, p. 40. Reprinted as "The Art of Expediency." *Will*
      They Ever Finish Bruckner Boulevard? pp. 143-47.

      New York's Pennsylvania Station has been pulverized and
      has been replaced by "chill, bleak anonymity of twentieth
      century transit catacombs. Some misguided people want to
      recreate the past, but why do that when the past, in its
      original form, is preservable."

313. "Culture Is as Culture Does." June 2, 1968, Section 2,
      p. 25. Reprinted in *Will They Ever Finish Bruckner*
      Boulevard? pp. 228-32 (wrongly dated there as June 21,
      1968).

      Many modern culture centers are being built throughout
      the country, sometimes in place of old centers which in-
      variably have many positive features, including good
      acoustics. The Chicago Auditorium is a case in point.

314. "Architecture: Grotesquerie Astride a Palace." June 20,
      1968, p. 37. Reprinted as "Grand Central Tower Gro-
      tesquerie." *Will They Ever Finish Bruckner Boulevard?*
      pp. 82-86.

      "Give a grotesquerie to a good architect and you are
      going to get a better grotesquerie, like a better mouse-
      trap. Mr. Breuer has done an excellent job with a dubious
      undertaking"--a second Grand Central Tower, 221 feet away
      from the Pan Am Building and 150 feet higher, astride the
      station's concourse. The project would be expensive and,
      according to Mr. Breuer, a romantic whim. He would pre-
      fer demolition of the concourse area of the station.

315. "Everybody Back into the Old Rut." June 23, 1968, Section
      2, p. 28. Reprinted as "The Federal Image: Everybody
      Back into the Old Rut." *Will They Ever Finish Bruckner*
      Boulevard? pp. 153-56.

      President Kennedy made a serious attempt to improve
      the design of government buildings and projects. After
      his assassination his ideals in quality architecture
      were shelved. Good designers have been employed, but
      the general run of federal buildings fit into a pattern
      of the cost-per-square-foot principle.

316. "Grand Central. Its Heart Belongs to Dada." June 23,
      1968, Section 4, p. 10.

      Problems and solutions relating to Breuer's $100 million

design for a fifty-five-story building above Grand Central's south mezzanine concourse.

317. "It Can Happen Here." June 30, 1968, Section 2, p. 18.
      Reprinted as "Riverbend Houses; It Can Happen Here."
      Will They Ever Finish Bruckner Boulevard? pp. 73-77.

      Good housing at reasonable costs and rents can be real-
      ized in New York City under the Mitchell-Lama Law, espec-
      ially when good architects and builders collaborate with
      the sponsoring city agency. Planning arrangement, space,
      texture, materials, color, landscaping, and supergraphics
      make the project, by Davis, Brody and Associates, look
      better than speculative housing and render it unrecog-
      nizable as subsidized residential architecture.

318. "Architecture by Entrapment." July 7, 1968, Section 2,
      p. 18.

      Edward Durell Stone has designed the new General Post
      Office, New York City, a $100 million structure "just as
      big as the Pan Am building laid on end." This is another
      of Stone's candy box designs.

319. "Where Did We Go Wrong?" July 14, 1968, Section 2, p. 24.
      Reprinted in *Will They Ever Finish Bruckner Boulevard?*
      pp. 221-24.

      Mrs. Huxtable parodies Lewis Carroll's *Through the Look-
      ing Glass* in making a point concerning the reconstruction,
      in Baltimore, of Babe Ruth's birthplace. "The purpose of
      preservation is not to re-create the past, a laughable
      impossibility filled with booby traps.... What preservation
      is really all about is the retention and active relation-
      ship of the buildings of the past to the community's func-
      tioning present."

320. "This Time Everyone Wins." July 21, 1968, Section 2, p.
      29. Reprinted in *Will They Ever Finish Bruckner Boule-
      vard?* pp. 224-28.

      The New York Bar Association purchased three 1830s houses,
      numbered 2, 3, and 4 Elk Street in Albany, New York, with
      the idea of demolition and the construction of a modern
      headquarters building on the site. The Albany Historic
      Sites Commission objected, as did numerous other public-
      minded bodies. Architect James Polshek retained the old
      houses and introduced a new structure at their rear. Credit
      should go to the Bar Association for spending more to pre-
      serve and add, rather than taking the cheaper way of total
      destruction.

321. "The American Image Abroad."   July 28, 1968, Section 2,
      pp. 21-22.

      The United States Congress reduced the amount of money
      to be spent on the American pavilion for the 1970 fair at
      Osaka, Japan, from $16 million to $10 million.   Davis,
      Brody and Associates are having to change their original
      design, which consisted of clusters and bubbles.

322. "Washington's National Gallery Engages Pei for New Build-
      ing."   July 30, 1968, p. 31.

      An announcement with all the facts.

323. "That Silly Time of Year."   August 4, 1968, Section 2,
      p. 20.

      August is no longer the silly season now that "violence
      stalks the summer streets."   But it is the silly season
      with regard to some crazy ideas concerning preservation.
      Examples provided.

324. "New Federal Office Building: A Capital in Microcosm."
      August 29, 1968, p. 37.

      "The story of a new Federal office building in New York
      City by Eggers and Higgins, to house fifty-five agencies."
      About one-third the square footage of Washington's Penta-
      gon Building, it outscales everything in the immediate
      area.

325. "Architecture: The House That HUD Built."   September 22,
      1968, Section 2, pp. 37-38.

      Marcel Breuer's Department of Housing and Urban Develop-
      ment building, in Washington, D.C., "is a handsome, func-
      tional structure that adds quality design and genuine
      20th century style to a city badly in need of both."

326. "A Start on Cities of 'Quality and Style.'"   September
      23, 1968, p. 34.

      The Johnson Administration gave us the Department of
      Housing and Urban Development, but the agency lacks
      adequate funding.

327. "Architecture: A Museum Is Also Art, Exhibition Shows.
      71 Buildings in Diverse Styles House Treasures."
      September 25, 1968, p. 40.

      "Architecture of Museums" was the title of an exhibition

of seventy-one museums in twenty-two countries, held at
the Museum of Modern Art. Some are listed.

328. "How to Impoverish City at $400 a Square Foot." September
      29, 1968, Section 2, pp. 31, 33. Reprinted as "How to
      Bankrupt a City at $400 a Square Foot." *Will They Ever
      Finish Bruckner Boulevard?* pp. 60-64.

      "New York's Villard house group ... is one of the few
      places in the city that makes sense, visually, architec-
      turally and historically." All the signs of the process
      toward razing the building were present in 1968: one
      owner moved out, development possibilities were instiga-
      ted by real estate men, and the Roman Catholic Archdio-
      cese, part owner, was in desperate need of money. If it
      is ultimately sold for development, "all New York will be
      poorer on the profits made."

329. "The Newest Skyscraper in Manhattan. G.M. Building Draws
      Crowds But Gets Mixed Reviews." October 1, 1968, p.
      57. Reprinted as "The Parthenon Comes to General Motors."
      Will They Ever Finish Bruckner Boulevard? pp. 92-95.

      The General Motors Building on Fifth Avenue between
      Fifty-eighth and Fifty-ninth Streets, by Edward D. Stone,
      has "small-town developmental styling" and "G.M.-Hilton"
      styling. Pentelic marble, from which the Parthenon was
      sculpted, was used as a veneer on and in this building,
      but internally, only as far as the eye can see.

330. "Architecture: Atlanta's Arts Center." October 5, 1968,
      p. 31.

      Atlanta's $13 million Memorial Arts Center, containing
      a variety of teaching and entertainment facilities, covers
      six acres. It is "a prime example of the Big Box School.
      ... It satisfies the sponsor's requirements for that
      pointless classical recall ... a more sophisticated Soviet
      Palace of Culture."

331. "Strictly from Hunger." October 6, 1968, Section 2, p.
      34. Reprinted in *Will They Ever Finish Bruckner Boule-
      vard?* pp. 64-68.

      "After you've built up on all the avenues, there is no
      place to go but the side streets. Now the peculiarity of
      New York is that while the avenues are its show, the side
      streets are its soul." Zoning laws give greater height
      for plazas, and the urban character of shops and other
      neighborhood amenities will disappear.

332. "All of the Arts But Architecture." October 13, 1968,
      Section 2, p. 40. Reprinted in *Will They Ever Finish
      Bruckner Boulevard?* pp. 191–95.

      The appearance of the Atlanta Memorial Arts Center
      (that it was designed by a computer to be contained
      within a box) is due in part to a financial squeeze
      and in part to bad taste; but all this is commonplace--
      it happens everywhere.

333. "Plan for Jewish Martyrs' Monument Here Unveiled."
      October 17, 1968, p. 47. Reprinted as "Of Art and
      Genocide." *Will They Ever Finish Bruckner Boulevard?*
      pp. 108–110.

      Kahn's scheme of seven glass blocks, 10x10 in plan,
      and 11 feet high, on a 66-feet-square grey granite base,
      was designed to commemorate the death of six million
      Jews during World War II. Mrs. Huxtable questions whether
      the memorial should be located in New York's Battery
      Park as proposed.

334. "Metropolitan Museum to Get Costly New Facade. $1.6-
      Million Project Planned for Fifth Avenue Front--City
      Will Share Cost." October 22, 1968, p. 39.

      A cleanup of the physical appearance of the Fifth
      Avenue facade of the Met at a cost of $1.6 million.

335. "A Tale of Two Houses." October 27, 1968, Section 2,
      p. 27.

      Ernest Flagg designed the Lewis Gouverneur House, on
      the southeast corner of Park Avenue and Eighty-fifth
      Street. This house and a small frame row house at 312
      East Fifty-third Street are being sought by midtown
      side street assemblage developers.

336. "Architecture: Object Lesson in Art and Museology."
      October 29, 1968, p. 55. Reprinted as "Art, Architec-
      ture and Museology." *Will They Ever Finish Bruckner
      Boulevard?* pp. 198–201.

      Mrs. Huxtable suggests that I.M. Pei's Everson Museum
      of Art at Syracuse, New York, is so timeless in its
      design that it will be numbered with those buildings
      representative of our age in the architectural histories
      of the future. She likes the form, massing, space
      arrangements, materials, and textures.

337. "London Studying $300-Million Renewal of the Covent
      Garden Area." November 8, 1968, pp. 49, 95. Reprinted
      as "London: Renewing Covent Garden." *Will They Ever
      Finish Bruckner Boulevard?* pp. 129-33.

      Covent Garden is one of many areas throughout London
      planned for redevelopment, but in so doing the market
      and associated building uses, which are inherently a
      part of old London, will be lost. These groupings of
      historic structures create an idea of place and a total
      environment and should not be lost.

338. "London at Last Promised Elegant Skyscraper." November
      16, 1968, pp. 39, 41. Reprinted as "London: Skyscraper
      Asparagus." *Will They Ever Finish Bruckner Boulevard?*
      pp. 124-28.

      The theme of this article, centered around a proposed
      Mies van der Rohe structure in the financial district
      of the City of London, is the effect of the skyscraper
      on the urban environment of a horizontally organized
      city. Other slick highrises are listed and described.

339. "Mackintosh: A Genius to Be Reckoned With." November
      17, 1968, Section 2, p. 27. Reprinted as "Mackintosh:
      Revolution and the Scent of Heliotrope." *Will They
      Ever Finish Bruckner Boulevard?* pp. 249-52.

      At the Edinburgh Festival, 1968, a centenary exhibi-
      tion of the work of Charles Rennie Mackintosh (1868-
      1928) was staged. "This exhibition was indeed a reve-
      lation," consisting of recreated interiors designed by
      the architect, 1900-1917. The show was later taken to
      London, where it appeared at the Victoria and Albert
      Museum. "Mackintosh was involved in a reformation that
      was also a gentle exploration of beauty and a probing
      analysis of architectonic surfaces and space."

340. "London Puts Brakes on Private Development in Historic
      Areas. Projects Now Under Planners' Control in Eight
      Districts." November 19, 1968, p. 3. Reprinted as
      "London: Putting the Brakes on 'Progress.'" *Will
      They Ever Finish Bruckner Boulevard?* pp. 133-37.

      Town planning authorities in London can designate
      "conservation areas" in order to prohibit demolition or
      new construction, to protect "amenities." "As under-
      stood in England amenities in this sense covers a civil-
      ized concept of total environmental excellence."

341. "Architecture: Making the Scene with Sir John." November
      24, 1968, Section 2, p. 34. Reprinted as "The Curiously
      Contemporary Case of Sir John Soane." *Will They Ever
      Finish Bruckner Boulevard?* pp. 245-49.

      From 1812 to 1837 Sir John Soane lived in the London
      house which he designed for himself in Lincoln's Inn
      Fields. There is space, light, architectural poetry,
      and "architectural memorabilia [of] ... Soane's ...
      magpie acquisitiveness," which many of today's architects
      (and critics) make a pilgrimage to see.

342. "A Singularly New York Product. Co-op Monumental in
      Size, Minimal in Social Planning." November 25, 1968,
      p. 43. Reprinted as "Co-op City: A Singularly New
      York Product." *Will They Ever Finish Bruckner Boule-
      vard?* pp. 77-81.

      The United Housing Federation, noted for its lack of
      imagination in planning and architecture, has produced
      good examples of both at Co-op City. In addition to
      livable apartments, the project was also a low-budget
      success.

343. "An Exercise in Chinese Irony." December 1, 1968, Sec-
      tion 2, p. 40.

      Twenty-four windows by Frank Lloyd Wright were shown
      at the Richard Feigen Gallery, New York. Most of them
      were stripped from existing buildings, which means that,
      however magnificent, they are out of context.

344. "More Side Street Sabotage." December 15, 1968, Section
      2, p. 36. Reprinted as "Side Street Sabotage." *Will
      They Ever Finish Bruckner Boulevard?* pp. 68-71.

      Money-making schemes, tax benefits, and tax shelters
      have greater appeal to developers than do those civiliz-
      ing amenities which make the city what it is. The side
      streets are being developed as the avenues once were.
      Syracuse University has even got into the act with its
      endowment fund. In New York City, it purchased 12, 14,
      16, and 18 East Sixty-second Street and attempted to
      assemble the whole block for speculative purposes.
      "Greetings, New York City, from Syracuse University."

345. "Lessons in Urbicide." December 22, 1968, Section 2,
      p. 33. Reprinted as "Manchester, N.H.: Lessons in
      Urbicide." *Will They Ever Finish Bruckner Boulevard?*

pp. 111-15.

Urban renewal is destroying a heritage of mill structures built between 1838 and 1915 at Manchester, New
Hampshire. The method of this urbicidal ignorance is
described step by step.

1969

346. "Ground Is Broken for the $15 Million Hirshhorn Museum.
      Marble Home Seen as a Realization of American Dream."
      January 9, 1969, p. 20.

      "The one word to describe Washington's Hirshhorn
      Museum is formidable ... the biggest marble doughnut
      in the world." Skidmore, Owings and Merrill are the
      architects. The scale of the museum is compared to
      other large structures. A "splendidly engineered tomb
      second to nothing else on the Mall for Pop pomposity."

347. "Kicked a Building Lately?" January 12, 1969, Section
      2, pp. 25, 28. Reprinted in *Will They Ever Finish
      Bruckner Boulevard?* pp. 177-81.

      "Supermannerism" is here seen as part of "a rebellious
      attempt to expand experience by breaking down the tradi-
      tions of the Establishment.... The results range from
      godawful to the genuinely revelatory expansion of visual
      and sensuous experience." The other side of the coin is
      the work of the established professionals--dull, bland,
      computerized glass boxes.

348. "Don't Call It Kookie." January 19, 1969, Section 2,
      p. 27. Reprinted in *Will They Ever Finish Bruckner
      Boulevard?* pp. 181-84.

      A general introduction on megastructure leads to a
      description of a modified megastructure, reduced to the
      scale of buildings which can be readily comprehended--
      Scarborough College of the University of Toronto by
      John Andrews. Other influences and related buildings
      are noted and discussed.

349. "The Case for Chaos." January 26, 1969, Section 2, p.
      32. Reprinted in *Will They Ever Finish Bruckner
      Boulevard?* pp. 184-88.

      Considers the Venturian esthetic of including all
      architectural philosophies, even those which are usually

thought to be non-architecture. Venturi's manifesto, *Complexity and Contradiction in Architecture*, is reviewed, and Las Vegas, the Mecca for his students, is explained with relation to his article "... Learning from Las Vegas." *Architectural Forum*, 128 (March 1968): 36-43.

350. "Where It Goes Nobody Knows." February 2, 1969, Section 2, p. 29. Reprinted as "Lower Manhattan Expressway: Where It Goes, Nobody Knows." *Will They Ever Finish Bruckner Boulevard?* pp. 18-24.

Expressways destroy cities; thus, the Lower Manhattan Expressway was acceptable to New York City's administration only if it were depressed below street level. "Do you kill a city or maim it?" Thousands of people will lose their homes, adjacent properties will become blighted, and historic structures--in this case, the Cast-Iron District--will be lost.

351. "A Breakthrough in Planning. Water St. to Get Office Tower with Plaza." February 7, 1969, p. 39.

A building larger than the Pan Am Building is to be built at 55 Water Street, at a cost of $150 million. None of the fanfare and concern over Pan Am has been repeated for this oversized structure by Emery Roth.

352. "Boston's New City Hall: A Public Building of Quality." February 8, 1969, p. 33. Reprinted as "Boston City Hall: A Winner." *Will They Ever Finish Bruckner Boulevard?* pp. 167-71.

The building is described as "one of the handsomest ... around ... a solid impressive demonstration of creativity and quality." Expression and function of Kallman, McKinnell and Knowles' structure are explained.

353. "Kahn Plans Hall for Venice Biennale." February 8, 1969, p. 22.

Louis Kahn's model for the new Congress Hall in Venice was displayed in the Doge's Palace. Some believe Kahn to be the only modern architect capable of success in Venice because "he stays away from passing architectural fashions." Accommodations are described. Kahn states: "I was constantly asking each building I love so much in Venice whether they would accept me in their company."

354. "How to Love the Boom." February 16, 1969, Section 2,
      p. 34.

      About fifty-five acres of Lower Manhattan are being
      completely rebuilt at the expense of New York's Greek
      Revival heritage. Uris Building Corporation, for ex-
      ample, has erected 55 Water Street: Larger than the
      Pan Am Building, "it received no public attention" com-
      parable to the Pan Am furor.

355. "Politicalizing Architecture." February 23, 1969, Sec-
      tion 2, p. 33.

      Columbia University architecture students believe that
      the American Institute of Architects and its practicing
      membership are irrelevant. The students claim that
      businessmen, realtors, and accountants dictate to archi-
      tects.

356. "Pressing the Panic Button on City Zoning." February
      24, 1969, p. 33.

      Converting low-density residential and commercial
      areas to high-density office and luxury apartment areas
      plays havoc with social, cultural, and economic qualities
      in many New York neighborhoods. Zoning needs to be modi-
      fied.

357. "They Know What They Don't Like." March 2, 1969, Section
      2, p. 24.

      Montpelier's Pavilion Hotel, adjacent to the Vermont
      State Capitol, is not to be preserved. It would have
      cost $2.8 million to preserve it and $3.5 million to
      construct a new building. Thus, illogically, the legis-
      lature of Vermont will build a new one. (The end of the
      story, long after the publication of this article, is
      that the new building was modelled identically on the
      old Pavilion! See item 423.)

358. "New York, Life's Loser, Does It Again." March 9, 1969,
      Section 2, p. 28.

      The waterfront land of the Brooklyn meat market became
      available when the market moved. What was to become of
      the open space? The local residents wanted the site for
      housing or a new school. It is unlikely that either will
      be built. Rather, Bethlehem Steel will provide another
      Brooklyn site for the meat market in exchange for the
      waterfront site, on which they intend to build profitable
      housing. Could not the meat market be relocated in the
      old Brooklyn Navy Yard?

359. "How to Keep the Status Quo." April 6, 1969, Section 2,
     p. 23.

     Lincoln Square, New York, is likely to go the way of
     conventional development and become "conventional disaster."

360. "The Stakes Are High for All in Grand Central Battle."
     April 11, 1969, p. 28.

     Should a "certificate of appropriateness" be issued
     for Penn Central's proposed skyscraper over the Grand
     Central Terminal? Even the better of Breuer's two
     proposals would be nothing more than a dressed up com-
     mercial package. The landmarks law protects the exterior.
     What is more important about Grand Central is its spacious
     interior.

361. "Plan's Total Concept Is Hailed." April 17, 1969, p.
     49.

     Battery Park City, as proposed, does not merely juxta-
     pose housing and office blocks, it also expresses the
     ideals of the linear city. A certain amount of control
     over the bulk of some structures would be desirable.

362. "The View from the Mayor's Windows." April 20, 1969,
     Section 2, p. 26.

     Behind Boston's new City Hall, a cluster of the town's
     most historic structures will be preserved and adapted
     to modern use.

363. "Housing, the American Myth." April 21, 1969, p. 46.

     "Government programs have all slowed down housing and
     sent prices straight into the stratosphere while dampen-
     ing the most innovative spirit."

364. "The Old City of Jerusalem Is Getting a New Old Look."
     May 7, 1969, p. 49.

     Jerusalem's twenty-five-acre Old City is being restored
     at a cost of $5 million per year. Old Sephardic syna-
     gogues of the sixteenth century have been discovered and
     may ultimately be complemented by a new synagogue by
     Louis Kahn.

365. "Jerusalem: Vista of Two Worlds." May 12, 1969, p. 20.

     People of Israel are being moved into old areas of
     Jerusalem, won in the Six Day War, on a permanent basis.

But the 68,000 Arabs and 210,000 Jews will retain their own areas of the city, west and east, respectively.

366. "Israel Hopes to House Negev Bedouins, a People of Space and Sky." May 19, 1969, p. 22.

Tel Sheva, five miles from Beersheba, in the Negev of South Israel, is a new town planned initially for 500 families of skilled, hard-working Bedouins. It "is an architectural and social experiment, an exercise in desert urbanism."

367. "New Towns Bloom in Israeli Desert." June 1, 1969, Section 8, pp. 1, 7.

Beersheba, based upon the English town-planning concepts of the garden city, is "a museum of planning errors." Garden cities are not the solution to urban developments in the desert, where planning on any scale is a myth. Arad, a later new town begun in 1962, will have six neighborhoods to accommodate 25,000 people. Phosphate deposits ten miles away will provide an industrial base for the town.

368. "Tinker Toy City Hall in Israel Is Space Packed." June 5, 1969, p. 49.

Bat Yam, a suburb of Tel Aviv, has a new city hall. Designed by Alfred Neumann, it is composed of hexagonal units called cuboctahedrons. Ultimately, standardized prefabrication should result in cheap mass production.

369. "The Second Israel." June 8, 1969, Section 2, p. 26.

Tel Aviv of the 1920s was built by immigrant designers. There have been other generations since then, including the present one, which produces sensitive, handsome structures.

370. "Museums a la Carte." June 15, 1969, Section 2, p. 23.

Mrs. Huxtable prefers cities to museums, but admires those museums recently visited in Turkey, Israel, Greece, Yugoslavia, and England. They range from simple to brash, historic to modern.

371. "Two in Trouble." June 22, 1969, Section 2, p. 30.

The Hayward Gallery, in London, has "bad lighting, inept installation," and, because of its organized confusion, its entrance is not easily discovered. The extension to

the Tate Gallery, by Richard Llewellyn Davies and others,
is, by comparison, readily accessible.

372.   "Student Architects Ask Aid to Combat Urban Plight."
       June 27, 1969, p. 43.

       Student architects want the American Institute of
       Architects to cough up $15 million. To refuse would
       be to admit a failure by the profession, and the students
       intend to go ahead with their plans, whatever the out-
       come.

373.   "The City Dear Brutus." July 6, 1969, Section 2, p. 20.

       "Urban Design in New York" was the title of an exhibi-
       tion at the Architectural League of New York. It illus-
       trated projects of the Urban Design Group, a section
       within the City Planning Department and related to the
       Office of Lower Manhattan Development. Exhibits
       concerned the theater district, street parks, and new
       public and municipal projects, as well as plans for
       neighborhoods and other areas of comprehensive redevelop-
       ment.

374.   "Urban Planning Boasts a World Supersalesman." July 8,
       1969, p. 45.

       Constantinos Doxiadis heads the Athens-based Center of
       Ekistics (the science of human settlement). Although
       this non-profit-making concern works mainly with problems
       in South America, North American cities have also retained
       Doxiadis as consultant. His approach is to collect, ana-
       lyze, and synthesize data to produce proposals. "We must
       think of planning as a long-term process," he claims.

375.   "Politics of Expressways. Putting Highway Through City's
       Core Is Regarded as Poison to a Candidate." July 17,
       1969, p. 51.

       Mayor Lindsay announced the abandonment of two proposed
       expressways--the Cross Brooklyn and the Lower Manhattan.
       Progressive planning does not take "white man's roads
       through black man's bedrooms" or through areas of low
       property values.

376.   "He Was Not Irrelevant." July 20, 1969, Section 2, p.
       21.

       Wright, Mies, and Corbu were as great as any of the
       famed architects of history, but Gropius was uneven in

his contribution, collaborating with a whole range of
designers. His was the role of a "catalyst of ideas"
rather than that of a shatterer of "stylistic norms."

377.   "Barbarism Notes from All Over." July 27, 1969, Section
        2, p. 20.

        You lose some and you win some in the continuous battle
        of preservation. Examples of recently saved structures
        are provided, along with examples of recently demolished
        ones.

378.   "Building for the Space Age." August 3, 1969, Section
        2, p. 22.

        Architects, in addition to scientists and engineers,
        will be needed on the moon to provide for man's psycho-
        logical and environmental needs. The architect is con-
        tributing to the space-center needs on earth here and
        now, designing assembly buildings.

379.   "'Ominous' Outlook for Housing." August 4, 1969, p. 34.

        Federal limits on the cost of public housing brought
        some to a standstill in New York City, due to the rapidly
        increasing rate of inflation.

380.   "A Personal Inquiry into the Nature of Some Hotel Rooms
        Overseas." August 17, 1969, Section 10, p. 29.

        Subjective impressions by Mrs. Huxtable concerning
        eight hotels in five Middle Eastern and European countries.
        She likes comfort and amenity on a deluxe scale. "At
        Claridge's tapioca pudding can be divine."

381.   "Planning Tied to Policy Held Key to City's Quality."
        August 17, 1969, Section 8, pp. 1, 6.

        Planning has come to New York City only in the last
        five years. "It is concerned with the city's growth,
        development and health." A housing agency, community
        participation, scale, variety, open space, esthetics,
        special zoning, and numerous other aspects are part of
        the total package.

382.   "Soaring Towers Gave Form to an Age." August 19, 1969,
        p. 28.

        Mies knew exactly what his objectives were in each
        and every building he designed. The copyists, and those

designing utilitarian buildings, reduced his esthetic to
the commonplace. Written as part of an appreciation of
Mies, at the time of his death.

383. "Mies van der Rohe, 1886-1969." August 24, 1969, Section
      2, p. 24.

      "Mies's work is a system of thought and values," states
      Mrs. Huxtable in her obituary of the master.

384. "The Bucolic Bulldozer." September 14, 1969, Section 2,
      p. 28.

      The General Worth Hotel, built in Hudson, New York, in
      1837, is to be demolished. It is one of a group of Hud-
      son buildings which have been categorized as fire hazards.
      This is but one of many structures threatened with destruc-
      tion by developers and government agencies in New York and
      other states.

385. "Open Season on the Nation's Monuments." September 21,
      1969, Section 2, p. 30.

      The Union Bank and Trust Company of Grand Rapids, Mich-
      igan, proposed to demolish the Victorian city hall, built
      in 1888. It was the work of Elijah Meyers, who designed
      state capitols for Utah, Idaho, Texas, Colorado, and
      Michigan, and city halls for Richmond, Virginia, and his
      home town, Detroit. Other government structures elsewhere
      are threatened.

386. "Doomsday Notes on a Rotten Game." September 28, 1969,
      Section 2, p. 34.

      "It seems worth observing that the finger of God, or
      whatever force is at work, has unerringly struck down
      just those historic buildings that were being actively
      promoted for preservation," but also stood in the way of
      "development," public and private. Five are named, in-
      cluding the carriage house and barn by A.J. Downing, at
      Springside, Poughkeepsie, New York, about which there
      are lengthy comments.

387. "The National No-Building Program." September 29, 1969,
      p. 46.

      There will be need for ten times as much construction
      in the United States before 2,000 A.D. as has been built
      since the founding of the Colonies. But there is a sev-
      enty-five percent cutback in federal construction programs.
      Inflationary costs make delays exceedingly expensive.

388. "From a Coleridge Opium Dream." October 5, 1969, Section
      2, p. 27.

      Interior designs for John Nash's Brighton Pavilion were
      sold to New York's Cooper-Hewitt Museum in 1948. They
      were displayed during 1969 in an exhibition entitled "A
      Stately Pleasure Dome, The Brighton Pavilion." Historic
      background and research into the period are cited.

389. "Juilliard's New Building: Esthetic Reality." October
      8, 1969, p. 59.

      This last structure to open at Lincoln Center, New
      York, is free from gold leaf, pretentiousness, and
      pomposity. The five-story structure houses four theaters,
      including Alice Tully Hall, in a total of 490,000 square
      feet at a cost of $30 million. Belluschi is described
      as "an architect of notable sensibility who has worked
      most beautifully in wood, for almost 40 years."

390. "A Plan for Welfare Island Is Unveiled." October 10,
      1969, p. 49.

      Mayor Lindsay announced that Philip Johnson and John
      Burgee would plan a community and $200 million worth of
      development on the East River's 147-acre Welfare Island.
      Discusses the financial arrangements, zoning of the island,
      existing use, future plans, subway-tunnel link, and other
      general aspects.

391. "What's It Worth on the Market?" October 12, 1969, Sec-
      tion 2, p. 29.

      The National Association of Real Estate Boards is look-
      ing for large open sites with run-down old single houses
      on them, as a means of good investment in progressive
      America. Olana, the home of Hudson River painter Fred-
      erick Church, is one house and site that was saved before
      realtors could get their hands on it.

392. "This Time They Mean It." October 19, 1969, Section 2,
      p. 32.

      Welfare Island, in the East River, is the site for a
      proposed housing development for 20,000 people: the
      elderly; those of low, moderate, and middle incomes; and
      those desiring a luxury level. In addition, there will
      be parks and recreation areas, plus a variety of amenities
      and the existing historic structures. Compares what is
      being attempted to what a private developer might or
      might not do.

393. "The State Office Building Dilemma." November 2, 1969,
      Section 2, p. 32. Reprinted as "Hard Questions for
      Harlem: The State Office Building Dilemma." *Will They
      Ever Finish Bruckner Boulevard?* pp. 36-39.

      Revitalization of an area of New York City usually en-
      courages real estate speculators to follow and, thus,
      results in a general uplifting of an area. It was de-
      cided by New York State that Harlem should be revital-
      ized and get "a piece of the action" at 125th to 126th
      Streets, between Lenox and Seventh Avenues. But who
      would benefit except the real estate speculators? The
      Architects Renewal Committee in Harlem has attempted to
      inject into the program local amenities which would
      benefit Harlem.

394. "Beating the System." November 9, 1969, Section 2, p. 31.

      The $25 million police headquarters of New York City,
      completed by Gruzen Partners, involved several variant
      architectural partnerships. Under the Lindsay administra-
      tion, "The job has been done. It took a decade and seven
      Public Works Commissioners, of whom three died...." The
      cost, the increase in space needs, what was attempted and
      what was actually achieved, are the facts in the complex
      story of any major structure today.

395. "Proposed Monument Under Glass at the U.N. But Economic
      Value of Such a Structure Is Called Doubtful." Novem-
      ber 12, 1969, p. 37.

      Two blocks, 540 feet high and costing $300 million,
      represent the gigantic scale and cost of this Roche and
      Dinkeloo project, to include a hotel, apartments, and
      three office towers. Those displaced by the development
      will be relocated in Davis, Brody and Associates' Water-
      side housing, which the UN is likely to subsidize.

396. "Plan Is Regarded as Break with Tradition." November 16,
      1969, Section 1, p. 84.

      The *Plan for New York City* is described as unconventional
      and controversial. It deals with processes and recognizes
      realities.

397. "Souvenirs of a New Age." November 16, 1969, Section 2,
      p. 28.

      Reviews Eric Mendelsohn and his work and his famous
      thumbnail sketches, which were exhibited at the Museum

of Modern Art.   Relates Mendelsohn to European and
American twentieth-century movements.

398.   "US Pavilion at Osaka Fair Will Have Translucent Inflated
       Roof." November 21, 1969, p. 6.

       This air-inflated, vinyl-coated, fiber glass pavilion
       roof with perimeter berm is the size of two football
       fields and cost $10 million. Davis, Brody and Associates
       and others were the designers.

399.   "American Architecture and Urbanism." November 23, 1969,
       The New York Times Book Review, pp. 6-7, 52, 54.

       Reviews a book which "does not turn out to be the
       definitive volume on *American Architecture and Urbanism*
       that we have been waiting for, in spite of the promise
       of both in the title and the author ... this is not even
       a good book until we get half way through ... a brilliant
       man's lazy book." Mrs. Huxtable gives her reasons for
       such statements, and quotes from Vincent Scully's book.
       For Scully's reply, see item 947.

400.   "Planning Blueprint for City Designed for People." No-
       vember 23, 1969, Section 4, p. 7.

       Reviews the recently published *Plan for New York*, a
       comprehensive planning document required by the 1938
       City Charter. The plan suggested sweeping changes in
       welfare, education, and employment. Objectives in the
       plan are categorized under four headings: (1) National
       Center: The city has more office space than the nine
       next largest cities of the United States. (2) Oppor-
       tunity for more skilled employment. (3) Environment,
       particularly in urban housing. (4) Government and
       the machinery for implementing the plan, at an estimated
       cost of $54 billion.

401.   "About the Satisfaction of the Human Spirit." November
       30, 1969, Section 2, p. 25.

       New York's Master Plan is concerned with the total
       environment. The plan is controversial and misunderstood,
       since there are no readily available solutions to the
       problems of the city. The plan has no hope, and lacks
       understanding.

402.   "Lessons in the Death of Style." December 21, 1969,
       Section 2, p. 36.

       "The Railroad Age is over" and, thus, not only is New

York's Pennsylvania Station (1903-07, by McKim, Mead
& White) gone, but others are threatened and are not
replaced with anything resembling excellence. Daniel
Burnham's Pittsburgh Station, 1898-1902, has lost its
railroad sheds, and the new projected development may
not even include the station's famed rotunda.

403.   "Architecture: Yoo-Hoo, Abominable Snowman." December
       28, 1969, Section 2, p. 16.

       Holiday Inns has invaded Cambodia, and there will soon
       be one such motel (complete with giant sign) in Nepal,
       and others in half a dozen other countries of the Far
       East. They provide bowling alleys and eighteen-hole
       golf courses, and do not attempt to cushion the American-
       ization of other cultures.

404.   "The Crisis of the Environment." December 29, 1969, p.
       28.

       A diatribe against the bulldozer and its financial and
       bureaucratic backup.

405.   "In New York, a Losing Battle." December 30, 1969, p.
       18.

       An autobiographical sketch of Ada Louise Huxtable's
       love for Manhattan. Her way of life has changed over
       the years because of the rise in rents. She objects to
       not being able to choose her own way of life. Words of
       advice are given for coping with New York.

                              1970

406.   "Architecture: Seen Any Good Buildings Lately?" January
       11, 1970, Section 2, p. 27.

       A lament for the architecture of the 1960s, which has
       extended itself beyond esthetic considerations. "Social
       concerns alone will not produce a better physical world."
       Esthetics and function are equally a part of the process
       of design and should complement the safe and sanitary
       standards.

407.   "Heroics Are Out, Ordinary Is In." January 18, 1970,
       Section 2, p. 27.

       "Anti-architecture" is "in" as seen in the design awards
       in the January 1970 issue of *Progressive Architecture*.

Jury and winners are listed and their comments are quoted.

408.   "This Is Silver Lining Day." January 25, 1970, Section 2, p. 26.

Landmarks: you win some, you lose some; examples both ways.

409.   "Assembly Line for That Dream House." February 1, 1970, Section 4, p. 3.

"The purpose of Operation Breakthrough is to prod private business into producing housing on the industrialized scale that is the only realistic way to meet the national need." Cites problems.

410.   "Peacock Feathers and Pink Plastic." February 8, 1970, Section 2, p. 25.

The first Bruce Goff retrospective exhibition was held in 1970 at the Architectural League of New York. Goff is Midwestern and thus not easily appreciated by sophisticated architects of the eastern seaboard. His work is imaginative, and his drawings are meticulously rendered.

411.   "Sugar Coating a Bitter Pill." February 15, 1970, Section 2, p. 25.

The United Nations Development Corporation has proposed a $310 million development between First and Second Avenues from Forty-second to Forty-third Streets for mission space, apartments for personnel, and a hotel. Roche and Dinkeloo designed the forty-story glass interlocking boxes containing 4.2 million square feet. "The question is to what degree have costs been escalated by a monument fixation? What is being subsidized--the UN's functional needs or the architect's esthetic needs?"

412.   "Columbia Plan Includes Underground Expansion." February 18, 1970, pp. 1, 34.

Fifteen months were spent in consultation with local groups and members of the academic community, in order to produce a master plan for the university. To avoid expansion into local community areas, much has been planned on underground levels.

413.   "Fun City, No; Slob City, Yes." February 22, 1970, Section 2, p. 25.

Our breathing, walking, and looking may be in jeopardy
in New York City.

414. "Model Homes for Americans." February 28, 1970, p. 31.

Examples resulting from Operation Breakthrough are illustrated and listed, and the technological aspects are
discussed.

415. "Handling a Hot Potato." March 1, 1970, Section 2, p.
27.

Adler and Sullivan's Chicago Stock Exchange, 1893, was
one of the seventeen structures proposed by the Chicago
Landmarks Commission for designation as landmarks. The
Chicago City Council would have to have compensated the
owners if it accepted the designation status. The Stock
Exchange is functional and rents well, but yields less
than would a new building on the same site designed to
a maximum zoning height. Mrs. Huxtable suggests that
the "air rights" above the building should be salable,
as in New York City, thus alleviating the need for demolition.

416. "Blue Monday in Los Angeles." March 8, 1970, Section 2,
p. 23.

After stating that Irving Gill's Dodge House, Los Angeles, 1916, was "one of the 15 most significant houses in
the history of American domestic architecture," Mrs. Huxtable relates the tragedy of its demolition. It was
compulsorily purchased by the Los Angeles Board of Education so that it could be razed and the site used for a
school, which was never built.

417. "Tale of a Few Cities--Everywhere." March 9, 1970, p.
36.

"It is one thing to erode Third Avenue for common
commercialism," but such development should not be allowed to spread to Paris or London.

418. "Prophet in the Desert." March 15, 1970, Section 2, p.
26.

A justification of Soleri's work and a survey of his
achievements. Includes discussion of an exhibition at
the Corcoran Gallery, Washington, D.C., in the Spring of
1970, and an MIT Press publication, *The City in the Image
of Man*. Soleri's "arcology" is compared to other mega-
structural schemes throughout the world. His mega-city,

Arcosanti, is to be constructed on 800 acres of land
seventy miles north of Phoenix, Arizona.

419. "It's a Long Way from 1900." March 22, 1970, Section 2,
      p. 31.

      Hector Guimard died in New York in 1942. After the war,
France showed little interest in preserving his Paris
home or its furnishings and, thus, several examples of
that furniture were purchased by the Museum of Modern
Art. The Museum's 1970 exhibition on Guimard displayed
these examples. Mentions modern research, collections,
and sponsors of the exhibition.

420. "A New City Is Emerging Downtown." March 29, 1970,
      Section 8, pp. 1, 4.

      Lower Manhattan, below Brooklyn Bridge, is being re-
vitalized in more ways than one. Housing, preservation,
and the fifty million square feet of additional office
space are explained; commercial structures are explained
in detail.

421. "Whither World's Fairs?" March 29, 1970, Section 2, p.
      32.

      Preparations are going ahead for America's bicentennial
in 1976, whatever form it may take, but how much time is
available to do something urbanistically significant?
Describes proposals by various cities which are vying
for the privilege of participating.

422. "To See Ourselves." April 5, 1970, Section 2, p. 20.

      A visitor to the United States is quoted as saying:
"American cities are in permanent process of renewal.
But they are destroying their urbanity without recreat-
ing a new one.... Cities must change, but you cannot
abandon them." Other allied attitudes are expressed.

423. "Having It Both Ways in Montpelier." April 12, 1970,
      Section 2, p. 23.

      Montpelier, Vermont, lost its 1875 Pavilion Hotel to
the wreckers in December 1969, only to have it replaced
by a replica to accommodate state offices. The reason?
It was cheaper to rebuild, or so it was originally thought.
See the article of March 2, 1969 (item 357), which suggests that preservation would have been cheaper than the
construction of a new building.

424. "Metropolitan Museum Plans Centennial Expansion." April
      13, 1970, pp. 1, 53.

      Roche and Dinkeloo are to expand the Metropolitan
      Museum of Art by thirty-three percent. The additions
      will complete the perimeter on the north, south, and
      west sides of the building.

425. "The Revolution Was Real." April 19, 1970, Section 2,
      p. 23.

      An exhibition entitled "Theo van Doesberg: The Develop-
      ment of an Architect" was held at the Museum of Modern
      Art in the Spring of 1970. Mrs. Huxtable expounds on
      the de Stijl Movement, the influences on it, and its
      subsequent impact.

426. "A Happy Marriage on the Hudson." April 26, 1970, Sec-
      tion 2, p. 29.

      Sherwood, Mills and Smith Partnership of Stamford,
      Connecticut, has designed a small concrete museum,
      planetarium, and library to complement an 1876 Victorian
      house at Yonkers, New York, which houses the Hudson River
      Museum. Comments on space, cost, and esthetics.

427. "The Black Man and His Architecture." May 3, 1970,
      Section 2, p. 25.

      Reviews an exhibition on the work of black architects
      at the New York Chapter of the American Institute of
      Architects. "The work ranges from pedestrian to excel-
      lent." Black architects have usually been trained in
      the same manner as white architects, but their role in
      dealing with government and community may require a dif-
      ferent educational background. The black architects
      realize this and are doing something about it.

428. "It's Hard to Despise Victorian Houses Anymore." May 3,
      1970, Section 8, pp. 1, 6.

      Reviews "The Rise of an American Architecture," an
      exhibition at the Metropolitan Museum of Art. One of
      the four sections of the exhibit, the Victorian house,
      is lauded as one of America's most noteworthy contribu-
      tions to architectural history.

429. "Bending the Rules." May 10, 1970, Section 2, p. 23.

      Westbeth, bound by West, Bank, Washington, and Bethune
      Streets, is a conversion from the former Bell Telephone

Laboratories into non-profit middle-income artists'
housing. Describes the purchase of the premises and
all the side-stepping through red tape necessary to
achieve the realization of this project. Richard Meier's
solution is described as "exemplary" because of his innovative planning, which has been achieved at reasonable
cost.

430. "The Tower, the House and the Park." May 17, 1970, Section 2, p. 23.

Two exhibitions are reviewed: "Back Bay Boston: The
City as a Work of Art," at the Boston Museum of Fine Art,
and "The Rise of an American Architecture," at the Metropolitan Museum of Art. Displays, catalogues, and con-
tent are surveyed.

431. "Dissimilar Buildings, Similar Awards." May 24, 1970,
Section 8, pp. 1, 7.

Pietro Belluschi's Juilliard School in Manhattan, and
Hardy Holzman Pfeiffer Associates' Brooklyn Children's
Museum are two winners of the Bard Award. Each is briefly
described.

432. "Good Buildings Have Friends." May 24, 1970, Section 2,
p. 26.

The twenty acres of the area of Manhattan south of
Houston Street is popularly known as SoHo. It is called
Hell's Hundred Acres by those who have worked there, and
is known as the SoHo Cast-Iron Historic District by the
Landmarks Preservation Commission. Most of the cast-iron
structures there were built from the 1860s to the 1890s,
in what is termed the "palazzo" style. All are architect designed. Lofts in the area are admirable as spacious living quarters, although residential use is fre-
quently illegal in terms of zoning. But now that the
speculators are moving in and values are rising, artists
are being forced out and are being replaced by the chic
set.

433. "Finnish Master Fashions Library for Abbey in Oregon.
Aalto Blends Wood, Lighting and Hills in Ageless Style."
May 30, 1970, p. 50. Reprinted as "Art and Building:
Alvar Aalto: Mt. Angel Library." *Kicked a Building
Lately?* pp. 92-95.

Dedicated in May 1970, the Mount Angel Benedictine
Monastery Library in Oregon, by Alvar Aalto, is an essay

in wood, Finnish lighting fixtures, Finnish furniture,
natural lighting effects, external brickwork blending
into the Oregon countryside, natural colors and textures,
and fan-shaped free-form architecture.

434. "No Time to Joke." May 31, 1970, Section 2, p. 16.

"Huxtable's law: Every program or procedure set up
with laudable aims and intentions produces uncalculated
side effects that sabotage the original goals," and
this is the case in urban renewal and slum clearance.
In the eyes of developers, historic structures in older
communities are obsolete, and ripe for demolition. The
Lexington, Kentucky, urban renewal project has taken
this attitude.

435. "In Portland, Ore., Urban Decay Is Masked by Natural
      Splendor." June 19, 1970, pp. 39, 74.

With sixty percent of Portland's downtown covered by
automobile-related acreages, one would expect humanizing
elements to be introduced into the remaining areas, but
new highrise structures ignore the problem. "The new
Portland, then, consists largely of towers, bunkers and
bomb sites."

436. "Coast Fountain Melds Art and Environment." June 21,
      1970, Section 1, p. 53.

Portland's fountain, cascade, and waterfall, one block
square and eighteen feet high, will begin to circulate
13,000 gallons of water per minute. This people's park
cost $12,000. It is Renaissance Rome in concept.

437. "Design by Rethink." June 28, 1970, Section 2, p. 22.

Simon Frazer University, Vancouver, British Columbia,
has a megastructure by Erickson and Massey. Winning
design in a 1963 competition, this structure acts as a
covered plaza tying many elements of the campus together.
The plaza has become a center for student protest and
thus it has been modified to some extent by the college
administration.

438. "A Tale of Three Cities." July 5, 1970, Section 2, p.
      18.

Seattle, Portland, and Vancouver are losing their
identities as cities. "The automobile is the destroyer
everywhere.... the skyscraper is killing the life of
the streets ... parking garages proliferate."

439. "The Architects Design Their Dream Home." July 12, 1970,
    Section 2, p. 20.

    The American Institute of Architects headquarters, in
    Washington, D.C., needed to expand, so in 1962, the A.I.A.
    held a competition, and "all hell broke loose for eight
    years." Mitchell-Giurgola won the award. Changes were
    demanded by the Institute, and the Washington Fine Arts
    Commission rejected and condemned the design on two sep-
    arate occasions. "The Institute paid off its architects.
    It interviewed new ones. The office of Mies van der Rohe
    declined to be interviewed on the grounds that it did not
    feel the Fine Arts Commission would accept anything it
    would do. The job went to The Architects Collaborative
    of Cambridge, Massachusetts."

440. "The Battle of Murray Hill." July 12, 1970, Section 8,
    p. 1.

    Murray Hill Association, a local community group in
    Manhattan, and Laird Properties, Inc., real estate de-
    velopers, have mutually agreed to negotiate a reasonable
    solution to urban renewal. "Handsome restraint" replaced
    "tasteless bulk of Miami jazziness." "The results are
    good business and good urbanism."

441. "'The Revolution Grows Old Quickly.'" July 26, 1970,
    Section 2, p. 20.

    Henry Ford's 1,200-acre plant at River Rouge, Michigan,
    by Albert Kahn is an important structure to the architec-
    tural historian and an anathema to the workers who earn
    a living there. Describes the evolution of the plant and
    lists Kahn's accomplishments.

442. "City Landmark Gets a Chance for Survival." August 2,
    1970, Section 8, pp. 1, 7.

    Air-rights given to a forty-two-story office building
    could save Amster Yard, an historic landmark on Forty-
    ninth Street east of Third Avenue. The 30,697 square
    feet of air rights are worth $494,731. The office struc-
    ture is limited to an additional twenty percent area of
    space. "Air rights transfer may offer the city the dif-
    ference between saving and losing its unique architectural
    heritage."

443. "'No Canoeing Allowed Here.'" August 2, 1970, Section 2,
    p. 18.

    "The Old St. Louis Post Office has been running for its

life since 1959." It is government surplus, standing on
expensive downtown real estate. Mrs. Huxtable shows how
forces of city government and the "Feds," both with ul-
terior motives, have forwarded the demolition of the
building. Letters are quoted that "are either terribly
stupid or terribly clever ... to make preservation difficult and horsetrading easy."

444. "What a Little Taste Can Do." August 9, 1970, Section
      2, p. 18.

      A pedestrian mall has been created at City University
      Graduate Center, linking Forty-second and Forty-third
      Streets between Fifth and Sixth Avenues. Provides
      a history of this 1912 building and gives renovation
      costs.

445. "Creation of 3 Top Architects Shown." September 30,
      1970, p. 38.

      "Work in Progress: Architecture by Philip Johnson,
      Kevin Roche, Paul Rudolph" was an exhibition at the
      Museum of Modern Art. Twenty-five projects were dis-
      played, all reflecting "a commitment to the idea that
      architecture ... is worth bothering about," according
      to Arthur Drexler, the director of the Museum's Depart-
      ment of Architecture.

446. "Vision of a New Town on Welfare Island Is Unveiled Here:
      Quality Design with Amenities." October 7, 1970, pp.
      49, 57.

      "It is the showpiece and star performance of the New
      York State Urban Development Corporation, which was
      created by the State Legislature to expedite housing and
      urban renewal. As such, it can't do Governor Rockefeller
      any harm" in an election year. Philip Johnson and his
      partner, John Burgee, are the master planners, and ten
      noteworthy architectural firms are each to contribute
      a portion of the total plan.

447. "Show Offers 'Joy' of Hotel Architecture." October 15,
      1970, p. 60. Reprinted as "The Hospitality Industry:
      Every Little Room Is Lapidus in Bloom." *Kicked a
      Building Lately?* pp. 23-26.

      "The Architecture of Joy," an exhibition of the work
      of Morris Lapidus, was held at the Architectural League
      of New York. Lapidus gives the public what it wants, an
      approach which is fast catching on. "The effect on arrival"

at a Lapidus-designed hotel, "still vivid after seven years, was like being hit by an exploding gilded eggplant."

448. "You Can't Win 'Em All." October 25, 1970, Section 2, p. 25.

Comments on urban planning laws, mainly related to New York City, although other towns are mentioned.

449. "Passport to Power." November 1, 1970, Section 2, p. 25.

The New York Cultural Center staged an exhibition of the architecture of Hitlerian Germany, at the time of publication of *Inside the Third Reich*, by Albert Speer, Hitler's architect. All adds up "to a pretty depressing experience ... a classic tale of corruption, both of the man, and of the art of architecture." Mrs. Huxtable emphasizes Speer's "weak talent," the "total sterility of the neo classical wedding cake school," and "the cruel element in this architecture."

450. "Elegance Clinging to Avenue, But It Too May Pass." November 8, 1970, Section 8, pp. 1, 7.

"Madison Avenue ... is the New Yorker's street of steets," but glass box skyscrapers with street-level blandness are likely to replace the boutiques and the traditional type of stores common to "one of the finest pedestrian streets in the world." (See item 951.)

451. "Misgivings at the Metropolitan." November 8, 1970, Section 2, p. 27.

"For the record, this writer believes that the museum is superlatively and dangerously wrong" in its expansion program. But Mrs. Huxtable knew the museum as a child and is nostalgic about the splendor of the space of the great hall, the chandeliers, and the tapestries, especially as they are now being replaced by a style of "expensive bank with corporate accessories to match."

452. "How Doth Welfare Island Fare?" November 15, 1970, Section 2, p. 27.

Philip Johnson and John Burgee are the choreographers of a group of architects planning residential developments on Welfare Island in New York's East River. Each contributing architect is "doing his own thing."

453. "Britain Wins the Housing Race." November 16, 1970,
     p. 37.

     Not all British housing may be of high standard in
     design and location, but at least it is being built to
     permit economic rents, and there is a possibility of a
     six percent surplus by 1973!

454. "Architecture: How Not to Build a City." November 22,
     1970, Section 2, p. 25.

     "Battery Park City sprang full blown from Governor
     Rockefeller's head ... much to New York's surprise ...
     on landfill that would extend Manhattan's shoreline
     north from the Battery, in this case on the Hudson
     River side ... in which the firm of Philip Johnson and
     John Burgee was brought in as a kind of architectural
     marriage broker to promote a shotgun wedding between
     the Governor's architect, Wallace K. Harrison, and the
     city's chief architects for the Lower Manhattan Plan,
     Conklin and Rossant.... Battery Park City is a potential
     tragedy of errors."

455. "The Chicago Style--On Its Way Out?" November 29, 1970,
     Section 2, p. 27.

     Two buildings in the Chicago Loop, the Stock Exchange
     by Adler and Sullivan, and the Carson Pirie Scott store
     by Sullivan, are discussed with relation to preservation.
     The Chicago Historical and Architectural Landmarks Com-
     mission requested landmark status from the owners of
     the Stock Exchange, who refused. Because the city council
     (which grants landmark status) supports the realtors' lobby,
     the Stock Exchange will be lost, while landmark status
     has been approved for the store, since it is in no im-
     mediate danger.

456. "Concept Points to 'City of Future.'" December 6, 1970,
     Section 8, pp. 1, 7.

     The first zoning ordinance for New York City came in
     1916. The most recent zoning code provides bonuses to
     developers who provide pedestrian and other amenities for
     the public. These bonuses are spelled out in a detailed
     manual. An explanation is given in an accompanying
     article (not by Mrs. Huxtable) on pp. 1, 4.

457. "Ode to Manhattan's Spires and Shards." December 6,
     1970, Section 1A (Special Section), p. 16.

     An essay on the generation of photographers who parallel

the twenty-year spurts of skyscraper construction in
Lower Manhattan. Examples of most recent highrise office
buildings are listed, with the comment that "a building
decreases in practicality and increases in cost as it
rises in height."

458.   "For a New and Presumably Better City." December 13,
       1970, Section 4, p. 12.

The 440,000-word study of New York City's master plan
has been finalized with the publication of the sixth
volume, on Manhattan. Some of the proposals may sound
utopian but most are realistic, if not immediately so.

459.   "Hands Across the Bureaucracy." December 20, 1970,
       Section 2, p. 26.

The Washington Market urban renewal area of Lower
West Side Manhattan, consisting of thirty-eight acres,
was demolished to make way for 1,335 housing units.
Three thirty-nine-story towers, plus town houses, were
planned at a total cost of $57 million. Additionally,
ten landmark 1820s Federal-style houses were incorporated into the scheme, six retained in their original
positions and others wheeled in. Gruzen, with others,
was the architect.

460.   "A Funny Roll of the Dice." December 27, 1970, Section
       2, p. 27.

The old Boston City Hall was saved from destruction
by converting it to commercial uses, thus producing
revenue for its upkeep. Mrs. Huxtable praises this
approach, as opposed to that of the United States General Services Administration, which prohibits commercial
uses for buildings no longer in use by the federal government. This article discusses other preservation
projects.

1971

461.   "Missing the Point (and Boat) at City Hall." January
       3, 1971, Section 2, p. 22.

The Astor Library, converted by Giorgio Cavaglieri, is
now the New York Shakespeare Festival Public Theater.
The city government threatens withdrawal of public funds
on the grounds of poverty (after investing $200 million
in Lincoln Center).

462.   "Bank's Building Plan Sets Off Debate on 'Progress.'"
        January 17, 1971, Section 8, pp. 1, 4.

        Because of real estate development, the $22 million
        First and Merchant's National Bank of Richmond, Virginia,
        wants to demolish some nineteenth-century cast-iron fronts.
        The problem of tax structure in relation to the regenera-
        tion of dying downtown areas is typical of that of many
        cities; the need for preservation goes hand in hand with
        redevelopment.

463.   "It's So Peaceful in the Country." January 17, 1971,
        Section 2, p. 29. Reprinted as "Art and Building:
        American Can: It's So Peaceful in the Country."
        Kicked a Building Lately? pp. 71-74.

        Discusses not only Gordon Bunshaft's American Can Co.,
        in Greenwich, Connecticut, but also the reality that
        many offices of prestige companies are moving from New
        York City into the countryside, usually in the direction
        of the residence of the president of the company. "The
        building is a beauty. A lot of people would call that
        irrelevant, but they shouldn't. American Can has not
        participated in the Rape of the Environment." The build-
        ing is in Bunshaft's favored form, that of a rectangular
        doughnut. Other aspects of the design are highly praised.

464.   "Library as Friend." January 24, 1971, Section 2, p. 22.
        Reprinted as "Pleasures: A Hard Act to Follow." *Kicked
        a Building Lately?* pp. 221-24.

        A love affair between Mrs. Huxtable and the New York
        Public Library with all its amenities. Financial troubles
        stem the purchase of books and the facility is closed on
        weekends. So, do become a friend and give a contribution
        to the library, especially "if the library has been a
        friend to you."

465.   "'Social Significance' Qualms Overcome in Design Awards."
        January 24, 1971, Section 8, pp. 1, 2.

        In the twelfth annual *Progressive Architecture* design
        awards, 1965, private housing was not a "valid architec-
        tural problem.... it had no social significance," accord-
        ing to the jury. But by 1971 things had changed again.
        Other building types receiving awards are discussed.

466.   "Not for the Medici." January 31, 1971, Section 2, p. 28.

        The Clinton Youth and Family Center at 314 West Fifty-

fourth Street, New York, an old District Police Court,
has been used as a center for six years. "A one million
dollar renovation job was begun in 1969 [by architect
James Polshek], producing well-programmed spaces and a
conscious style, but the building's uses and character
are dynamic rather than static." The Center is located
in an area called Hell's Kitchen, where "poverty, crime,
narcotics, alcoholism, bitterness and hate" exist.

467. "The Plot Thickens." February 14, 1971, Section 2, p.
25.

A synopsis of the attitudes of the present owners of
the Villard houses toward preservation. Much wheeling
and dealing seems to have been perpetrated during 1971
in order to sell the properties for maximum financial
gain without regard for the national significance of
the houses as a contribution to late nineteenth-century
American architecture.

468. "A Nation of Shopbuilders." February 21, 1971, Section
2, p. 20.

Several subjects of preservation are touched upon but
the salvation of the Art Nouveau shopfront on Massachusetts Avenue (facing Harvard Yard), in Cambridge, Massachusetts, gains most attention.

469. "Museum Exhibit Evokes a Lost Grace." March 7, 1971,
Section 8, pp. 1, 7.

"How Green Was My City," comparing scenes in New York
whose appearance has changed drastically over the years,
is the theme of an exhibition at the Museum of the City
of New York.

470. "Thinking Man's Zoning." March 7, 1971, Section 2, p.
22.

"Zoning does not solve social, racial and other urban
ills; it tells builders how they can build," but it could
help New York's Fifth Avenue to remain the major shopping
boulevard that it is. Commercial offices, banks, and
airlines pay higher rents than specialty shops, but the
shops are the essence of New York—its interesting di-
versity. Fifth Avenue has been designated a zoning
district (one of two in the city at present, the other
being Lower Manhattan) whereby all new buildings from
Thirty-eighth to Fifty-ninth Streets must have two floors
of retail space.

471.   "Compatibility Called Key to Building Plan." March 10,
       1971, p. 45.

       The house at 18 West Eleventh Street, New York, was
       inadvertently blown up by the daughter of the owner (with
       the assistance of her fellow Students for a Democratic
       Society). Architect Hugh Hardy purchased the site and
       wanted to build a sympathetically designed twentieth-
       century residence for two families. Greenwich Villagers
       wanted an 1844 house again. (See item 516.)

472.   "A Solid Dross City?" March 14, 1971, Section 2, p. 16.

       Air rights over a low-rise existing building, especially
       a structure designated a landmark, can be transferred to
       an adjoining site to permit added height on new construc-
       tion, beyond that scheduled by zoning. The code could
       apply equally to air rights over highways. "The quality
       of that urban experience is a calculated element of the
       new regulations." If it works in New York, why not also
       Chicago?

473.   "Pow! It's Good-bye History, Hello Hamburger." March 21,
       1971, Section 2, p. 23. Reprinted as "Failures: Good-
       bye History, Hello Hamburger." *Kicked a Building Lately?*
       pp. 254-56 (wrongly dated as March 31, 1971).

       "Mapleside," a pleasant mid-nineteenth-century house in
       Madison, Wisconsin, was demolished for a Burger King, which
       then received an award from an environmental-action group
       known as Capital Community Citizens of Dade County! This
       is one of several such examples cited.

474.   "Quiet Rules in Charleston as Bridge Plan Is Stayed."
       April 2, 1971, pp. 41, 78.

       Charleston, South Carolina, has 412 acres of historic
       downtown, preserved as a zone in 1931. The three main
       streets of this area would have an increase in the number
       of vehicles from 3,600 to 17,000 per day if the new bridge
       from suburban James Island were constructed. There are
       legal ways of preserving historic Charleston.

475.   "Charleston: Call It Making the City Work." April 4, 1971,
       Section 2, p. 23.

       The city fathers of Richmond, Virginia, could learn the
       art of preservation by taking a trip to Charleston, South
       Carolina. Charleston has found modern uses for old build-
       ings, in addition to the preservation of notable historic
       structures by nationally known architects.

476. "Anyone Dig the Art of Building." April 11, 1971, Section
      2, p. 26. Reprinted as "Art and Theory: Architecture
      in the 1970's." *Kicked a Building Lately?* pp. 42-44.

      In writing about the key monuments of architecture, Mrs.
      Huxtable states: "The history of architecture has been
      taught as a progression of monuments. Thank God for them.
      Without them, we would have a hard time claiming a civili-
      zation. In New York, the towers of the mammoth World
      Trade Center rise aggressively over everything else,
      gleaming like new minted money—the architecture of power.
      But what is built for the ordinary people and ordinary
      purposes, like a place to live or the pursuit of happi-
      ness?" This is the general theme of the article.

477. "Not for City Planners." April 18, 1971, Section 2, p.
      22.

      "Will Insley: Ceremonial Space," an exhibition at the
      Museum of Modern Art, illustrates in a sculpturesque
      manner the visionary, almost mystical, eschatological
      ideas of space and city. "The gap between vision and
      reality grows constantly."

478. "Only You Can Help Yourselves." April 25, 1971, Section
      2, p. 21.

      "Every preservation project is a cliff-hanger." The
      article explains which authorities to contact, where to
      do research, where to submit material, and to whom one
      should write.

479. "'You Have a Friend ...' Maybe." May 2, 1971, Section 2,
      p. 22.

      "The destruction of American towns of beauty or char-
      acter follows a predictable pattern," as in the case of
      Exeter, New Hampshire, where drive-in banks and gas sta-
      tions are likely to replace Federal and other nineteenth-
      century structures. Other towns with similar problems
      are cited.

480. "A Lot Happens in Ten Years." May 9, 1971, Section 2,
      p. 21.

      A lament for the possible passing of Richardson's
      Union Station, New London, Connecticut, 1885, scheduled
      for demolition in the 1961 urban renewal plan to provide
      a view of the river. According to architectural histor-
      ian Henry-Russell Hitchcock, this station was "the best
      of its type."

481. "Keeping the There There." May 16, 1971, Section 2, p. 21.

The Chicago Chapter of the American Institute of Architects leased Richardson's Glessner House, Chicago, and thus ensured that the structure would not be demolished. The article lists the Glessner House as one of many successful preservation projects.

482. "A Success as Architecture and as Monument. A Texas-Big Library Houses Impressive Exhibit of Era." May 23, 1971, Section 1, p. 39.

Gordon Bunshaft, of Skidmore, Owings and Merrill, has designed the latest of presidential libraries on the University of Texas campus at Austin, to house the papers of President Lyndon Baines Johnson. Such libraries satisfy presidential egos, a few researchers, and many memorabilia-viewing visitors. "It will be a long time before another presidential library is opened with a barbecue for 3,000."

483. "Too Bad About the Mall." May 23, 1971, Section 2, p. 29.

The State of New York is spending $4 billion on university campuses. 752 projects have cost about $1 billion, and others are in progress, notably one at Purchase designed by a host of outstanding architects.

484. "Covent Garden Plan: It Just Isn't Loverly." June 4, 1971, p. 9. Reprinted as "London: Covent Garden 1." *Kicked a Building Lately?* pp. 185-88 (wrongly dated June 14, 1971).

The Countess of Dartmouth, chairman of the Covent Garden Joint Development Committee of the Greater London Council, advocated preserving Covent Garden's charm by constructing a hotel and convention center. This would be at the expense of the area's low-rent business and residential mix, and its artistic, cultural, and architectural heritage. (See item 638.)

485. "London's New Buildings Are Closer to Miami." June 12, 1971, pp. 31, 58. Reprinted as "London: How Far from the Ocean." *Kicked a Building Lately?* pp. 182-85.

Richard Seifert and Partners are building many of the new London skyscrapers in a Pop Art style, and in so doing are making London look more like the worst of the United States.

486. "It's Hawksmoor's Day Again in London Town." June 13,
      1971, Section 2, p. 25. Reprinted as "Pleasures:
      Hawksmoor London." *Kicked a Building Lately?* pp. 193-
      96.

      Christ Church, Spitalfield's, London, 1729, needs
      $160,000 for refurbishing. Mrs. Huxtable, admitting
      "I joined the Hawksmoor buffs," describes Hawksmoor's
      professional background.

487. "London's Shops--Part Oriental Bazaar, Part Lower East
      Side." June 22, 1971, p. 40.

      London has American, French, youth-culture, boutique,
      and Oriental-bazaar type stores. "Everything must Pro-
      claim the Hip."

488. "London's Second Blitz." June 27, 1971, Section 2, p.
      25. Reprinted as "London: The Second Blitz." *Kicked
      a Building Lately?* pp. 179-82.

      London has been laundered to a middlin' cream color
      instead of the soft chiaroscuro black of yesteryears.
      Gone, too, is some of the character, destroyed partially
      by the new scale of the skyscraper.

489. "Next Crisis: A Loss of Faith." July 4, 1971, Section
      2, p. 20. Reprinted as "Art and Theory: A Loss of Faith."
      Kicked a Building Lately? pp. 48-50.

      The twentieth-century British architect has become
      technician in place of artist. He works with "arrogant
      detached disregard." The article is, in part, a review
      of Martin Pawley's new book *Architecture Versus Housing.*
      "Mr. Pawley may be the Jane Jacobs of architectural theory."

490. "London: A Design That Soured." July 11, 1971, Section
      8, pp. 1, 11.

      A grass roots movement in London is attempting to save
      Covent Garden. Britishers are no longer willing to accept
      what paternalistic planners consider to be good for them.
      Other historic structures and areas in London are also
      listed, including the famed Barbican area, north of St.
      Paul's. "And yet, no one has approached planning with
      more dedication and intelligence than the British. No
      country has had the idealism, the talent and conviction."

491. "Mr. Pei Comes to Washington." July 11, 1971, Section 2,
      p. 24. Reprinted as "Art and Building: The National

Gallery: Breaking the Role of Mediocrity." *Kicked a Building Lately?* pp. 84-87.

The East Building of the National Gallery of Art is "a great building for all time." The enhancement of an awkward site by a work of architecture in scale with the existing gallery is something that Washington deserves.

492. "There's More to a Pub Than Meets the Lips." August 8, 1971, Section 8, pp. 1, 7.

Mrs. Huxtable likes the authentic atmosphere of London pubs, especially those in old buildings. They are comparable to New York's Third Avenue bars, and so different from the fake superficiality of the New York "pub." The atmosphere in several London pubs is described and some are named. Maurice Gorham and H. McG. Dermott's *Inside the London Pub* (London: Architectural Press, 1950) is quoted.

493. "The Big Tent: Structural Be-All?" August 15, 1971, Section 2, p. 18.

Tensile and pneumatic structures by the German architect Frei Otto were exhibited at the Museum of Modern Art. His work from 1955 was illustrated, and a fifty-foot-high, 2,300-square-foot structure exhibited. Mrs. Huxtable doesn't take the tent or any other flash-in-the-pan structure as the answer to the future. Neither simple, nor cheap, they are expensive in their testing and development.

494. "Sorry Wrong Number." August 22, 1971, Section 2, p. 18.

The proposed New York Telephone Building at Pearl and Madison Streets is to be 540 feet high and cost $80 million. Although overly close to the Brooklyn Bridge, it is acceptable to the city because New York needs the service provided and the new school which will be incorporated into the scheme. It will cost the Telephone Company $4 million for air rights. "No one has beat the soul-selling rap yet."

495. "Architecture: A Look at the Kennedy Center." September 7, 1971, pp. 1, 46. Reprinted as "The Monumental Muddle: The Kennedy Center, 1." *Kicked a Building Lately?* pp. 3-5.

Edward D. Stone's superbunker, 300x630 feet, and 100

feet high, has a corridor 60x600 feet, containing eighteen chandeliers, plus Hall of State and Hall of Nations,
plus concert hall, opera house, and theater. It is
brash, gargantuan, and a national tragedy. "It is a
cross between a concrete candy box and a marble sarco-
phagus in which the art of architecture lies buried."
An award-winning article. (See item 954.)

496. "Some Sour Notes Sound at the Kennedy Center." September
      19, 1971, Section 2, p. 25. Reprinted as "The Monu-
      mental Muddle: The Kennedy Center, II." *Kicked a
      Building Lately?* pp. 6-8.

      Mrs. Huxtable laments the fact that in a country of
      tremendous architectural potential, Washingtonians
      should accept the Kennedy Center because it fills a
      cultural void. Mr. Stone is a talented, charming friend
      who forged ahead in the Modern Movement in the 1930s,
      and reappeared in the 1950s and 1960s with a new and
      highly successful philosophy of design: Modern archi-
      tecture can be decorative and timeless. "Decorative
      recall is no substitute for a creative act. The Ken-
      nedy Center makes one sad, angry and considerably
      ashamed.... And Mr. Stone ... owes himself more."

497. "New Prison Designs Emphasize Human Elements." September
      21, 1971, p. 74.

      In an era of needed prison reforms and new design
      concepts in prison facilities, Gruzen Associates has
      made the attempt. A $12 million building to house 400
      detainees has been designed for Park Row, New York City.
      Another, to house 504 men, was built by the same firm at
      Leesburg, New Jersey, in 1958, at a cost of $16 million.
      Good planning, landscaping, and an attitude of rehabilita-
      tion are forward-looking attitudes.

498. "New Bar Center Offers Lesson in Civilized Architecture."
      September 25, 1971, p. 33. Reprinted as "Successes:
      Albany: A Happy Alliance of Past and Present." *Kicked
      a Building Lately?* pp. 240-42.

      The new headquarters of the New York Bar Association,
      in Albany, consists of refurbished nineteenth-century
      row houses, plus a new structure at the rear. It would
      have been cheaper to demolish and forget, but preserva-
      tion, not merely of facades, but interior spaces, too,
      won out.

499. "Celebrating 'Dumb, Ordinary' Architecture." October 1,
      1971, p. 43.

      An architectural billboard of Venturi's work, slogans,
      and philosophy was exhibited at the Whitney Museum, New
      York City. "If you like it, you like the Venturis. If
      not, this way out."

500. "The Endless Search." October 3, 1971, Section 2, p.
      25.

      Piano and Rogers won the competition for the Beaubourg,
      near Les Halles, Paris, for their scheme of "non-archi-
      tecture," as one juror described it. But is it non-
      architecture or "a monument to end all monuments"?

501. "Plastic Flowers Are Almost All Right." October 10,
      1971, Section 2, p. 22. Reprinted as "Art and Theory:
      Buildings You Love to Hate." *Kicked a Building Lately?*
      pp. 45-47.

      Mrs. Huxtable expresses "some personal feelings and
      guarded opinions about the work and theory of Venturi
      and Rauch." They are the heretics to modern doctrine,
      but their theories are down to earth and practical. They
      preach and practice the art of the possible. Their archi-
      tecture is the "mediocrity with which America has housed
      and serviced itself."

502. "Albia, Iowa, Has Lessons to Teach City." October 24,
      1971, Section 8, pp. 1, 8.

      Albia was founded in 1859, has a population today of
      4,500, and has recently spent $150,000 on "common sense
      restoration." Mrs. Huxtable feels that this could serve
      admirably as a model for Long Island towns, where old
      houses are demolished as bad, and brand-new ones erected
      as good. Albia is not fake modernization but the real
      thing, well done. Credit is given to those involved.

503. "Co-op City's Grounds: After 3 years a Success." October
      26, 1971, p. 43.

      Co-op City, on the Hutchinson River Parkway in the
      Bronx, is a success, unbelievable as it may seem. $5.4
      million worth of landscaping by Zion and Breen serves as
      a foil to 15,372 well-planned apartments.

504. "If It's Good, Leave It Alone." October 31, 1971, Sec-
      tion 2, p. 22.

      A tale of two hotels: the Plaza, New York City, by

Henry Janeway Hardenberg, which was being unsympathetic-
ally remodelled; and the Mohonk Mountain House, an 1880s
Catskills retreat in "austere Victorian plain," with the
help of Napoleon Le Brun. (See the Plaza's response, item
956.)

505. "An Edwardian Splendor or Green Tulip Modern?" November
      5, 1971, pp. 45, 47.

      The Green Tulip is the name given to the refurbished
      Edwardian Room at Hardenberg's Plaza Hotel. It has
      desecrated the Edwardian feeling of the original, however,
      and it is to be hoped that the Landmarks Preservation Com-
      mission will have power in the future to prevent such
      acts of vandalism.

506. "Cooper Union Projects Vary Architecture Show." November
      13, 1971, p. 24.

      Reviews an exhibition at the Architectural League of
      New York called "Education of an Architect--a Point of
      View." The work exhibited will be admired for its esthetic
      qualities, but should also be appreciated for the related
      interdisciplinary studies which have an effect upon today's
      architecture. "The Cooper Union program also begets a
      product, something currently unpopular as a skill."

507. "Non-Fables for Our Time." November 14, 1971, Section
      2, p. 22.

      The Lincoln Memorial, Washington, D.C., seems to be dis-
      integrating "like a giant Alka-Seltzer tablet." Although
      this article begins with this lament, and the moralization
      that "A country gets the monument it deserves," the major
      portion is concerned with the Chicago School and the sky-
      scraper, notably those that have been demolished. "Final
      moral: We get the cities we deserve."

508. "Architectural Study Says City Gets Poor Service at High
      Cost." November 23, 1971, pp. 1, 45.

      The problem with planning and architectural design in
      New York City is that plans and budgets are unrealistic.
      Delays, contracts, bidding, reviews, poor design, and
      poor site supervision are some of the basic problems of
      construction in the city, as outlined in an architectural
      study by the Urban Design Council.

509. "The Federal Funnybone." November 28, 1971, Section 2,
      p. 22.

The General Services Administration is having a change
of heart concerning its surplus buildings. Mullett's St.
Louis Post Office precipitated this change of attitude.
Formerly, old buildings owned by the government have
been sold to state or local authorities for non-profit
uses. An airport passenger terminal in downtown St.
Louis would be profit making, but this, or a similar
use, may be the only feasible means of utilizing the
old structure and thereby preserving it.

510. "The Building You Love to Hate." December 12, 1971,
        Section 2, p. 29.

Rudolph's Art and Architecture Building at Yale acci-
dentally burned in 1969, at an appropriate moment from
the point of strained student-administration relations.
Space, both physical and ideological, was considered
too dominant by students of painting, sculpture, and
architecture.

511. "Architects Unit Endorses City Master Plan--with Qualifica-
        tions." December 19, 1971, Section 1, p. 46.

The New York Chapter of the American Institute of
Architects supports the New York City Master Plan as "a
vital organic framework," but with the proviso that amenities must grow with higher densities.

512. "A Vision of Cities Revived in a Book." December 19,
        1971, Section 8, pp. 1-2.

Gordon Cullen's *Townscape* praised the relationship within the city. Ten years later, *The Precise Townscape* re-
emphasizes these relationships, especially of space between
buildings. New York City has lost many of its intimate
town-type streets and has replaced them with open areas
between high structures.

513. "American Place Theater Finds a Cozy Home Under New City
        Code." December 21, 1971, pp. 39, 51.

The American Place Theatre has been built at 111 West
Forty-sixth Street in an attempt to retain a theater
district in the city, under a pioneer project of Mayor
Lindsay for special theater-district zoning (1967).
Three other new theaters are projected, and existing
theaters will be preserved. "This is a remarkable planning package, and New York is way out in front in the
creative and constructive use of zoning." Describes the
American Place Theatre and gives credits.

514. "A Bad End and a Good Idea." December 26, 1971, Section
     2, p. 24.

     Chicago has done little to preserve its heritage, least
     of all in respect to the Stock Exchange, but when New
     York's Metropolitan Museum of Art wanted the Exchange's
     large entrance arch and adjoining colonnade to incorpor-
     ate into its new extensions, Chicago objected to the arch's
     leaving the Windy City. "This unwillingness to see the
     arch go was not, of course, matched by an equal unwilling-
     ness to see the building go."

                           1972

515. "Architecture in '71: Lively Confusion." January 4,
     1972, p. 26.

     "Today the architect is in the process of painful
     professional soul-searching." Social process, style,
     and other current trends, together with architectural
     examples, are discussed.

516. "The Landmark Hole in the Ground." January 9, 1972,
     Section 2, p. 25.

     "This is a saga of an unbuilt house, and also a tale
     of the odds against you in New York. It is about the
     house on West 11th Street--the one that was to be built
     on the site of No. 18, which achieved a kind of national
     fame when it was blown up by young revolutionaries almost
     two years ago. The original house dated from 1844-5 and
     the present design [by Hugh Hardy] was to be a house for
     two families." Thus began the story of the opposition
     and red tape and the increase in the cost of construction
     from $125,000 to $175,000 minimum, which prevented the
     owners from building. (See item 471.)

517. "Where They Do It Right." January 23, 1972, Section 2,
     p. 23.

     Having seen much of Aalto's work in the United States
     and Finland, Mrs. Huxtable admires his newest design,
     the Finlandia Hall, Helsinki. She likes the elements,
     relationships, light, color, and detail--all subtle,
     restrained, and "painstakingly beautiful." It is admired
     and described, and compared to similar halls in the United
     States.

518.   "The F.B.I. Building: A Study in Soaring Costs and Capital
       Views on Beauty." January 24, 1972, p. 16.

       "Anonymous Federal construction" continues in Washington
       with the new $126 million, 2.5 million-square-foot FBI
       Building on Pennsylvania Avenue between Tenth and Eleventh
       Streets. Murphy Associates has built several notable
       civic buildings; this is not one of them, although "it
       could be a lot worse. It could have looked like the Ray-
       burn Building." The complex and its varied facilities are
       described.

519.   "$5-Billion Urban Reform Proposed by Architects." January
       25, 1972, pp. 37, 39.

       The American Institute of Architects has, by a $5 bil-
       lion public land-purchase program, forwarded a policy of
       involvement by the federal government in urban develop-
       ments. Called "A Strategy for Building a Better America,"
       the report is described in detail.

520.   "Renwick Gallery Wins Survival Battle." January 28, 1972,
       p. 24. Reprinted as "Successes: Washington: Victoriana
       Lives." *Kicked a Building Lately?* pp. 245-48.

       Scheduled for demolition in 1958, the Corcoran Gallery,
       Washington, D.C., commissioned in 1858 and opened as a
       gallery in 1871, has been restored at a cost of $2.8
       million. The spirit of Renwick's day and age seems to
       have been recaptured--"a jewel setting for the arts of
       design."

521.   "Forest Hills: Innovation vs. Red Tape." February 8,
       1972, pp. 35, 66.

       Ulrich Franzen's original idea for a scatter-site
       housing project in Forest Hills, Queens, was for a mix
       of lowrise and highrise apartments. Financial expediency
       resulted in the abandonment of the idea and the architect,
       in preference for the housing authority's more standard
       norm. Details of the financial and design aspects are
       provided. (Had Franzen's ideas been taken seriously,
       Forest Hills' later social problems might not have
       arisen.)

522.   "Cultural Shock Anyone?" February 13, 1972, Section 2,
       p. 22.

       The Museum of Modern Art exhibited projects for the
       Beaubourg site in Paris. The prize-winning design in

this international competition was of a modifiable building, all elements of which could be changed to suit varying conditions, designed by Renzo Piano and Richard Rogers. "These are not just the affectations of youth: they are in many ways the realities of today's existence."

523. "Bicentennial Panel Urges Network of Parks. Project Could Cost Up to $1.2-Billion, Commission Says." February 23, 1972, p. 18.

The federal government is likely to spend $1.2 billion on small parks, 100 to 500 acres in extent, to be planned by the states as part of the 1976 program.

524. "Your Friendly Bank Knows Best." March 5, 1972, Section 2, p. 23.

"Main Street everywhere" is being dominated by local banks and their financial policies. The Vermont National Bank bought the 1835 Greek Revival Windsor House at Windsor and wanted to demolish it. They later agreed to sell it to any non-profit organization, a virtual impossibility. Gives similar examples of banks' attempts to dictate, on behalf of their shareholders, to local communities.

525. "It's All in the Mind--and Eye." March 19, 1972, p. 22.

"Oh modernity what crimes are committed in thy name?" is the theme of this article on preservation. Lists arguments and ploys used to destroy America's heritage.

526. "Piranesi's Roman Grandeur on Show." March 22, 1972, p. 58. Reprinted as "Pleasures: Piranesi's Rome." *Kicked a Building Lately?* pp. 197-98.

Columbia University's Piranesi exhibition illustrated the "phantasmagoric, ... overscaled ... panoramas" of one of the many eras of creative Rome. On display were 110 items, including twenty-three drawings.

527. "Carnegie House Given to Cooper-Hewitt Museum." April 1, 1972, pp. 1, 11.

Gifts from various donors have made the re-use of the Carnegie Mansion a reality, with the conversion in the hands of Hardy Holzman Pfeiffer. Provides background material on the museum.

528. "A Place of Genuine Joy." April 2, 1972, Section 2, p. 21.

This is the second article on the Piranesi exhibition at Columbia University (see item 526), sponsored by the Avery

Architectural Library. Mrs. Huxtable praises the re-
sources and the librarians of this, the most prestigious
architectural library in the world.

529. "Architect Selected by Jury for City Convention Center."
      April 6, 1972, p. 45.

      Twenty-seven architectural firms submitted designs
      for New York City's proposed $100 million Convention
      Center, to be built along the Hudson River between
      Forty-fourth and Forty-seventh Streets. Skidmore,
      Owings and Merrill were chosen from a short-list of six
      firms. Excellence in design was the first criterion,
      with cost a close second. The firm is analyzed with
      relation to Gordon Bunshaft, the designer of the center.

530. "Environment Key to Downtown Plan. Concept Called Good
      Because of Care in Its Design." April 13, 1972, p.
      48.

      The Office for Lower Manhattan Development aims to
      improve the "quality of the environment." This will be
      possible if realtors realize that they can turn a profit
      by so doing. Zoning variances are used in giving planning
      permission in exchange for amenities for people (open
      space, covered walkways, galleria, shopping, etc.).

531. "Some Awful Building Truths." April 16, 1972, Section
      2, p. 21.

      Various agencies, corporations, and development programs
      established by state or city governments tend to produce
      mediocrity in architectural design. This mediocrity is
      frequently tied to scandalous corruption. In 1972, a
      New York Council on Architecture was formed. It recog-
      nizes the problems and hopes to do something about them.

532. "And This Time--The Good Banks." April 30, 1972, Section
      2, p. 22.

      Gives examples of good conversions of historic properties
      into banks, but is essentially concerned with the Security
      Bank and Trust Company, Owatonna, Minnesota, 1908, by
      Sullivan, aided by George Grant Elmslie. Provides a
      brief sketch of this particular bank up to the period of
      its restoration in 1958 by Harwell Hamilton Harris.

533. "The Decline (and Fall?) of Italy's Cultural Environment."
      May 12, 1972, p. 43.

      "Visit Italy Now, Before the Italians Destroy It," a

poster title which Mrs. Huxtable came across, is linked
to an exhibition entitled "Art and Landscape of Italy--
Too Late to Be Saved?" at the Metropolitan Museum of Art.
The exhibition represents how "industry, expansion and
migration have totally dislocated the traditional Italian
society and scene." Oil refineries along the coast, the
automobile in the tightly knit towns, and the abandon-
ment of old buildings spell decline, but "the exhibition's
organizers say No."

534.   "Metropolitan to Set Up Wright Interior." May 15, 1972,
       p. 42.

       The Francis W. Little House, Wayzata, Minnesota, 1912-
       15, has been demolished and one room will be installed
       in the American Wing of the Metropolitan Museum of Art.
       It is the "first museum display of a major, original
       room to document the work of the American master archi-
       tect."

535.   "Two Buildings Win Design Awards." May 19, 1972, p. 18.

       Kennedy Airport's National Airlines Terminal, by I.M.
       Pei, was given the prestigious Bard Award (which is also
       described).

536.   "It Isn't Green Cheese." May 21, 1972, Section 2, p. 25.

       During 1972, the 150th anniversary of Frederick Law
       Olmsted's birth, numerous exhibitions and sesquicentennial
       celebrations were staged. The article outlines Olmsted's
       career, his successes, his interest in national, phil-
       anthropic, and city concerns, and his contribution,
       specifically to New York City.

537.   "Italian Design Show Appraised--Ambiguous But Beautiful."
       May 26, 1972, p. 43.

       A show at the Museum of Modern Art entitled "The New
       Domestic Landscape" includes 180 objects, eleven com-
       missioned for the architectural environment from Italian
       designers.

538.   "Designing the Death of Design--But Stylishly." June 4,
       1972, Section 2, p. 23.

       When Mrs. Huxtable returned with material from Italy
       in 1952, she and it were more or less ignored. In 1972,
       the high quality of Italian design was discovered and
       was exhibited at the Museum of Modern Art in a show

entitled "Italy: The New Domestic Landscape." The
material is "all style and none of it is quite real."

539. "New Bronx Zoo Building a Rara Avis." June 14, 1972,
      p. 40.

      Impressive buildings for the birds were designed by
      Morris Ketchum, Jr., with attention to the natural en-
      vironment. A history of the older buildings is given.

540. "The Old Lady of 29 East Fourth St." June 18, 1972,
      Section 2, p. 22.

      This is a Greek Revival residence of 1832, which has
      almost self-destructed from lack of care. Funds have
      been provided from several public and private sources.
      Mrs. Huxtable raises the question of interior spaces,
      which are not protected in the Landmarks Preservation
      Law, as are the exteriors of structures. Gives examples
      of preserved landmarks in which the interiors are as
      important as the exteriors.

541. "Stein's 'Sunnyside' Left a Permanent Imprint." June
      25, 1972, Section 8, pp. 1, 10.

      As Clarence S. Stein reaches his ninetieth birthday,
      he is remembered for garden city suburbs "that believed
      simply, brilliantly and without cynicism or fear of
      future shock, in a better world." Land was not owned
      by individuals in these garden communities. Thus, they
      were carefully planned rather than speculative, and
      institutionalized healthy features which in other com-
      munities today are accepted as standard. Describes the
      planning and the individual residences.

542. "Putting Together a Perfect Doomsday Package." July 2,
      1972, Section 2, p. 16.

      The First National Bank of Oregon, Portland, 1916, in
      all its Doric splendor, is being threatened with demoli-
      tion to provide space for a parking lot for a new eye-
      catching, status-seeking highrise bank building by Charles
      Luckman. Will the low image of the bank's intentions
      save the dignified old structure?

543. "Open Space Designs Breathing New Life Into Smothered
      Blocks." July 6, 1972, pp. 39, 74.

      New York is not dying. This optimism comes from the
      new trends in open spaces, revitalized streets, parks,

and plazas. They create a compromise between the sterile glass box with a bank at ground level, and the stimulating variety of the old lowrise buildings with a multitude of stores at ground level. Lists numerous examples.

544. "Lights Out?" July 16, 1972, Section 2, p. 22.

The energy crisis of 1972 and after is likely to play havoc with buildings that rely upon the controlled environment--sixty-seven million square feet of them since 1952. We rely too much on glass, air-conditioning, aluminum (six times as costly in electric power to produce as steel), and the enclosure of buildings. Does a building need to be sealed, conditioned, or heated continuously? Do we need to rethink?

545. "How a Pool Grew in Brooklyn." August 13, 1972, Section 2, p. 18.

Alan Lapidus, son of Morris Lapidus, designed the 2.3-acre pool in the Bedford-Stuyvesant section of Brooklyn. It took six years of battling through a maze of red tape. Service stacks have become sculptures, planning and layout have been imaginatively handled, and the tall lighting stands provide for night-time activities.

546. "New Boston Center: Skillful Use of Urban Space." September 11, 1972, pp. 39, 73.

The Boston redevelopment plan by Pei comprises "thirty coordinated buildings" in a variety of architectural expressions. Discussion centers around the achievements, admitting, however, that the new grows from the rubble of demolished structures which gave the old Boston a character of its own. Several buildings of landmark status have been retained and refurbished. Lists the new structures and their designers.

547. "Doing the Hard Things First." September 24, 1972, Section 2, p. 26.

Graphics of all types, small parks, new housing, transportation, and the landscape are being revitalized in various ways in New York City. The New York Cultural Center has an exhibition illustrating the methods by which designers in all fields are "Making New York Understandable."

548. "Architecture at the Head of Its Class." September 27,

1972, p. 38. Reprinted as "Art and Building: Princeton Institute: At the Head of Its Class." *Kicked a Building Lately?* pp. 88-90.

Princeton's Institute for Advanced Study contains new facilities for eating and administration, by Geddes Brecher Qualls Cunningham. It is a functional building, designed with taste and integrated into the landscape. Briefly describes the workings of the Institute and of the building itself.

549.   "You Win Some, You Lose Some." October 8, 1972, Section 2, p. 29.

Cites several examples of historic structures saved and lost, but concentrates on two Fifth Avenue houses opposite the Metropolitan Museum of Art which were razed. Explains loopholes in the Historic Landmarks Preservation Law which allow demolitions.

550.   "2 Shows Celebrate Olmsted's Talent." October 19, 1972, p. 54.

The sesquicentennial celebrations of Olmsted's birth were acknowledged in numerous ways, including two exhibitions, one at the Whitney Museum of Art, New York, and one at the National Gallery, Washington, D.C. Provides a summation of Olmsted research sources and publications, in addition to details of his life and his work in the field of landscape architecture.

551.   "Old City Hall in Boston Gets a New Life." October 21, 1972, p. 39.

Instead of being demolished, the Boston City Hall, 1862-65, by Bryant and Gilman, has been refurbished into modern offices, with a French restaurant in the basement (the basement walls are those of an earlier city hall by Charles Bulfinch). Provides a detailed account of the steps taken in preserving the building. "Those who said it couldn't be done are enjoying tournedos and a good little Burgundy at Maison Robert."

552.   "The Past Is a Moment Ago." October 22, 1972, Section 2, p. 27.

In other words, the past is a preface to the present, but let's be careful that we don't recreate a replica of what we feel the past should have been. This is almost as bad as demolition of the past. Examples to support this thesis are taken from Boston.

553. "New Exeter Library: Stunning Paean to Books." October 23, 1972, p. 33. Reprinted as "Art and Building: Louis Kahn: Exeter Library." *Kicked a Building Lately?* pp. 95-98.

The new library for Phillips Exeter Academy, Exeter, New Hampshire, cost $3.8 million and was built of local brick; it thus blends. The bricks talked to Kahn and said that they enjoyed working with the huge internal areas of concrete, because both are part of a modern structure.

554. "Megalopolis' Show: Artists and the Urban Scene. Hans Haacker's Exhibit Looks at Real Estate." October 31, 1972, p. 54.

Columbia University School of Architecture has sponsored a chronological presentation of work by Walter Gropius from 1906 to 1969. Mention is also made of "Making Megalopolis Matter," a show on real estate at the New York Cultural Center.

555. "A Prescription for Disaster." November 5, 1972, Section 2, p. 23.

Pruitt-Igoe housing, St. Louis, Missouri, by Hellmuth, Yamasaki and Leinweber, "one of the great American social reforms--safe and sanitary housing in exchange for slums --has obviously gone off the rails." Draws on Oscar Newman's *Defensible Space: Crime Prevention Through Urban Design*, which basically claims that vandalism and crime increase with the height of highrise structures built by public authorities. Lists other projects in New York City and elsewhere.

556. "New Harvard Hall: Drama and Questions." November 8, 1972, p. 52.

The Graduate School of Design at Harvard has moved into its new home, Gund Hall, by John Andrews, a Toronto architect. Built in an age of conflict, it perhaps reflects the derisive attitudes of instructors and students at the school, all of whom work under a single sloping glass roof, in a school without walls.

557. "The Bigger They Are...." November 19, 1972, Section 2, p. 22.

The Art Deco Railroad Station at Cincinnati by Fellheimer and Wagner, 1933, is the subject of this article on preservation, since the station is scheduled for demolition.

558. "Illuminating Show of Breuer's Work." November 30, 1972,
      p. 54. Reprinted as "Art and Building: The Work of
      Marcel Breuer." *Kicked a Building Lately?* pp. 90-92.

      An exhibition covering fifty years of Breuer's work was
      held at the Metropolitan Museum of Art. Discusses Breu-
      er's background, his furniture designs, and his archi-
      tecture in France, England, Israel, and the United States.

559. "What's Higher Than Highest? Wait and See." December 3,
      1972, Section 2, p. 23.

      The race to build taller buildings after they first
      reached 100 feet in the 1930s resulted in a series of
      new buildings throughout Manhattan. They seek prestige,
      high density, and economy of land, but have decided dis-
      advantages. They are not generally popular as living
      environments, but there are those who will always have
      the desire to build them.

                              1973

560. "Nothing Is the Way It Was." February 11, 1973, Section
      2, pp. 25, 27.

      Architecture can be many things. It can be a magnifi-
      cent structure or, equally, an answer to a social need.
      An architect can serve the private or the public sector,
      as in the case of the Office of Lower Manhattan Develop-
      ment.

561. "That Was No Lady in Hoopskirts." February 25, 1973,
      Section 2, pp. 23, 25.

      Cooper Union, at Astor Place, Manhattan, 1853-58, is
      the subject of this article. A history of the building
      is given, including Peter Cooper's innovative step of
      producing the first wrought iron I-section beam of any
      significant length made in the United States.

562. "Must Bad Buildings Be the Norm." March 11, 1973, Sec-
      tion 2, pp. 23-24.

      $100,000 was appropriated to improve the design standards
      of the federal government in the sphere of architecture,
      products, and graphics, all of which are briefly discussed.

563. "Architecture: Washington Never Slept Here." March 25,
      1973, Section 2, pp. 25-26.

      A general review of vernacular industrial architecture,

usually utilitarian in form, and the materials used in
its construction. Describes various mill towns, the
buildings in them, and the preservation programs related
to them.

564.   "Big But Not So Bold. Trade Center Towers Are Tallest,
       But Architecture Is Smaller Scale." April 5, 1973,
       p. 34. Reprinted as "New York: Big But Not So Bold:
       The World Trade Center." *Kicked a Building Lately?*
       pp. 122-23.

       Discusses the New York Port Authority twin tower World
       Trade Center by Minoru Yamasaki. Its structure and modu-
       lar grid are of interest, but the building must be judged
       in relation to its environment.

565.   "Architecturally, a Promise in Use of 'Found Space.'"
       April 13, 1973, p. 41.

       City Center Cinemathèque, a museum and exhibition
       center costing $6.5 million, is to be built under the
       Queensborough Bridge in Manhattan. Architect Pei is
       using the "found space" under this historic bridge for
       a sympathetic new Space-use-area. Mel Gussow's article
       in the same issue provides additional information.

566.   "A Plan for Chicago." April 15, 1973, Section 2, p. 23.

       Chicago is losing some nationally known structures at
       an alarming rate. A proposal is therefore being for-
       warded that air rights above historic structures should
       be sold by owners of the buildings to offset the loss
       of retaining the structures (rather than demolishing
       them and building more profitable pieces of real estate
       on their sites).

567.   "Architects, in Show, Face Energy Crisis." April 19,
       1973, p. 50.

       "The Architect and the Energy Crisis" was a travelling
       photographic show of the New York Chapter of the American
       Institute of Architects. The exhibition questioned the
       sealed-in glass box attitude of design in which the
       environment is dehumanizingly controlled.

568.   "Revolt in London." April 29, 1973, Section 2, pp. 21,
       23.

       The subject is Picadilly Circus and the grass roots
       movement (new in England) to save it "like-it-is!" There

have already been fifty proposals for Picadilly in a space of fifteen years.

569.   "Roosevelt Memorial Design Hits Snags." May 1, 1973, p. 48.

An FDR Memorial on Welfare Island, in New York's East River, apparently hit some snags but will be going ahead, although only twenty instead of sixty feet in height.

570.   "Wright Show Tells of the Wrangles in Creation of a Landmark House." May 5, 1973, p. 41.

"An Architect and His Client," an exhibition on Wright at the Metropolitan Museum of Art, related to the future installation in the American Wing of two rooms from the Francis W. Little House at Wayzata, Minnesota, 1912-14. One of the two rooms is the living room, which measures 35x35 and is 14.5 feet high.

571.   "Only the Phony is Real." May 13, 1973, Section 2, p. 24.   Reprinted as "Failures: Only the Phony Is Real." *Kicked a Building Lately?* pp. 256-59.

Nashville, Tennessee's Union Gospel Tabernacle, 1892, was converted to Ryman's Auditorium in 1904, and from 1925 has been known as the Grand Old Opry House.   The National Life and Accident Insurance Company is to demolish it to build a new Opry House, costing $12 million, as part of Opryland, a $38 million amusement park.

572.   "Lessons in How to Heal the City's Scars." May 27, 1973, Section 2, p. 19.

The National Endowment for the Arts has provided $1 million in grants for the "City Edges" program.   City edges are those awkward spots edging railroad yards, canals, and the like.   Cities which have been awarded such grants are listed, together with particular projects.

573.   "Innovative Design and Planning Takes Shape in Lower Manhattan." June 8, 1973, pp. 41, 48.

Praises the innovations of the Office of Lower Manhattan Development and the way in which it is helping to shape the city.   Several noteworthy developments are listed.

574.   "Anti-Street, Anti-People." June 10, 1973, Section 2, p. 24.

Something has gone wrong at Skidmore, Owings and Merrill.
Is it hardening of the arteries or just arrogance? Mrs.
Huxtable praises the Hancock and Sears towers in Chicago,
but questions the blindness of the anti-environment structures on Forty-second and Fifty-seventh Streets, Manhattan.
This criticism of Gordon Bunshaft claims that "good taste,
superior technology and impeccable execution," ignoring
the immediate and general surroundings, are not good enough.

575. "Pei's Bold Gem--Cornell Museum." June 11, 1973, p. 47.

Ours is an age of housing projects and museums, the
latter building type, private and public, seeming to
sprout all over the country, designed by all the well-
known names in architecture. Cornell's museum, donated
by Herbert F. Johnson of Johnson Wax fame, is meant not
only to house a collection; its giraffe-like form is
meant also as a viewing platform for the campus and the
Finger Lakes Region.

576. "Architecture: 6 Designs Win Bard Merit Awards." June
     14, 1973, p. 58.

A report on who received the 1973 Bard Awards for
Excellence in Architecture. Lists the jurors along with
the winners and their schemes.

577. "Another Chance for Housing." June 24, 1973, Section 2,
     p. 23.

Low-income housing, accompanied by the usual trend of
poor design, has proved to be anti-social in the United
States. Arthur Drexler of the Museum of Modern Art
staged an exhibition entitled "Another Chance for Housing:
Low Rise Alternatives." Discusses various schemes illustrated in this exhibition, their aims, and their qualities.

578. "Good Buildings Are Hard to Get." July 8, 1973, Section
     2, p. 19.

Historic structures are demolished in urban areas, but
so, too, are notable old halls on college campuses. Cites
several examples of both types of destruction.

579. "54-Story Hotel Expected to Revitalize Times Square."
     July 11, 1973, pp. 43, 50.

A new hotel at Times Square, on the west side of Broadway between Forty-fifth and Forty-sixth Streets, is to
begin in 1974, for completion in 1977. Three theaters

will be demolished and will be replaced by one. There
will also be a covered throughway. Perhaps the hotel
will revitalize the Times Square area. Gives background
on architect John Portman and his operation.

580. "Battery Park City, in 3d Plan, Hovers Between Dream and
      a Disaster." July 14, 1973, pp. 27, 37. Reprinted as
      "New York: Battery Park City: Dream or Disaster?"
      Kicked a Building Lately? pp. 118-22.

      Describes the plan for the "city" to be built on land
      fill from the Battery to Forty-second Street along the
      Hudson River. Lists the governmental and organizational
      agencies, and the architects involved. Discusses the
      pros and cons of the scheme, the compromise plans, the
      battles between the various developers and architects,
      and the question of whether or not it will ever material-
      ize.

581. "'Uglification Has Followed Ruin.'" July 22, 1973, Sec-
      tion 2, p. 15.

      Bath, England, has destroyed 308 of its recognized
      landmarks, leaving a few showplace pieces, and all in the
      guise of development; "uglification has followed ruin."

582. "Local Workshops to Study Residential Zoning Plan."
      July 23, 1973, p. 35.

      Workshops are to be held in New York City to consider
      "height-to-openland ratio" of highrise apartment struc-
      tures. Gives background to the numbers game of zoning.
      Errors of the past educate us to the needs of the future;
      some of those needs are human and environmental.

583. "Standing Room Only." September 16, 1973, Section 2,
      p. 26. Reprinted as "Marblehead, Mass.: Spirit of
      '76." *Kicked a Building Lately?* pp. 175-78.

      Marblehead, Massachusetts, has become a bedroom com-
      munity within easy reach of Boston and has thereby almost
      suffocated its historic area. "The old houses are beau-
      ties and the new ones are bastards." The bastards are
      fake! The flavor of historic Marblehead is compared to
      the crass commercialism of Salem, where most of its heri-
      tage has been destroyed by the same exploiters who adver-
      tise the town as "Historic Salem."

584. "New Wing of Boston's Public Library Quietly Embodies

Architecture's Best." September 24, 1973, p. 35.
Reprinted as "Successes: Boston: A Sensitive Succes-
sion." *Kicked a Building Lately?* pp. 242-45.

The title is a give-away; she likes the building. Com-
plementing the earlier structure of 1895, which will be
used for research, the wing by Philip Johnson has sim-
plicity, refinement, compatibility, "sophisticated
visual expression of an unusual structural system, ...
well worked out, technically and esthetically."

585. "Selling the President, Architecturally." September
      30, 1973, Section 2, p. 28. Reprinted as "The Monu-
      mental Muddle: The Kennedy Library." *Kicked a Build-
      ing Lately?* pp. 18-19.

After an introduction concerning future and past presidential libraries in general, the article zooms in on
the Kennedy Library for Harvard by architect Pei, a
truncated pyramid of glass, eighty-five-feet high; it
is a shrine for visitors as much as a research facility
for scholars.

586. "New Custom House: Modern, Functional, No Match for the
      Old." October 4, 1973, pp. 47, 90. Reprinted as
      "Dilemmas: An Exercise in Cultural Shock." *Kicked a
      Building Lately?* pp. 262-66.

The new Custom House, part of the World Trade Center,
is standard, efficient, mechanical, and bland. Mrs.
Huxtable realizes that this is a sign of the times, but
laments that it lacks the grandeur of the old Custom
House, Cass Gilbert's historic, elaborately classical
building of 1907, with its numerous sculptures and
paintings and its rich array of finishes and materials.

587. "Hospitality and the Plastic Esthetic." October 14, 1973,
      Section 2, p. 27. Reprinted as "The Hospitality Indus-
      try: Stale Air and the Plastic Esthetic." *Kicked a
      Building Lately?* pp. 20-23.

Hotel architecture tends to be mediocre, impersonal,
standard, and uniform, and has very little sense of iden-
tity. Most of this can be blamed on the 4,000 items sold
by the Institutional Mart of America and on the hotelier
training at Cornell!

588. "They Finally Got It Right." October 21, 1973, Section
      2, p. 25. Reprinted as "Art and Building: Akron Arts

Center: At Last They've Got It Right." *Kicked a Building Lately?* pp. 75-80.

Mrs. Huxtable likes the new Edwin J. Thomas Performing
Arts Hall at Akron, Ohio. She states that "the performance halls of Lincoln Center look, and are, provincial
by comparison." She is bamboozled by the technology of
acoustics, even though "we cannot pretend to judge" the
sound factors. The questions of financial support and
of the standard of quality of performance are also raised.

589. "You Can't Go Home to Those Fairs Again." October 28,
1973, Section 2, p. 27. Reprinted as "Pleasures: Art
and Nostalgia and the Great World's Fairs." *Kicked a
Building Lately?* pp. 207-12.

The New York Cultural Center held an exhibition called
"1930's Exposition," consisting of large photographs plus
memorabilia originating from the Dallas Museum of Fine
Arts. Describes the five major fairs of the 1930s and
their exhibits.

590. "Antonio Gaudi: Genius and Sorcerer." November 11, 1973,
Section 2, p. 16. Reprinted as "Pleasures: The Sorcery
of Gaudi." *Kicked a Building Lately?* pp. 202-204.

Reviews "The Furniture of Antonio Gaudi," an exhibition
of photographs plus one piece of furniture, at New York's
Spanish Institute. Surveys and describes Gaudi's life
and work, in reference to the photographs exhibited.

591. "Farewell, Old New York." November 18, 1973, Magazine
Section, p. 102.

Dutch and Georgian New York has just about disappeared.
Now, Greek Revival and Victorian structures are also
being demolished at such an alarming rate that one can
only ponder the ultimate fate of this historic city.
It is not merely the buildings and their contribution
to the environment that are disappearing, but the types
of stores they contained and their related atmosphere.
Lists several examples of lost notable vernacular groups
and areas and relates them to what has replaced them.
New structures and developments are necessary to the
city's economic growth, but at what a price.

592. "How to Build a Civic Center." November 18, 1973, Section
2, p. 28. Reprinted as "New York: How to Build a Civic
Center." *Kicked a Building Lately?* pp. 107-11.

Gruzen and Partners' $58 million Police Headquarters for

New York City is the realization of ten years of planning
waivers and maneuvering through red tape. Sheer tenacity!

593. "Revitalization of Cleveland at a Turning Point." Novem-
      ber 23, 1973, pp. 37, 70.

      "The battle for center-city survival will be won or
      lost in the next few years.... Clevelanders ... have
      traditionally written off their city," and at first
      glance this may seem to be a justifiable attitude. Hous-
      ing has been integrated into the downtown commercial area,
      and thus part of the center-city is being revitalized.

594. "How We See, or Think We See the City." November 25,
      1973, Section 2, p. 26. Reprinted as "New York: Per-
      spective on the City: The Photographer's Eye 1."
      Kicked a Building Lately? pp. 133-37.

      The Metropolitan Museum of Art held an exhibition of
      photographs called "Landscape-Cityscape." The photographs
      are as much art history as are the famous paintings of
      the period. "In both literature and art the image of
      the city has always been subject to philosophical and
      emotional manipulation ... the city as ugly and evil,
      the country as beautiful and good. American photography
      treats them equally, as art objects."

595. "Just a Little Love, a Little Care." December 9, 1973,
      Section 2, p. 28.

      The argument is in the title; that is, if continuous
      maintenance were provided for Central Park, there would
      be no need to spend $21,000, plus labor, for the renova-
      tion of a 9x15-feet ladies pavilion originally designed
      by Calvert Vaux. Likewise, repairs to a ninety-foot
      bridge would not be necessary, at a cost of $327,000.

596. "Art and Building by the System." December 16, 1973,
      Section 2, p. 28. Reprinted as "Art and Theory: Build-
      ing by the System." *Kicked a Building Lately?* pp. 38-
      41.

      Modern technology has swept away traditional modes of
      building construction. But the new technology brings
      with it new problems concerning construction, fire codes,
      performance standards, and the use of glass, steel, and
      concrete. The energy crisis has made us rethink our at-
      titudes toward modern architecture.

597. "Measuring the Dream." December 23, 1973, Section 2,
      p. 16. Reprinted as "Housing the American Dream:
      Measuring the Dream." *Kicked a Building Lately?* pp.
      27-30.

      Cites and assesses several reports, emanating from gov-
      ernment and research agencies, on a variety of topics
      related to housing and American cities. "These reports
      rarely, if ever, give answers to anything. Each in its
      own way states a problem." People seem to like to live
      in neighborhoods that offer a quality of life related
      to their own.

                              1974

598. "The New Urban Image? Look Down Not Up." January 6,
      1974, Section 2, p. 21.

      The First National City Bank of New York, or Citicorp,
      as it is now known, is constructing a forty-six-story,
      910-feet-high tower on Fifty-third to Fifty-fourth Streets
      between Lexington and Third Avenues at the cost of $128
      million. "It seems to be very strong on urban design
      and very weak on architecture ... quite simply awful.
      It reaches weakly after an image.... The design is an
      unconvincing sandwich," built in place of a church which
      sold its land to Citicorp in exchange for a new church,
      plus. Hugh Stubbins, architect.

599. "Some Handsome Architectural Mythology." January 13,
      1974, Section 2, p. 8. Reprinted as "Housing the
      American Dream: Some Handsome Housing Mythology."
      Kicked a Building Lately? pp. 30-33.

      A review of the work of Moshe Safdie on the occasion
      of an expansive exhibition in New York, entitled "Moshe
      Safdie: For Everyone a Garden," at the Jewish Museum.
      Only Habitat, in Montreal, has been built, although
      many habitats have been projected elsewhere; systems
      buildings are generally questioned since few ever seem
      to get off the ground. General solutions apparently
      do not work, because of the variety of individual needs.

600. "Adding Up the Score." January 20, 1974, Section 2, p.
      24.

      City planning's aim is to cater to future needs of the
      people, the environment, and the physical form of the
      city, before problems allied to these forces arise. This

can be done by several tools, such as zoning, special
districts, and air rights. Various examples are introduced to illustrate the viewpoint.

601. "From Sentiment to Social Force." February 3, 1974,
      Section 2, p. 26.

      The Landmarks Commission of New York City was estab-
lished in 1965, and since that time has designated twenty-
four historic districts and 406 buildings--a total of
10,000 properties--most by popular demand of citizens
who realize that a neighborhood remains healthy when it
has a sense of place and that historic structures tend
to provide that quality. The Landmarks Commission has
had problems and lawsuits, but its work is worthwhile.

602. "Breaking the Mold." February 10, 1974, Section 2, p. 22.

      Praises nine projects by Davis, Brody and Associates for
New York City, where residential architecture is, by tradition, cramped and high priced, but that's the cost of living in the city. Collaboration with the various authorities
and with the building contractors has produced far better
results than the average. "There should be penalties for
architects who do less."

603. "A Little Museum That Teaches." February 17, 1974,
      Magazine Section, pp. 65, 70.

      Everyone has his favorite small museum. Renwick's Cor-
coran Gallery, Washington, D.C., recently refurbished is
highly praised. The restoration was by John Carl Warnecke.
The new interiors are described.

604. "There But for the Grace...." February 17, 1974, Section
      2, p. 29.

      Renwick built Grace Church, 1843-46, and added clergy
houses and other accommodations in the 1880s facing Fourth
Avenue at the rear of the church. The buildings form a
total group in the Gothic Revival style, but the need for
additional and changing facilities has led the church
toward the inevitable idea of demolition of part of the
Fourth Avenue buildings (not the church on Broadway).
To preserve and refurbish the houses would be expensive,
but really not as expensive as the proposed new structure.

605. "In St. Louis, the News Is Better." March 10, 1974, Sec-
      tion 2, p. 21.

Adler and Sullivan's Wainwright Building is being
preserved as a part of the center city revitalization
in St. Louis. Other examples of successful and not so
successful preservation in other cities are mentioned.

606. "Of Capital Failure and Capital Crimes." March 17, 1974,
      Section 2, p. 27. Reprinted as "Washington: Capital
      Failures." *Kicked a Building Lately?* pp. 171-74.

Washington is being destroyed by private and public
agencies and their bland architecture. Each act of
demolition and erection is justified and supported, but
the residents realize that each new structure produces
a more sterile city. Several examples are cited. The
saga of the new headquarters of the American Institute of
Architects is recounted.

607. "Kahn's Buildings Blended Logic, Power and Grace." March
      20, 1974, p. 64.

In a series of brief quotations from Louis Kahn's writings and lectures, Mrs. Huxtable has captured the spirit
of the man and his philosophy of design. "In one sense,
his work was timeless, in another daringly contemporary.
... Slow to mature, late to be recognized, Mr. Kahn
evolved in his 60's as one of the great architects and
teachers of this century."

608. "Garden of Eden--Updated." March 24, 1974, Section 2,
      p. 24.

The conservatory of the New York Botanical Garden in
the Bronx, 1899, is being repaired with additions by
Edward L. Barnes, over a five-year period at a cost of
$2.5 million. The new building will cost $7.5 million
in private funds and its form will consist of glass hexagonal clusters.

609. "The Meaning of a Wall." April 7, 1974, Section 2, p.
      26. Reprinted as "Art and Building: Louis Kahn: The
      Meaning of a Wall." *Kicked a Building Lately?* pp.
      98-101.

Kahn "was a fundamentalist, seeking beginnings and
meanings ... a promising talent ... that flowered late."
He utilized materials in a logical manner, the way that
was right for the inherent qualities or characteristics
of each material.

610. "The Skyscraper Style." April 14, 1974, Magazine Section,
     pp. 58-59, 66-68. Reprinted as "Pleasures: The Sky-
     scraper Style." *Kicked a Building Lately?* pp. 213-17.

     America has produced the skyscraper and, during the Art
     Deco period, some of the more outstanding examples of that
     building type. The qualities of the style, the background
     influences, the materials used and expressed, the impact
     upon recent stylistic trends, the exhibitions and their
     organizers, and the architectural historians interested
     in this style are all listed and described.

611. "New Orleans: Boom or Bust." April 21, 1974, Section 2,
     p. 23. Reprinted as "New Orleans: The Old American
     City." *Kicked a Building Lately?* pp. 166-70.

     The French Quarter of New Orleans is protected as a
     district, but no other area of the city is, except for
     those buildings and sites listed on the National Register.
     One-fifth of the business district has disappeared since
     1970; forty-two percent is used for parking. A nine-
     month moratorium has been imposed upon any type of demoli-
     tion, until a growth-management program has been completed.
     "Does anyone really have the right to destroy a city be-
     cause he owns the land it stands on?"

612. "The New American City." May 5, 1974, Section 2, p. 21.
     Reprinted as "Atlanta: The New American City." *Kicked
     a Building Lately?* pp. 161-65.

     Atlanta is the twentieth-century dream city for the
     realtors, the chamber of commerce, and John Portman, the
     new type of architect-developer. Commercial, recreational,
     and entertainment facilities are there, and Atlanta has
     become the third most important convention center in the
     country. Universities, housing developments, and general
     amenities complete the picture. It is to be hoped that
     this go-ahead attitude will aid the socially underprivi-
     leged of Atlanta, too.

613. "A Few Signs of Spring and Other Good News." May 12,
     1974, Section 2, p. 23.

     Several notes of preservation interest are introduced,
     but the major thrust is devoted to the successful con-
     version of one of New York's largest and finest cast-iron
     buildings from commercial to residential use. The build-
     ing, by John Kellum, is at 67 East Eleventh Street.

614. "The Kickback Game." May 14, 1974, p.37.

      "The Kickback system ... is a thoroughly rotten, eternal
      political verity." Architectural firms from Baltimore
      to California, Nassau County to New Orleans, are cited.

615. "The Letterhead Is Solidly Male." May 19, 1974, Section
      2, p. 26.

      "Women in Architecture," an exhibition at the New York
      Chapter of the American Institute of Architects, includes
      the work of fifty-eight women. Vital statistics are
      given on foreign born, foreign educated, married versus
      single, those acting as partners, and reasons for the
      emergence of women in the architectural profession.

616. "A Sense of Manhattan as Reflected in Landscape Design
      and Photography." June 2, 1974, Section 2, p. 22.
      Reprinted as "Perspective on the City: The Photographer's
      Eye II." *Kicked a Building Lately?* pp. 137-39.

      Reviews photographic exhibitions in New York, including
      one entitled "Central Park's Calvert Vaux," at the Museum
      of the City of New York. Provides background information.

617. "Construction in the Capital." June 9, 1974, Section 2,
      p. 19.

      The theme of the American Institute of Architects'
      conference in Washington, D.C., was "humane architecture."
      A tremendous amount of construction was going on in Wash-
      ington and much was being demolished which could have
      been preserved; the spirit of L'Enfant's plan was also
      being lost.

618. "What's a Tourist Attraction Like the Kennedy Library
      Doing in a Nice Neighborhood Like This?" June 16, 1974,
      Section 2, pp. 1, 28.

      Smaller in size and cost than originally proposed by
      Pei, this presidential library on the Charles River caters
      to the environment and is not a structure designed to
      glorify the architect. Cambridge, Harvard University,
      and the Kennedy family must cooperate to provide what is
      best for the area. "Mr. Pei could goof, but it is 99 per-
      cent unlikely with this talented and tasteful man."

619. "How to Slipcover a Building, Washington Style." June 23,
      1974, Section 2, p. 23. Reprinted as "Art and Building:
      The New Senate Office Building: How to Slipcover a Block-
      buster." *Kicked a Building Lately?* pp. 80-83.

A proposed new Senate Office Building is being discussed openly. It is huge in scale, as most governmental
buildings are, and has classical proportions slipcovered
on to a well-planned structure, in lieu of the usual
classical detailing. "The result is an esthetic bastard.
... The Warnecke design is more skillful than many."

620. "Can a Symbol of Graft Be an Architectural Landmark?"
     July 7, 1974, Section 2, p. 19. Reprinted as "Dilemmas:
     Can Anyone Use a Nice Anglo-Italianate Symbol of Graft?"
     Kicked a Building Lately? pp. 266-69.

     John Kellum's $10 or $12 million Tweed Court House,
     1861-72, just north of the older New York City Hall, is
     again threatened with demolition. It is a fine example
     of the Italianate style and, like so many other comparable
     structures of the same style which have been threatened
     and then saved, should be studied as a piece of architec-
     ture, and not related to the false economics of its wasted
     space-use.

621. "The Bulldozer Approaches a Historic Block." July 14,
     1974, Section 2, p. 21.

     The Fraunces Tavern block in Lower Manhattan is signif-
     icant, not so much for the reconstructed tavern as for
     the totality of an intact block comprising a scale of
     buildings that are representative of old New York. "Be-
     cause the block is a historic unit, demolition of any
     part of it destroys the whole."

622. "Eads Bridge--Engineering Miracle and Work of Art." July
     21, 1974, Section 2, p. 19.

     This year is the 100th anniversary of the completion
     of the Eads Bridge, St. Louis, begun in 1867. It pioneered
     the use of steel and of pneumatic caissons in the United
     States. Recounts the difficulties of erection. (Material
     from *Progressive Architecture*, April 1957. See item 870.)

623. "Going the Way of the Dinosaur." July 21, 1974, Magazine
     Section, pp. 38-39.

     The modern period has produced new building types, in-
     cluding the factory, the skyscraper, and the railroad
     station, the latter of which is going out of style. Some
     are, however, being revitalized, especially the small
     ones. Mentions Hardy Holzman Pfeiffer Associates' report,
     "Re-using Railroad Stations," and lists successful restor-
     ations.

624. "Public Sculpture--A City's Most Pervasive Art." September 15, 1974, Section 2, p. 29. Reprinted as "Pleasures: Friends in Public Places." *Kicked a Building Lately?* pp. 228-30.

Mrs. Huxtable has always admired nineteenth-century heroic sculptures scattered around New York City, so that she is completely in accord with the Metropolitan Museum of Art exhibition "New York City Public Sculpture." Many of the works are described, but so too are recent additions commissioned to complement architectural designs.

625. "How Salem Saved Itself from Urban Renewal." September 29, 1974, Section 2, p. 27.

Traffic improvements could have destroyed Salem, but opponents of the Redevelopment Authority's plan have ensured that the vernacular infrastructure as well as the monuments will remain.

626. "The Hirshhorn Museum: An 'Important' Collection in a 'Bomb Shelter.'" October 6, 1974, Section 2, pp. 1, 20. Reprinted as "The Monumental Muddle: The Hirshhorn Museum." *Kicked a Building Lately?* pp. 8-12.

Gordon Bunshaft of SOM has gone awry in the design of the $16 million Hirshhorn Museum, Washington, D.C., "a maimed monument and a maimed Mall." It is a bulky "gun emplacement" which demands attention and is a disaster.

627. "MOMA's Immortal Pots and Pans." October 6, 1974, Magazine Section, pp. 74-76.

Reviews the collection of 2,100 objects in the Museum of Modern Art Design Collection.

628. "Surviving Downtown 'Progress.'" October 20, 1974, Section 2, p. 33.

Progress means investing money in prime downtown land to make money. "The battles are legion." Minoru Yamasaki is panned for a building in Seattle, and John Carl Warnecke for the demolition by Neiman-Marcus of San Francisco's City of Paris, 1909.

629. "Once There Was a Palace on 42d Street." October 27, 1974, Section 2, pp. 33, 35.

"The Crystal Palace on 42d Street, 1853-54: A Graphic Presentation" was an exhibition held at the Graduate

Center of City University, on Forty-second Street just
opposite the original site. Comments on the area in
general.

630.   "Believe It or Not, Highways Don't Have to Be Ugly."
       November 10, 1974, Section 2, p. 30.

       Sensitive highway design was the aim of the Department
       of Transportation's Highway Administration, as seen in
       "The Highway and Its Environment," an exhibition at the
       McGraw-Hill Building, New York. Examples are provided
       and discussed.

631.   "The Public Building: From Soaring Statements to Shoddy
       Mediocrity." November 10, 1974, Magazine Section, pp.
       86-87, 89.

       Traditionally, public buildings emphasized design,
       materials, details, setting, and style; but today the
       emphasis is on the shoddy, fast-buck expedient, with a
       few notable exceptions.

632.   "Skyscraper Art Rides High." November 17, 1974, Section
       2, pp. 37-38. Reprinted as "Pleasures: The Skyscraper
       Style." *Kicked a Building Lately?* pp. 213-17.

       In praise of the Art Deco skyscrapers throughout the
       United States, at a period when interest in Art Deco is
       in full flood. Finch College Museum of Art, New York,
       adds to the celebration with an exhibition on "American
       Art Deco Architecture."

633.   "Chairs Not Meant for Sitting." November 24, 1974,
       Section 2, p. 29. Reprinted as "Pleasures: The
       Chairs of Mackintosh." *Kicked a Building Lately?*
       pp. 205-207.

       Twenty "re-creations" or reproductions of chairs by
       Mackintosh were shown at the Museum of Modern Art.
       Mackintosh's impact on the Modern Movement is emphasized.

634.   "The New Cooper Union Still Evokes the Past." December
       8, 1974, Section 2, p. 36. Reprinted as "Successes:
       New York: The Creative Continuity of History and Art."
       Kicked a Building Lately? pp. 233-36.

       John Hejduk has refurbished Fred A. Peterson's Cooper
       Union Building of the 1850s. The shell remains, but the
       internal accommodation has been altered slightly to meet
       present-day needs.

635. "Art, Money and Impotence in New York." December 15,
      1974, Section 2, pp. 1, 40.

      The Mayor's Committee on Cultural Policy examined how
      New York City organized its cultural affairs. The Com-
      mittee, realizing that art and business are inseparable,
      came to the conclusion that the City's efforts were in-
      effective.

636. "Landmarks Are in Trouble with the Law." December 22,
      1974, Section 2, p. 39.

      New York's landmarks laws recognize that they must
      be economically fair. The New York State Court of Ap-
      peals has decided against the forced preservation of
      the J.P. Morgan house because it looks upon it as an
      uncompensated taking. The Landmarks Commission is fight-
      ing to save Grand Central.

1975

637. "They Call This 'Saving' a Landmark?" January 5, 1975,
      Section 2, p. 29. Reprinted as "Dilemmas: Kicking a
      Landmark." *Kicked a Building Lately?* pp. 269-72.

      Emory Roth and Sons have designed a fifty-two-story
      hotel to be built for Harry Helmsley above the Villard
      Houses on Madison Avenue. Interiors will be gutted and
      will be replaced by "a pastiche of token vulgarities."
      (See item 1031.)

638. "The Ludicrous Relocation of Covent Garden Market."
      January 12, 1975, Section 2, p. 24. Reprinted as
      "London: Covent Garden II." *Kicked a Building Lately?*
      pp. 188-90.

      It was decided in 1957 to move Covent Garden Market
      from the center of London. A site was chosen at Nine
      Elms in 1964, and the new market opened there in 1974.
      The old market was to be comprehensively developed;
      that is, bulldozed except for monuments and one or two
      token streets. (See item 484.)

639. "Looking Back at the World of Tomorrow." January 26,
      1975, Magazine Section, pp. 40-43. Reprinted as "Look-
      ing Back at the Future: The City as Dream: Hugh Ferriss."
      Kicked a Building Lately? pp. 291-95.

      Drawings by Hugh Ferriss (1889-1962) of New York

structures designed during the 1920s, a transitional
period between the Beaux Arts and the Modern Movement,
are our legacy.

640. "New York Can Learn a Lot from St. Louis." January 26,
      1975, Section 2, p. 30.

      McKim, Mead & White's Villard Houses, New York, and
      Adler and Sullivan's Wainwright Building, St. Louis,
      are being threatened by injudicious remodelling. A
      national competition has provided an enlightened
      solution for the Wainwright Building as a State Office
      Building, but the Villard Houses will be exploited
      because of mediocre architects, in league with lawyers
      and financiers.

641. "Why Did We Lose Grand Central as a Landmark?" February
      2, 1975, Section 2, p. 26 (correction: March 2, 1975,
      Section 2, p. 33).

      The New York Supreme Court has decided against landmark
      designation for Grand Central Terminal. Mrs. Huxtable
      admits that she cannot judge the legalities of the case,
      but she does raise some significant arguments and issues.

642. "Preserving Noo Yawk Landmarks." February 4, 1975, p. 33.

      A reply to Professor Herbert Gans, who has accused the
      Landmarks Preservation Commission of elitism at the ex-
      pense of popular architecture, including the tenement.
      Mrs. Huxtable points out that historians and preservation-
      ists are dedicated to such vernacular items.

643. "More Bad News about Times Square." February 9, 1975,
      Section 2, p. 32. Reprinted as "New York: Bad News
      about Times Square." *Kicked a Building Lately?* pp.
      112-15.

      "The future of Times Square seems to depend on one
      large tide-turning project: the $160 million hotel planned
      by the Atlanta architect-entrepreneur John Portman."
      Immediate planning prospects, including the destruction
      of buildings, look depressing.

644. "One Look at Charlottesville Is Worth 3,000 Bicentennial
      Projects." March 2, 1975, Section 2, p. 33.

      A trip to Charlottesville is worth all the remainder
      of the bicentennial projects, which are briefly discussed
      with relation to the organizations involved.

645. "Thomas Jefferson's Grand Paradox." March 9, 1975, Sec-
       tion 2, pp. 1, 36. Reprinted as "Pleasures: Jefferson's
       Virginia." *Kicked a Building Lately?* pp. 198-202.

       The campus of the University of Virginia is described
       in order to show the "values to which American democracy
       aspired." Mrs. Huxtable asks: "What has happened to the
       values that infused the life, art, and politics of the
       new nation?"

646. "Urban Progress Doesn't Always Make Things Better."
       March 16, 1975, Section 2, p. 34.

       "How Grim Was My City," an exhibition at the Museum of
       Modern Art, compared the bad old days of nineteenth-cen-
       tury New York with today, which isn't quite as bad.

647. "The Blooming of Downtown Brooklyn." March 30, 1975,
       Section 2, pp. 1, 32. Reprinted as "New York: The
       Blooming of Downtown Brooklyn." *Kicked a Building
       Lately?* pp. 115-18.

       Brooklyn is described as a steady progression of urban
       renewal with numerous underpublicized landmarks, some
       modern successes, and a few disappointments.

648. "What's Best for Business Can Ravage Cities." April 6,
       1975, Section 2, pp. 1, 30. Reprinted as "New York:
       Dead or Alive." *Kicked a Building Lately?* pp. 139-42.

       Adler and Sullivan's Stock Exchange, Chicago, was de-
       molished because it was economically unviable, but its
       forty-three-story replacement is also unviable, because
       of the recession. New York similarly has big money losers.
       Other buildings are still being destroyed, not for new
       buildings, however, but for more parking lots.

649. "For Those Who Sit and Wait." April 13, 1975, Magazine
       Section, pp. 74-76.

       A general article on the corporate reception area in
       modern designs.

650. "Poetic Visions of Design for the Future." April 27,
       1975, Section 2, p. 32. Reprinted as "Art and Theory:
       Visionary Architecture." *Kicked a Building Lately?*
       pp. 51-53.

       "Architectural Studies and Projects," an exhibition at
       the Museum of Modern Art, includes fifty imaginary drawings

by American and European architects. Most of them are poetic fantasies which "can be a lot better than building in a bankrupt society."

651. "Theaters Recycled." April 27, 1975, Magazine Section, pp. 74-75.

"Recycling" is the term used to describe the restoration of old buildings to save money, energy, and the national heritage. Several examples are provided.

652. "A Recession-Proof Plan to Rescue Little Italy." May 4, 1975, Section 2, p. 29.

The Little Italy Restoration Association will attempt neighborhood rehabilitation and "restoration in intimate detail" in the 125-acre area bounded by Bleeker Street, Bowery, Canal Street, and Broadway, which houses a population of 14,500.

653. "Transforming the Avant-Garde into an Instant Landmark." May 18, 1975, Section 2, p. 36. Reprinted as "Pleasures: The Future Grows Old." *Kicked a Building Lately?* pp. 224-27.

Walter Gropius's house at Lincoln, Massachusetts, designed in 1937 and constructed in 1938, has been given to the Society for the Preservation of New England Antiquities by his wife, Ise. House, furnishings, fittings, and Bauhaus objects are described.

654. "The New Lehman Wing--Does the Met Need It?" May 25, 1975, Section 2, pp. 1, 27. Reprinted as "The Monumental Muddle: The Lehman Wing of the Metropolitan Museum." *Kicked a Building Lately?* pp. 13-17.

The Lehman Wing of the Metropolitan Museum of Art, by Roche, Dinkeloo Associates at a cost of $7.1 million, has been completed. Along with a top-lighted central space, it contains unlighted domestic-scaled rooms which simulates Lehman's house. Mrs. Huxtable explains why she believes "that the Met has done the wrong thing impeccably."

655. "Chicago: A City of Architectural Excellence." June 8, 1975, Section 2, p. 31. Reprinted as "Chicago: A Pride of Buildings." *Kicked a Building Lately?* pp. 155-60.

Although Chicago and New York have many common denominators, the former "is a city of architectural excellence,

which New York is not." One of Chicago's most recent
successes is SOM's Sears Tower, 110 stories high and
containing five million square feet of space. Other
buildings in Chicago are mentioned.

656. "Recycling a Landmark for Today." June 15, 1975, Section
      2, p. 29.

      Friends Meeting House, Gramercy Park South, New York,
      1859, by Gamaliel King and John W. Kellum, has been sold
      and resold three times, but its most recent purchaser
      is the Brotherhood Synagogue, an appropriate similar-
      use buyer. Renovation by James Polshek cost $180,000,
      but another $75,000 is needed.

657. "The Needless Sacrifice of the Villard Houses." June 22,
      1975, Section 2, p. 31. Reprinted as "Dilemmas: ...
      With the Other Foct." *Kicked a Building Lately?* pp.
      272-75.

      The New York Landmarks Commission wants to preserve the
      interiors as well as the facades of the Villard Houses,
      when an adjoining hotel is built which will incorporate
      the air rights above its roof. The Gold Room is especially
      worth saving. (See item 1031.)

658. "A Delightful Walk Downtown." July 20, 1975, Section 2,
      pp. 1, 23. Reprinted as "New York: An Urban Spectacu-
      lar." *Kicked a Building Lately?* pp. 105-107.

      Streetscape, preservation areas, stylistic developments,
      modern art, and modern buildings are all part of Downtown
      New York. "New York, thy name is irreverence and hyper-
      bole. And grandeur."

659. "Henry Street's New Building--An Urban Triumph." August
      10, 1975, Section 2, p. 25. Reprinted as "New York:
      Small But Significant: Henry Street Settlement."
      Kicked a Building Lately? pp. 126-29.

      The Henry Street Settlement, founded in 1893, has added
      The Arts for Living Center by Lo-Yi Chan of Prentice,
      Chan, Ohlhausen, for their visual arts program.

660. "Voodoo Signs of the Business World." August 10, 1975,
      Magazine Section, pp. 42-45.

      A discussion of the need for corporate symbols, name
      changes, and face-lifts.

661. "Good News from the Witch of Salem." September 7, 1975,
     Section 2, pp. 1, 39. Reprinted as "Salem, Mass.:
     Renewing It Right." *Kicked a Building Lately?* pp. 150-
     54.

     Salem, a town of 40,000 people and a disappearing eco-
     nomic base, has problems keeping its historic areas alive.
     The Witch of Salem in 1965 was Mrs. Huxtable, when she
     objected to the proposed rape of the town. Ten years
     later the rebuilding was being done well.

662. "A Happy Turn for Urban Design." September 14, 1975,
     Section 2, p. 31.

     A general lament about architecture, mainly in New York
     City, where even the museums seem to ignore or shun archi-
     tectural shows.

663. "Another Chapter in the Urban Saga—How Three Lost Causes
     Were Saved." September 21, 1975, Section 2, p. 31.
     Reprinted as "Dilemmas: A Hopeful Toast." *Kicked a
     Building Lately?* pp. 275-77.

     (1) "To Mr. Helmsley ... we raise a glass" for his
     cooperation concerning the attempt to preserve the in-
     teriors of the Villard Houses. A good solution is likely.
     (2) Facades of property at Grace Church, New York, will
     be retained. (3) The Fraunces Tavern Block, New York,
     has retained buildings and stepped up maintenance. (See
     item 1031.)

664. "Money—The Root of All Preservation." September 28,
     1975, Section 2, p. 25.

     Fiscal retrenchment by the city of St. Louis, after it
     purchased the Wainwright Building, by Adler and Sullivan,
     to prevent its demolition, may act adversely for the
     building.

665. "Serlio Influenced Five Centuries of Architecture."
     October 5, 1975, Section 2, p. 34.

     An exhibition was held at the Low Memorial Library,
     Columbia University, to celebrate the 500th anniversary
     of the birth of Sebastiano Serlio (1475-1555), whose
     manuscript *On Domestic Architecture* is to be published
     for the first time, in facsimile. The manuscript is
     owned by the Avery Memorial Architectural Library.

666.   "How Great Buildings Shape a City's Soul." October 19,
       1975, Section 2, p. 32. Reprinted in "New York: Per-
       spective on the City: Three Buildings." *Kicked a Build-
       ing Lately?* pp. 129-33 (wrongly dated November 6, 1975).

       "Three Buildings," an exhibition at the City University
       Graduate Center, emphasizes the form and content of the
       Library at Fifth Avenue and Forty-second Street, Grand
       Central Terminal, and Times Tower. Comments are made
       concerning the landmark designation of the Terminal and
       the shocking refacing of the Tower.

667.   "Beaux Arts--The Latest Avant-Garde." October 26, 1975,
       Magazine Section, pp. 76-82. Reprinted as "Art and
       Theory: Rediscovering the Beaux Arts." *Kicked a
       Building Lately?* pp. 58-66; and *The New York Review*,
       November 27, 1975, pp. 6-7.

       "The Architecture of the Ecole des Beaux Arts," an
       exhibition at the Museum of Modern Art, included build-
       ings which were rejected by the Modern Movement. The
       exhibition is revisionist history and is part of an
       attempt to re-examine the tenets of the Modern Movement.
       In rejecting the Beaux Arts approach, had the modernists
       ignored aspects of design which are valid? There are
       also pitfalls for the unwary, notably in the excessive
       cost of monumental buildings.

668.   "Growing Up in a Beaux Arts World." November 9, 1975,
       Section 2, pp. 1, 33. Reprinted as "Pleasures: Beaux
       Arts Buildings I Have Known." *Kicked a Building Lately?*
       pp. 217-21.

       The Museum of Modern Art, which used to be opposed to
       the Beaux Arts tradition, has featured an exhibition on
       "The Architecture of the Ecoles des Beaux Arts." In her
       discussion, Mrs. Huxtable includes New York examples
       which she has always enjoyed.

669.   "Games Gnomes Play with the Urban Landscape." November
       16, 1975, Section 2, pp. 1, 33. Reprinted as "Failures:
       Of Landmarks and Litter or The Games Gnomes Play."
       Kicked a Building Lately? pp. 259-61.

       Gnomes "are creatures specializing in acts of perverse
       illogical or malevolent nonsense that results in situa-
       tions of consummate absurdity in which the rest of us
       are trapped." Several examples of gnomery are provided,
       including the 2,200 concrete trash containers, each weigh-
       ing 500 pounds, which litter New York City!

670.   "The Housing Crisis." November 18, 1975, p. 37.

New York is losing housing at the rate of 12,000 units
a year and the Mitchell-Lama program is ending because
of mortgage default. Other programs are being cancelled.
A general discussion on the housing problem.

671.   "Keeping up to Date with the Outskirts." November 23,
1975, Section 2, p. 25.

(1) The State of Pennsylvania has acted responsibly
in purchasing Louis Kahn's drawings. (2) The Architect
of the Capitol has been given an appropriation to provide a Master Plan for Capitol Hill, Washington, D.C.
(3) Buford Pickens of St. Louis is concerned with the
Wainwright block, and not just the building. (4) Cincinnati's Union Terminal is to be renovated by Hardy
Holzman Pfeiffer.

672.   "Our 'Expendable' Churches Are Too Good to Expend."
November 30, 1975, Section 2, p. 33.

Churches are increasingly becoming underused, super-
fluous, redundant, including the Greek Revival Village
Church on West Thirteenth Street. New uses are needed
for churches of this type, as indicated by publications
and conferences on the subject. Eighty of New York's
150 landmark churches are in trouble.

673.   "A Bizarre Monument to Non-Architecture." December 14,
1975, Section 2, p. 39. Reprinted as "Art and Theory:
A Bizarre Monument to Non-Architecture." *Kicked a
Building Lately?* pp. 34-37.

"Non-architecture wins over architecture, hands down."
Even a just completed but now defunct $5.7 billion ABM
site at Grand Forks, North Dakota.

674.   "Grooms's Zany 'Manhattan' Puts the City in Focus." De-
cember 21, 1975, Section 2, pp. 1, 41. Reprinted as
"The Near Past: Through the Artist's Eye." *Kicked a
Building Lately?* pp. 285-87.

"Ruckus Manhattan" is a Red and Mimi Grooms exhibition
in I.M. Pei's new Downtown Manhattan skyscraper at Pine
and Water Streets. It covers all the Downtown landmarks,
including Cass Gilbert's Woolworth Building.

675.   "Sprucing Up the Bank of Tokyo." December 28, 1975, Section 2, p. 28. Reprinted as "Successes: Sprucing Up

the Bank of Tokyo." *Kicked a Building Lately?* pp.
236-39.

The Bank of Tokyo occupies thirteen of the twenty-one
floors at 100 Broadway, the old American Surety Building,
built 1894-96 by Bruce Price. The bank, as tenant, and
the owner of the building have shared an $11 million
recycling, especially of the handsome interior.

1976

676. "This Is the Bank That Zoning Built." January 11, 1976,
      Section 2, p. 32.

      A product of New York City's special zoning ordinances
      of 1971, the Bankers Trust Building by Shreve, Lamb and
      Harmon is practical and is a positive addition to the
      townscape. Even so, it is not great architecture.

677. "Japan Builds the Ultimate Megastructure." January 18,
      1976, Section 2, p. 30.

      "Shinjuku--the Phenomenal City," a show held at the
      Museum of Modern Art to illustrate the twentieth century's
      confused environment, consisted of transportation, com-
      mercial development, and entertainment, one-third of a
      square mile in extent, in Tokyo. Chaotic and unplanned
      it is, but interesting!

678. "A Skyscraper Fit for a King (Kong)?" February 1, 1976,
      Section 2, p. 31. Reprinted as "The Near Past: Reflec-
      tions on the Near Past." *Kicked a Building Lately?*
      pp. 278-80.

      The remake of the film *King Kong* utilizes the twin
      towers of the World Trade Center instead of the Empire
      State Building, a significant pointer to our day and
      age. "The skyscraper's immense, efficient and impersonal
      blandness is a perfectly accurate picture of much of the
      architectural art of our age."

679. "Drawings from a Lost World." February 8, 1976, Section
      2, p. 35.

      Describes and evaluates "Architecture and Ornament
      Drawings: Juvarra, Vanvitelli, the Bibiena Family and
      other Italian draughtsmen," an exhibition at the Metro-
      politan Museum of Art.

680. "Deep in the Heart of Nowhere." February 15, 1976,
        Section 2, pp. 1, 36. Reprinted as "Houston: Deep
        in the Heart of Nowhere." *Kicked a Building Lately?*
        pp. 143-49.

        Houston is a modern, instant, nowhere city which has
        no zoning regulations. It covers 500 square miles and
        has a population of 1.4 million. "Houston is all pro-
        cess and no plan ... it works remarkably well." Modern
        additions are described.

681. "Houston's Towering Achievement." February 22, 1976,
        Section 2, pp. 1, 31. Reprinted as "Art and Building:
        Pennzoil: Houston's Towering Achievement." *Kicked a
        Building Lately?* pp. 67-71.

        Pennzoil Place, by Philip Johnson and John Burgee at a
        cost of $45 million, is dramatic, beautiful, and profitable.
        It is described and all its positive points are emphasized.

682. "What's in a Wall." February 29, 1976, Magazine Section,
        pp. 52-53, 56. Reprinted as "Art and Theory: What's
        in a Wall." *Kicked a Building Lately?* pp. 54-58.

        A wall can be "decorative, witty, sardonic or sad"
        and today it can be used for environmental-esthetic
        ends. Numerous examples country-wide are cited, but
        notably those by Sculpture In The Environment (SITE), who
        "specialize in a kind of constructivist-nihilist treatment"
        for Best Products Corporation.

683. "Federal Buildings Need Not Be Ho-Hum." March 7, 1976,
        Section 2, p. 31.

        Davis, Brody and Associates are part of a team which
        produced the design for an air structure called Mega-
        structure Environment Group 2, 100,000 square feet in
        extent. It has been designed to all General Service Ad-
        ministration regulations and standards and would serve as
        an economical office building.

684. "Rediscovering Chicago Architecture." March 14, 1976,
        Section 2, p. 30. Reprinted as "The Near Past: Re-
        discovering Chicago Architecture." *Kicked a Building
        Lately?* pp. 281-84.

        "Chicago Architects" is the title of an exhibition of
        rediscovery and re-evaluation held at New York's Cooper
        Union. It juxtaposes the skyscraper-engineering esthetic,
        the Beaux Arts of the Columbian Exposition of 1893, and
        more.

685.   "The Pop World of the Strip and the Sprawl." March 21,
       1976, Section 2, p. 28.

       Venturi and Rauch have analyzed America's Pop environ-
       ment in the exhibition "Signs of Life: Symbols in the
       American City," at the Old Corcoran building, Washington,
       D.C. Venturi and Rauch claim that "People are more inter-
       ested in representing their ideals and aspirations through
       architecture than they are in noticing how well a build-
       ing expresses its structure and function."

686.   "Budget Cutters Are Undermining Historic Buildings."
       April 4, 1976, Section 2, p. 29.

       Congress is cutting preservation funds by fifty percent,
       to $10 million. Renovation of landmarks, generally, has
       been a positive aspect of numerous towns and cities.
       Seattle, Cleveland, and Tampa are cited, to emphasize
       the point that too little money is being spent on nec-
       essary recycling.

687.   "Can New York Save the Schomburg Center?" April 25, 1976,
       Section 2, p. 31.

       The Schomburg Collection of black history, literature,
       and art, at the Harlem branch of the New York Public
       Library, is in an incredible condition even though it
       caters to 30,000 people per year. A new building for
       the Schomburg Center has now been shelved.

688.   "A New Twist to the Old Awards Game." May 2, 1976, Sec-
       tion 2, pp. 30, 38.

       General comments on awards and specifically about those
       of the American Institute of Architects, especially one
       given to David Kenneth Specter for the Galleria, New York.

689.   "From Genteel Mud to Showy Glitter." May 9, 1976, Section
       2, pp. 31-32. Reprinted as "Successes: Philadelphia:
       The Bizarre and the Beautiful." *Kicked a Building Lately?*
       pp. 249-53.

       Frank Furness's Pennsylvania Academy of Fine Arts,
       Philadelphia, 1876, was reprieved from likely demolition
       in 1973, and has been restored at a cost of $5.1 million.
       Furness was highly favored in the Victorian period, was
       rejected in the early twentieth century, and is now, much
       to the delight of Mrs. Huxtable, being re-evaluated.

690. "A Master Builder Who Left Poetry and Art--Not Monuments."
      May 23, 1976, Section 2, p. 35.

      Aalto's modern contribution has never been questioned,
      but since he is not in the mainstream he is difficult
      to classify. His works, in general, are discussed. They
      are never bombastic but have "only a quiet beauty."

691. "A Building That Looks Like a Loser." May 30, 1976, Sec-
      tion 2, pp. 23, 29.

      Ulrich Franzen has been added to the team which is
      developing the Dodge House site, 800 Fifth Avenue, at
      Sixty-first Street, a sensitive area for a block-buster
      if ever there was one!

692. "The Fall and Rise of Main Street." May 30, 1976, Maga-
      zine Section, pp. 12-14.

      The post-World War II suburban explosion dealt a lethal
      blow to Main Street in many towns, but nostalgia has made
      recycling fashionable. Modernization of the 1950s was
      destructive, but restoration of the 1960s, tied to eco-
      nomic revitalization, led to commendable recycling (numer-
      ous examples provided)--beware, however, of amenity pack-
      ages of the 1970s.

693. "Design (Good and Bad) down by the Levee." June 6, 1976,
      Section 2, pp. 27-28.

      Downtown St. Louis "clearly demonstrates that this is
      no way to rebuild a city's heart." New construction ex-
      emplifies esthetic and environmental poverty. The Wain-
      wright Building, by Adler and Sullivan, will be saved,
      but at the expense of the De Menil Building.

694. "Help Is on the Way for Discouraged Taxi Riders." June
      20, 1976, Section 2, pp. 41-42.

      There is hope for New York's travelling public, as seen
      at the Museum of Modern Art exhibit "The Taxi Project:
      Realistic Solutions for Today."

695. "The Gospel According to Giedion and Gropius Is under
      Attack." June 27, 1976, Section 2, pp. 1, 29.

      Modernism, as expressed in concrete by Le Corbusier
      or in steel and glass by Mies van der Rohe, is under
      attack. The Museum of Modern Art exhibit on the Beaux
      Arts and the Chicago exhibit "What the Chicago School Left

Out" are discoveries of what the Modern Movement discarded.
The new heretics were led by Louis Kahn, Philip Johnson,
Charles Moore, and Vincent Scully. Ornamentation is no
longer a crime, and form does not have to follow function.
Mannerism, rather than Puritanism, prevails. The new,
uninhibited generation includes Richard Meier, Venturi
and Rauch, and Hardy Holzman Pfeiffer. Revisionism,
romanticism, and inclusionism are the key words. (See
item 969.)

696. "Supermuseum Comes to the Mall." July 4, 1976, Section
      2, p. 22.

      The Air and Space Museum of the Smithsonian Institution,
      by Hellmuth, Obata and Kassabaum, "is sober, non-shock
      modernism." This $41.4 million museum for Washington,
      D.C., measures 685x225 feet and is a revised design of
      a more expensive scheme projected in the 1960s.

697. "New York Rediscovered." July 18, 1976, Magazine Section,
      pp. 32-33.

      New York City has numerous unrecorded and unsung publicly
      owned buildings. The New York Landmarks Conservancy lists
      4,000 of them, 744 of which are classed as exceptional.
      A photographic exhibition of 105 was held at Cass Gilbert's
      Custom House, of 1907, itself an endangered public build-
      ing.

698. "Splendor Overcomes Snafu in Battery Park City." July
      25, 1976, Section 2, p. 24.

      Banal Battery Park City didn't get built, but some
      state-aided housing has risen out of the ashes. Max
      Abramovitz has designed neighborhood groups, consisting
      of 1,642 units, which rival Roosevelt Island or Waterside.

699. "The Greening of Liberty Park." August 29, 1976, Section
      2, p. 27.

      Liberty Park, 800 acres of New Jersey shoreline fronting
      on New York Harbor, will be part of a clean-up operation.

700. "Why You Always Win and Lose in Urban Renewal." September
      19, 1976, Section 2, p. 34.

      Alexander Parris designed the Quincy Market, Boston,
      1824-26. Recently restored, as one of the first of such
      projects, it is a winner, though something is lost in
      any preservation project.

701. "Grand Hotel." October 3, 1976, Magazine Section, pp. 68-70.

The United Nations Plaza Hotel "is both a surprise and a delight. It bears no resemblance to the hospitality-industry formula." The new hotel, designed by Roche, Dinkeloo, and Associates, carries the address of "1 United Nations Plaza."

702. "The 'Miracle' of Cooper-Hewitt." October 3, 1976, Section 2, pp. 31, 33.

The Carnegie Mansion at Fifth Avenue and Ninety-first Street, by Babb, Cook and Willard, 1901, has been rescued after a thirteen-year saga. It will become the Cooper-Hewitt National Museum of Design, of the Smithsonian Institution, and will house the collection of decorative arts disposed of by Cooper Union in 1963. Hardy Holzman Pfeiffer have completed the renovation.

703. "Taking the Wraps Off of Egypt." October 10, 1976, Section 2, pp. 1, 23.

"For years I have been a closet Egyptologist." The new installation at the Metropolitan Museum of Art is a "model of scholarship and beauty ... [an] exemplary balance between art and information."

704. "The Master Builder." October 17, 1976, Section 2, pp. 27-28.

"Palladio in America" is the title of an exhibition which is travelling to various centers, but from New York's major museums is heard a "thundering silence." It will appear there at the Cooper-Hewitt Museum. "Palladio was the most influential architect who ever lived."

705. "Fisher Hall Is Alive with Grace." October 20, 1976, p. 56.

Acoustics have been a problem at Avery Fisher Hall since it opened in 1962. Now Philip Johnson and John Burgee have done it right.

706. "This Time Avery Fisher Looks Beautiful." October 24, 1976, Section 2, pp. 29-30.

This is a totally remodelled interior, including some of the structure. It cost $6.4 million and was designed by Philip Johnson and John Burgee.

707. "The Troubling Legacy of Ralph Adams Cram." November 7,
      1976, Section 2, p. 23.

      The Cathedral of St. John the Divine, New York, has
      organized an exhibition on Cram, who designed seventy
      cathedrals and churches in thirty-five states, from
      1900 to 1930. Mrs. Huxtable finds St. John the Divine
      "as cold as it is competent.... it touches the mind
      rather than the heart."

708. "Shlockton Greets You." November 23, 1976, p. 33.

      Most of "downtown" St. Louis has moved ten miles away
      to Clayton, "a universal speculative pattern in American
      cities.... the single most destructive force oper-
      ating in American cities."

709. "'One of Our Most Important Public Buildings.'" November
      28, 1976, Section 2, pp. 1, 39.

      Dallas, Texas, "willed itself into being," 135 years
      ago. The new Municipal Building scheduled to open in
      1977 measures 560x200 feet and is one of "the most
      interesting urban constructions of the 20th century."
      I.M. Pei, architect.

710. "The Trashing of Fifth Avenue." December 5, 1976,
      Section 2, pp. 33-34.

      "The mutilation of Fifth Avenue ... is a continuous
      event." Among the numerous examples provided, the latest
      mutilation is the fifty-two-story Olympic Tower, at
      Fifty-first Street. Its nondescript glass is to extend
      to Olympic Airways next door, as a facade to a building
      in scale with Fifth Avenue.

711. "Salvaging Ornaments from New York's Past." December 12,
      1976, Section 2, p. 29.

      "New York's Stepchildren" is a small photographic
      exhibition organized by the New York Chapter of the
      American Institute of Architects. It features the un-
      loved small public buildings of New York City, which will
      soon be under the control of the City Art Commission.

712. "The Revealing Art of Architectural Drawings." December
      19, 1976, Section 2, pp. 31, 35.

      Forty-five outstanding drawings from the Avery Archi-
      tectural Library are exhibited at the Low Memorial Library,
      Columbia University. The span the years from 1798 to the
      present.

713. "Skyscrapers, a 'New' Esthetic and Recycling." December
      26, 1976, Section 2, pp. 29–30.

      "The big building jobs go to the big names.... There
      is just too much money involved" for it to be otherwise.
      Pennzoil Building, Houston, Texas, by Philip Johnson, is
      one such building where the architecture of excellence
      and the establishment meet. Other buildings are men-
      tioned.

                              1977

714. "Clarence Stein--The Champion of the Neighborhood."
      January 16, 1977, Section 2, pp. 23, 28.

      Stein died in 1975 at the age of ninety-three and the
      American Institute of Architects, Washington, D.C., orga-
      nized a commemorative exhibition on his work as planner
      and humanist, champion of the neighborhood. His work
      is analyzed. (See also Lewis Mumford, Donald Haskell,
      and Marjie Bughman, *American Institute of Architects
      Journal*, 65 [December 1976]: 19–33.)

715. "Will Westway Turn Into the Opportunity of a Century."
      January 23, 1977, Section 2, pp. 25, 29.

      Westway, the proposed replacement for New York's West
      Side Highway, has just received $1.16 billion in federal
      funds. The Westway scheme provides the opportunity to
      reclaim the Hudson River Waterfront of Manhattan, 242
      acres of it if one includes landfill. "It could be
      New York's planning opportunity of the century."

716. "Unbuilt Buildings." January 30, 1977, Magazine Section,
      pp. 44–45, 49.

      Alison Sky and Michelle Stone edited *Unbuilt Buildings:
      Forgotten Architecture in the United States from Thomas
      Jefferson to the Space Age*, illustrating "models, draw-
      ings, archives and designers' fantasies. But they tell
      us a great deal about our taste, standards and values."

717. "The Venturi 'Anti-Style' of Architecture." January 30,
      1977, Section 2, pp. 27, 36.

      Cass Gilbert designed Oberlin College's Allen Memorial
      Art Museum, 1915–17, in the Beaux Arts style. Venturi
      and Rauch's addition is sophisticated, subtle, sympathetic,
      and not what one would perhaps have expected from a Pop
      guru such as Robert Venturi.

718.   "When Things Get This Bad You Have to Laugh."   February
       6, 1977, Section 2, p. 31.

       A general article on the fate of historic buildings in
       our "Catch 22 environment."

719.   "Greenfield, Mass., Gains a Bank and Loses a Museum."
       February 13, 1977, Section 2, pp. 33-34.

       Greenfield wanted to convert its Franklin Savings
       Institution, built in 1911 and recently vacated, into
       a museum but couldn't raise the money. Country Trust
       Company did, however, so a fine building has been pre-
       served. Franklin's new building is "decent but bland."

720.   "A Sense of Crisis about the Art of Architecture."
       February 20, 1977, Section 2, pp. 33, 36.

       The conference "After Modern Architecture" discussed
       architectural theory, which "is just a game for intel-
       lectuals to play." It "is indeed a game of ideas." The
       conference was organized by the International Conference
       of Little Magazines.

721.   "Enduring Splendor of Mies van der Rohe."   February 27,
       1977, Magazine Section, pp. 70-71, 80.

       Mies van der Rohe's furniture is now being expensively
       reproduced and is exhibited together with the originals
       at the Museum of Modern Art.

722.   "The Last Profession to Be 'Liberated' by Women."   March
       13, 1977, Section 2, pp. 25, 33.

       "Women in American Architecture: A Historic and Con-
       temporary Perspective" is an exhibition at the Brooklyn
       Museum. "All those bloody houses!" Discusses the accep-
       tance of women into schools of architecture and into the
       profession.

723.   "Three Different Apartments--One Classic Style."   March
       17, 1977, Section C, pp. 1, 12.

       Home in New York City is what you can find and afford.
       Mrs. Huxtable describes the three apartments that she
       and her husband have lived in; two are illustrated.

724.   "The Maverick Who Created Palm Beach."   March 20, 1977,
       Section 2, pp. 27-28.

       "Palm Beach ambience is largely the work of one maver-
       ick architect Addison Mizner (1872-1933) ... in the boom

years of the 1920's." The architect was eccentric, and
his buildings Hispano-Moresque. There is now a four-
part exhibition of his work entitled "Addison Mizner,
Architect of Dreams and Realities."

725. "A Marriage of Flamboyance and Delicacy of Taste."
     May 1, 1977, Section 2, pp. 29, 34.

     "The Royal Pavilion at Brighton" is the name of the
     exhibit at the Cooper-Hewitt Museum. Designed by John
     Nash, 1787-1822, the Pavilion is "one of the great exotic
     pleasure palaces of the world."

726. "A Landmark Before Its Doors Open." May 8, 1977, Section
     2, p. 25.

     Richard Meier's Bronx Development Center, for handi-
     capped patients, is eagerly awaited by architects, while
     most laymen see it as "unhomelike."

727. "A Spectacular Museum Goes Up in Washington." May 22,
     1977, Section 2, pp. 1, 29-30.

     Washington, D.C., has moved into the twentieth century
     with I.M. Pei's new East Building for the National Gallery.

728. "An Acrobatic Act of Architecture." June 5, 1977, Section
     2, pp. 27, 33.

     The acrobatics are the four structural legs, freestanding
     for the equivalent of nine of the Citicorp Building's
     forty-six stories. Mrs. Huxtable isn't too happy con-
     cerning any aspect of the design of this building by Hugh
     Stubbins.

729. "A Happy Birthday to the Carnegie Mansion." June 9,
     1977, Section C, p. 10.

     Photographs of all three phases of the house are shown:
     (1) Carnegie residence, 1909-46; (2) Columbia University
     School of Social Work, 1946-71; and (3) Cooper-Hewitt
     Museum, 1976.

730. "Architectural Drawings as Art." June 12, 1977, Section
     2, p. 25.

     The Cooper-Hewitt Museum exhibition "Two Hundred Years
     of American Architectural Drawings" contains 200 drawings
     by eighty architects. The drawings are described and
     discussed. So, too, is an exhibition on the drawings
     of Antonio Gaudí at The Drawing Center.

731. "Personal Landmarks along the Highway." June 26, 1977,
      Section 2, p. 25.

      Mrs. Huxtable has noticed the Colt Firearms Building
      each time she has passed Hartford en route to the New
      England shore. This industrial building of 1854 has
      changed from "shabby relic to renewed splendor," re-
      constructed in 1974. A few other similar buildings
      are noted.

732. "A Dramatic Example of Architectural Recycling." July
      3, 1977, Section 2, p. 17.

      Arthur Loomis Harmon's Shelton Hotel on Lexington
      Avenue, a winner from its inception in 1924, has fallen
      on hard times. Now the hotel is to be recycled by Ste-
      phen B. Jacobs for Halloran Properties and "hoked up"
      by Inn Keepers Supply Company of Memphis, Tennessee.

733. "The Case of the Stolen Landmarks." July 11, 1977, p. 24.

      The James Bogardus building at Washington and Murray
      Streets was dismantled and the 1849 cast-iron framework
      stored for re-erection. "Some interested observers of
      the process made off with most of them." Could Louis
      Sullivan's Prudential Building, Buffalo, 1894, also be
      dismantled?

734. "The Fun and Seriousness of Resort Design." July 17,
      1977, Section 2, p. 21.

      America at play or "Palaces for the People" is the
      title of the latest Cooper-Hewitt Museum show. Many
      resort hotels are gone and others are struggling for
      survival, but fantasy and escape were as much the theme
      then as now.

735. "The Most Influential Architect in History. Andrea
      Palladio Took the Lessons of Classical Antiquity
      and Turned Them into Some of the Most Beautiful Build-
      ings of the Renaissance." July 17, 1977, Magazine
      Section, pp. 22-25.

      For those who cannot savor Palladio's architecture in
      person, there is the "Andrea Palladio" show at the Cooper-
      Hewitt Museum, where sixteen huge models are on display,
      along with drawings, books, photographs, and other illus-
      trations.

736. "A Temple of Justice That Inspires." July 24, 1977,
      Section 2, p. 19.

      James Brown Lord designed the Appellate Division Court-
      house on Madison Square, and it is now the subject of an
      exhibition called "Temple of Justice," at the Bar of the
      City of New York. The 1896 building is richly decorated
      inside and out. All is described in the exhibit, but
      the Courthouse, itself, really should be seen.

737. "A Graceful Break with Tradition on Fifth Avenue." July
      31, 1977, Section 2, p. 20.

      A pair of town houses on Fifth Avenue, opposite the
      Metropolitan Museum, were demolished for new construction.
      The builder went bankrupt. H.J. Kalikow Company then
      developed the site with Philip Johnson and John Burgee
      as architects. It is Post-Modern creative eclecticism,
      twenty-three stories high.

738. "A Dubious Plan for the Modern." August 7, 1977, Section
      2, pp. 1, 20.

      The Museum of Modern Art is planning a luxury tower
      adjacent to the museum, on Fifty-third Street. "The
      tower is bad news, urbanistically, even though it is for
      a good cause."

739. "Has Mansard Mania Reached Its Peak?" September 18, 1977,
      Section 2, p. 29.

      Mansardmania, the decorative, slipcover double-pitched
      roof shape, is reaching epidemic proportions in Massa-
      chusetts and Connecticut. It has popular appeal and
      thus is today's vernacular. The form derives ultimately
      from François Mansart.

740. "The Fine Points of Drawings." September 25, 1977,
      Section 2, pp. 33, 36.

      "Drawing Toward a More Modern Architecture" is one of
      numerous exhibitions on architectural drawings, this one
      at the Cooper-Hewitt Museum; another is at The Drawing
      Center.

741. "A House Rewards Affection." September 29, 1977, Section
      C, pp. 1, 10.

      The Huxtables enjoy their rented New England vacation
      home. The hassle of New York is temporarily gone, but
      small town virtues are largely of the mind.

742. "Good News and Bad News from Buffalo." October 2, 1977,
       Section 2, pp. 35, 42.

       Three of America's greatest architects, Richardson,
       Sullivan, and Wright, built in Buffalo. Buildings
       there by the first two are in danger: Sullivan's Pru-
       dential Building and Richardson's State Hospital. Other
       notable Buffalo buildings are mentioned.

743. "The Fountain--A Deliberate Act of Fantasy." October
       16, 1977, Section 2, p. 31.

       Designs of forty French Rococo fountains are exhibited
       at the Metropolitan Museum of Art. Enchantment is the
       word to describe the poetry and magic that links water
       and architecture.

744. "Fame Is a Bust." October 17, 1977, p. 30.

       Busts of ninety-seven Americans represented at Stanford
       White's Hall of Fame, on the old Bronx campus of New York
       University, can no longer be maintained; the National
       Sculpture Society is doing its best to save them.

745. "Architectural Drawings as Art Gallery Art." October
       23, 1977, Section 2, p. 27.

       The Leo Castelli Gallery is exhibiting "Architecture 1,"
       its first exhibit on such a subject. Seven architects of
       international repute are being shown; their drawings illus-
       trate imaginary schemes as well as actual projects.

746. "A Subtle Counterchic." October 27, 1977, Section C, pp.
       1, 10.

       Made with Oak, 1975; *Living Places*, 1976; and *Good Lives*,
       1977, are three paperbacks on interior design by Herbert
       H. and Jeffrey Weiss. Most of the homes illustrated in
       these books represent good design without necessarily
       having been designed by professional designers.

747. "Old Magic and New Dreams on 42d Street." November 6,
       1977, Section 2, pp. 31, 39.

       "Forty-second Street--Theater and the City" is an ex-
       hibition at the Graduate Center of the City University of
       New York which deals with the street's legendary theaters.
       Photographs and films are augmented by seminars and walk-
       ing tours.

748. "Updating Landmarks con Amore." November 13, 1977, Sec-
      tion 2, p. 35.

      A tribute to the Avery Architectural Library at Columbia
      University, which began in 1890 with 2,000 books (and now
      has 100,000 plus drawings and research material), and the
      Institute of Fine Arts, New York University--the old Duke
      House by Horace Trumbauer. Both were built in 1912 and
      have been remodelled: Avery, recently, by Alexander Kouz-
      manoff, and the Institute, twenty years ago, by Robert
      Venturi.

749. "Exquisite Things Made by Man." November 20, 1977, Sec-
      tion 2, p. 29.

      "More Than Meets the Eye" was an exhibition of 400 ob-
      jects from the Cooper-Hewitt's permanent collection.

750. "Exhibit Captures Great Moments in Their Souvenirs."
      November 24, 1977, Section C, p. 10.

      The Cooper-Hewitt Museum's "To Celebrate the Moment"
      shows objects which glorify the individual and his
      achievements.

751. "A Triumphant Renovation of Cooper Union." December 4,
      1977, Section 2, pp. 29, 32.

      Fred A. Peterson's Cooper Union, built in 1859. was
      renovated in 1974. Cast-iron elements would have been
      so expensive to reproduce that students cast them in
      silicone aluminum.

752. "A Stylish New Building at Columbia." December 11, 1977,
      Section 2, pp. 35-36.

      Mitchell-Giurgola's Sherman Fairchild Center for the
      Life Sciences at Columbia University is "one of the best
      buildings to go up on the campus in a long time." Built
      at a cost of $12 million, it is described in relation
      to other campus buildings.

753. "Controversy over Dulles Airport." December 18, 1977,
      Section 2, p. 33.

      Eero Saarinen's Dulles Airport is "a brilliant archi-
      tectural and functional breakthrough." After fifteen
      years of use, passengers have increased from 66,559 in
      1962-63 to 2,841,495 in 1976. The Federal Aviation Au-
      thority is at present fighting against designating the
      airport a protected national landmark because they wish
      to expand the facility.

754. "Tinsel in the Sky." December 19, 1977, p. 30.

      "If the avant-garde now admits the Empire State Build-
      ing to the architectural pantheon, can its Pop seasonal
      and special-event lighting effects be far behind?"

755. "The Latest Style is 'Jeweler's Mechanical.'" December
      25, 1977, Section 2, pp. 1, 27.

      "In 1977 modern architecture was declared dead" and
      was replaced by Post Modernism. "Established rules are
      ... jettisoned and taboo areas ... are explored." See
      Charles Jencks, *The Language of Post-Modern Architecture*.
      Several examples are discussed.

756. "At Smithsonian, Decorative Art of Architect Wright."
      December 29, 1977, Section C, p. 6.

      The Renwick Museum, Washington, D.C., staged a show
      entitled "The Decorative Designs of Frank Lloyd Wright."
      It was the first show devoted to Wright's decorative
      designs.

                                  1978

757. "An Underground Show Devoted to Subway Design." January
      15, 1978, Section 2, p. 21.

      "Subways: An Underground Exhibition" is on view at the
      Forty-second Street and Sixth Avenue subway mezzanine.
      It consists of photographs of examples worldwide and was
      organized by the Cooper-Hewitt Museum.

758. "The Sabotaging of Public Space." January 26, 1978,
      Section C, pp. 1, 8.

      Citicorp Building, New York, by Hugh Stubbins, has
      taken advantage of zoning options by providing a covered
      pedestrian space. This atrium captures the spirit of
      the law by providing more than minimum requirements. It
      is a resounding success. Less successful pedestrian
      spaces are cited.

759. "Grand Central at a Crossroads." January 29, 1978, Section
      2, pp. 25, 28.

      Penn Central is trying, through the courts, to overturn
      the New York Landmarks Preservation Commission's designa-
      tion of Grand Central Terminal as a landmark.

760. "Potted Palms and Wilted Roses." February 3, 1978, p.
      22.

      Groundbreaking has begun for the Palace Hotel, New
      York, a fifty-one-story appendage to the Villard Houses.
      Discusses the hotel industry in New York, in general.

761. "The Current Period of Rediscovery." February 5, 1978,
      Section 2, pp. 25, 27.

      Architectural history is going through a phase of respect-
      ability, and philosophy and style are "in" again. Briefly
      discusses "The Decorative Designs of Frank Lloyd Wright,"
      a travelling exhibition, Arthur Drexler's *The Architecture
      of the Ecole des Beaux Arts*, and "Richardson's Allegheny
      Courthouse and Jail," an article by Franklin K.B. Toker
      in the *Carnegie Magazine*.

762. "Architecture for a Fast-Food Culture." February 12,
      1978, Magazine Section, pp. 23-25, 30-32, 36.

      Robert Venturi was one of the first of many designers
      who saw an "aesthetic merit and cultural meaning in the
      vernacular environment" of junk architecture. Cooper-
      Hewitt Museum's exhibition "Place, Product, Packaging:
      A Look at Four Popular American Building Types: Fast Food
      Restaurants, Diners, Gasoline Stations and Museum Villages"
      forwards this attitude. (See items 974 and 975.)

763. "Discovering the Talent of Ivan Leonidov." February 12,
      1978, Section 2, pp. 19, 24.

      The Institute of Architecture and Urban Studies held
      an exhibition on the Soviet architect Ivan Leonidov (1902-
      59). It includes photographs of models, drawings, and
      paintings, since none of the original material is allowed
      out of the U.S.S.R. Most are of unbuilt projects.

764. "The Changing 'Truth' of Le Corbusier." February 19,
      1978, Section 2, p. 29.

      Eighty-eight drawings and a few models of fifty build-
      ings by Le Corbusier, 1912-62, were on view at the Museum
      of Modern Art.

765. "Award Winners--Outrageous Yet Appealing." February 26,
      1978, Section 2, pp. 25, 28.

      Progressive Architecture's annual awards for architectur-
      al design are now into their twenty-fifth year, and in
      1978 "are on the cutting edge of esthetic exploration."

766.   "All Three Artists Are Preoccupied with Images Drawn
        from a Memory of Home." March 2, 1978, Section C, p.
        10.

        "Image of the Home" at the Institute for Architecture
        and Urban Studies consists of forty-four drawings by
        Guilano Fiorenzoli, Nancy Goldring, and Michael Webb.
        The work is haunting, provocative, and appealing.

767.   "Art for Money's Sake." March 3, 1978, p. 24.

        Banks look like laundromats, so is it any wonder that
        there were forty-six percent more robberies in 1978 than
        in 1977? Older banks such as those of the 1920s had
        splendor and monumentality, which suggests security.

768.   "Atlantic City: Growth vs. Grandeur." March 19, 1978,
        Section 11, pp. 1, 20-21.

        There will be no instant new Atlantic City, because of
        zoning, preservation law, planning, and other needed ap-
        provals. The Blenheim Hotel, of 1906, by Price and McLan-
        ahan of Philadelphia, a structural concrete breakthrough,
        and one or two other notable hotels, should be preserved
        within the new development.

769.   "Is It Curtains for the Music Hall?" March 19, 1978,
        Section 2, pp. 1, 31.

        Radio City Music Hall, at New York's Rockefeller Center,
        is to close April 12, 1978, because of dwindling attend-
        ance and a large deficit, but also possibly because it
        stands on valuable real estate. (Rockefeller Center
        Management Corporation went into large-scale real estate
        in September 1976.)

770.   "Today the Cards Are All in the Builders' Hands." March
        26, 1978, Section 2, p. 29.

        There are many elegant and outstanding buildings de-
        signed for Manhattan but there is a sense of uneasiness.
        Why? "New York is so anxious to have large-scale building
        resume that it is going to be very difficult for the
        City Planning Commission to set and maintain standards
        for these huge projects."

771.   "A Tiffany Treasure Comes to Light." March 30, 1978,
        Section C, pp. 1, 12.

        Parts of the loggia of Tiffany's own home, "Laurelton,"

at Oyster Bay, Long Island, is to be installed in the
New American Wing of the Metropolitan Museum of Art.
Provides a background to Tiffany, his house, and his
work.

772. "Photographs Recall the Glories of Chicago's Columbian
      Exposition." April 9, 1978, Section 2, p. 28.

      Low Memorial Library, Columbia University, had an
      exhibition of photographs of "White City," the Chicago
      World's Columbian Exposition of 1893. The photographs
      are startling in their detail. Discusses buildings
      at the Exposition and their architects.

773. "Johnson's Latest--Clever Tricks or True Art?" April 16,
      1978, Section 2, pp. 26, 31.

      Philip Johnson's A.T.&T. Building proposed for Madison
      Avenue between Fifty-fifth and Fifty-sixth Streets is to
      be a 645-foot-high Chippendale skyscraper, "a pastiche of
      historical references." Good analysis and criticism.

774. "The N.Y. Convention Center--Too Big to Be Bad." April
      30, 1978, Section 2, pp. 1, 25.

      A convention center is essential to New York City,
      which has procrastinated, over a ten-year period, in
      considering five different sites. Skidmore, Owings and
      Merrill have designed a scheme for the Penn Central Rail-
      road Yards at Thirty-fourth Street. "It is all a matter
      of design. That is the challenge now."

775. "Spring-Cleaning: A Bustling Tradition." May 4, 1978,
      Section C, pp. 1, 8.

      "It is no coincidence that the First Liberated Age
      came in the 1920's, when production of both washing ma-
      chines and refrigerators soared."

776. "A Capital Art Palace." May 7, 1978, Magazine Section,
      pp. 58-60.

      The National Gallery's East Building, by I.M. Pei, is
      "what Washington needed and what Washington got: a genuine
      contemporary classic."

777. "A Wrongheaded Museum." May 14, 1978, Section 2, pp. 27,
      35.

      The 1880s Pension Building, in Washington, D.C., by
      Montgomery Meigs, is to be converted into a National

Museum of the Building Arts. It would not be an architectural museum, or a "collector of last resort" for
material too valuable to lose. Instead it would stress
computer and public relations gimmickry. Lists several
examples of lost and endangered architectural material of
the type that this "museum" would not help to preserve.

778. "Paris: The Grand Design." June 6, 1978, Section C, p.
      1.

The French-American Foundation of New York brought
together planners of Paris and New York City on the
subject of "Two World Cities, Paris and New York: an
Urban Plan for Survival." New York has the problems
and Paris has the financial wherewithal. Paris is briefly discussed.

779. "The Educated Eye of Louis Kahn." June 11, 1978,
      Magazine Section, pp. 120-21.

An exhibition of drawings by Louis I. Kahn toured the
United States during 1978. They span the years 1913-59
and "represent an odyssey of discovery and learning."

780. "Paris's La Defense Cluster: Coup of Drawing-Board Style."
      June 11, 1978, Section 1, p. 60.

La Defense is ten minutes from the heart of Paris and
"a world of tomorrow ... an esthetic outrage ... cultural
shock all the way."

781. "Washington Elitism Vs. Paris Populism." June 18, 1978,
      Section 2, pp. 1, 27.

Piano and Rogers's Centre Georges Pompidou, in Paris,
and I.M. Pei's eastern extension to the National Gallery,
in Washington, D.C., are compared: the former is populist
and tacky, the latter, elitist. "In sum, the National
Gallery has risked nothing and the Beaubourg has risked
everything."

782. "The Best of Edwardian London." July 2, 1978, Section
      2, pp. 19-20.

"London 1900," an exhibition staged at the Royal Institute of British Architects' Heinze Gallery, overviews
the prolific embellishment of the Imperial City at the
turn of the century.

783.   "The Future of the Past in Paris." July 2, 1978, Sec-
       tion 4, p. 14.

       On visiting Paris one realizes how much it has changed,
       but "even with change, the center of Paris holds; it is
       the edges that are vulnerable."

784.   "Streets of Dublin Show the Scars of Battle with Build-
       ers." July 3, 1978, Section C, p. 2.

       Economic growth bypassed Dublin in the nineteenth cen-
       tury, which means that the present boom in land values
       is endangering much of its Georgian heritage. At $175,000
       per acre the commercial area could be increased five or
       ten times.

785.   "A 'Landmark' Decision on Landmarks." July 9, 1978,
       Section 2, pp. 21, 24.

       The United States Supreme Court has upheld the landmark
       designation of Grand Central Terminal, New York. But this
       must not lead to irresponsible future designations. The
       court's arguments are explained.

786.   "Living in the Follies of the Past." July 13, 1978, Sec-
       tion C, p. 6.

       "Follies are the icing on the cake of architecture ...
       for purely ornamental purposes." Marion and David Cooper
       purchased a Georgian tower folly in Hertfordshire, England,
       and live in it.

787.   "A Tastemaker Rescued from History." July 16, 1978, Sec-
       tion 2, p. 23.

       Numerous exhibitions are planned to mark the 250th
       anniversary of the birth of Robert Adam. He is "being
       rediscovered by a generation that grew up without him."
       His work is described and assessed.

788.   "Cities within the City of London." July 23, 1978, Sec-
       tion 2, p. 23.

       There are the cities of Sir Christopher Wren, High Vic-
       torian London, Edwardian London, and also contemporary
       London's highrise clusters of modern structures. "Through
       Lutyens, a circuitous line leads back to Wren again, and
       splendor is the constant theme."

789.   "Kilkenny Design Workshops Use the Best Irish Artisans

and Designers." July 27, 1978, Section C, p. 11.

Kilkenny Design Workshop in Dublin "is a revelation of sophisticated design products for the home."

790. "Future Shock: The New French Towns." August 13, 1978, pp. 40-42. (*The New York Times* was on strike on August 13, and no paper was published, but galleys exist. This article, galleys 241-49. It appeared again in the issue of November 19, 1978, item 794, when publication resumed, under the title of "Cold Comfort: The New French Towns.")

From 1965 to 1975 France has built five new towns within a twenty-mile radius of Paris, each to house 200,000 to 300,000 people, but they "raise a great many questions about architecture and urban design." Some of the problems are outlined.

791. "A Feast of Victoriana." November 9, 1978, Section C, pp. 1, 8.

"The Gilded Age of Westchester" is a "modest but fascinating display" at the Hudson River Museum at Yonkers.

792. "Sir Edwin Landseer Lutyens and the Cult of the Recent Past." November 12, 1978, Section 2, p. 35.

The Museum of Modern Art exhibited "The Architecture of Sir Edwin Landseer Lutyens (1869-1944)," another revisionist show.

793. "Atlantic City--The Wrong Ticket." November 19, 1978, Section 2, pp. 31, 40.

Governor Brendan Byrne of New Jersey wants all-new construction in Atlantic City, to make it the Las Vegas of the East. In so doing many historic structures will be forfeited, including The Blenheim Hotel, 1906, a pioneer design in reinforced concrete.

794. "Cold Comfort: The New French Towns." November 19, 1978, Magazine Section, pp. 164-69. See item 790.

Old Paris was refined. New Paris, only five miles away in the new towns, is monstrous. How does one return, in the words of a French planner, to the "warm, enriching animation of the urban environment"?

795. "Viennese Style--And Function." November 26, 1978,
      Section 2, pp. 31-32.

      An exhibition entitled "Viennese Moderne; 1898-1918:
      an Early Encounter Between Taste and Utility" was held
      at the Cooper-Hewitt Museum to show the end of nineteenth-
      century tradition and the beginning of twentieth-century
      vision. The big names are Josef Hoffmann and Adolf Loos.

796. "High-Tech or the Handcraft Look?" November 30, 1978,
      Section C, p. 6.

      Discusses several new publications which serve social
      and design history, including *High-Tech* by Joan Kron
      and Suzanne Slesin.

797. "Provocative Public Housing." December 3, 1978, Section
      2, pp. 35-36.

      Neave Brown's megastructure housing built for the Lon-
      don Borough of Camden, 1,000 feet long and six stories
      high, for 1,660 people in 520 units, could be a success.

798. "As East 62d Street Goes, So Goes New York." December
      10, 1978, Section 2, pp. 39-40.

      Side Street Sabotage is what is likely to happen to
      French Renaissance, Beaux-Arts, Sixty-second Street be-
      tween Madison and Fifth Avenues. "Nothing like them
      will ever be built again." What is being proposed is
      "bad preservation, bad urbanism and bad architecture."

799. "Tut Tut." December 25, 1978, p. 18.

      The Tutankhamun show at the Metropolitan Museum is
      part of the supershow industry.

800. "Behind Dublin's Georgian Facades, Gay and Elegant Ceil-
      ings." December 28, 1978, Section C, p. 6.

      "Nowhere is there a greater richness of ceilings than
      in the city of Dublin, in terms of sheer numbers and
      consistency of style." But many are being destroyed,
      as the houses in which they are situated are demolished.

801. "'Towering' Achievements of '78." December 31, 1978,
      Section 2, pp. 21, 24.

      The new eclecticism is the theme of architecture in
      1978. A general article on architecture, preservation,
      exhibitions, and historian-critics.

802. "Dreams from the Drafting Board." January 14, 1979,
      Magazine Section, pp. 50-51, 53, 56.

      Architectural dreams are either of unbuilt buildings
      or of buildings which are designed but never built. This
      was the subject of an exhibition of "Visionary Drawings:
      Architecture and Planning" at The Drawing Center, New
      York.

803. "The Japanese New Wave." January 14, 1979, Section 2,
      p. 27.

      The most "stunning and provocative" expression of
      Modernism in architecture is to be found in Japan, where
      a large proportion of current work is coming from the
      drawing boards of the thirty to fifty age group.

804. "Selling Cities Like Soap." January 16, 1979, p. 14.

      Melbourne, Australia, wants an image-making landmark
      and has offered $100,000 in prize money for a winning
      idea. Images of other cities are discussed.

805. "Master Builder of the Modern Age." January 21, 1979,
      Section 2, p. 25.

      An obituary of Pier Luigi Nervi, who died in Rome last
      week at eighty-seven. "He was an engineer with an Italian
      sensibility."

806. "Office Landscapes and Inner Space." January 31, 1979,
      p. 22.

      Office workers are miserable in the numerous revamped
      office buildings. Workers "resent the slick, inflexible,
      impersonal arrangements."

807. "The Fantasies of Ludwig II." February 1, 1979, Section
      C, pp. 1, 10.

      Ludwig II's eccentricities in Bavaria are now being
      taken seriously in an exhibition of drawings and arti-
      facts at the Cooper-Hewitt Museum.

808. "The 'Pathetic Fallacy,' or Wishful Thinking at Work."
      February 11, 1979, Section 2, p. 29.

      The Architectural Pathetic Fallacy is when one inserts
      a skyscraper into a low-rise context and attempts to

marry it in. Ulrich Franzen's highrise on the Dodge
House site on Fifth Avenue doesn't go easy; it is
mannerist. Philip Johnson's 1001 Fifth Avenue is amus-
ing, but no more successful.

809.   "'Development' at the Seaport." February 25, 1979,
       Section 2, pp. 31-32.

       "Illusion becomes delusion" at New York's Peck's Slip
       where Richard Haas's mural of the eighteenth- and early
       nineteenth-century architecture replaces the real thing,
       demolished in the 1960s. Seaport Development is going
       to put the whole area on a firm financial and commercial
       footing but not without damage to the original buildings.

810.   "Mirrors of Our Time. 20 Years of Modern Building."
       February 25, 1979, Magazine Section, pp. 22-24, 28,
       32, 54.

       "Transformations in Modern Architecture," at the
       Museum of Modern Art, surveys twenty years of design.
       Arthur Drexler, the organizer, ignores innovation and
       quality for an objective reading of trends. "Transforma-
       tion is the one constant theme."

811.   "Advertising Art: Indelible Images and Cultural Commentary."
       March 1, 1979, Section C, p. 10.

       Advertising is based upon trivia "playing on every hope
       and fear." This is the theme of Cooper-Hewitt's exhibi-
       tion "Indelible Images: Contemporary Advertising Design."

812.   "Mutations in the Modern Movement." March 4, 1979, Section
       2, p. 29.

       "Transformations in Modern Architecture," a show at the
       Museum of Modern Art, illustrates how "the rules of mod-
       ernism have been bent or broken."

813.   "A Promising Scheme for Les Halles." March 11, 1979,
       Section 2, pp. 31, 37.

       Les Halles, Paris, were demolished in 1971, leaving a
       huge hole in the ground. Many projects, solicited and
       unsolicited, have been proposed for the site. Mrs. Hux-
       table agrees with President Giscard d'Estaing that it
       should be left green.

814.   "The Many Faces of 42d Street." March 18, 1979, Section
       2, pp. 31, 33.

Forty-second Street contains some distinguished architecture, and not just the facades but also the spaces
behind. In the Fall of 1978 an exhibition on this theme
was held at the Grace Building on Forty-second Street.

815. "On the Japanese Esthetic." March 25, 1979, Section 2,
     pp. 31, 34.

     "MA, Space/Time in Japan" was the title of an exhibi-
     tion at the Cooper-Hewitt Museum, which attempted to
     explain the basic tenets of Japanese culture.

816. "A House in the Spirit of Its Time." April 8, 1979,
     Section 2, p. 33.

     Pierre Chareau built the Maison de Verre, Paris, 1928-
     32, an essay in glass bricks and innovative technical
     details. It has been well publicized and many architects
     make the pilgrimage to see it.

817. "Update on the Music Hall." April 22, 1979, Section 2,
     pp. 33, 36.

     Rockefeller Center, Inc., wished to demolish the Radio
     City Music Hall, which is running at a loss, but changed
     its mind, deciding instead to subsidize the Music Hall
     by a national entertainment package for which Radio City
     would be the showcase. Mention is also made of a Davis,
     Brody and Associates' proposal to build on the air rights
     above the Music Hall.

818. "An Inclusive View of Design." April 29, 1979, Section
     2, pp. 31-32.

     How the new, revisionist way of looking at things is
     affecting the field of design is seen in a re-evaluation
     exhibit at the Cooper-Hewitt Museum called "Take Your
     Choice: Contemporary Product Design."

819. "Remodel the Subway Remodelling Plan." May 4, 1979, p.
     32.

     Federal grants amounting to $300 million are earmarked
     for subway modernization in New York, but "spot beauti-
     fication is not subway redesign."

820. "Philip Johnson and the Temper of These Times." May 13,
     1979, Section 2, pp. 27-28.

     "The name of the game in architecture right now is
     'Can You Top This?'" That Philip Johnson is master of

the game is shown in his latest design for P.P.G. Industries of Pittsburgh. "Like it or not, a spectacular addition to the skyline."

821.   "Industrial Design: Invented to Serve and Shape a 20th-Century Consumer Economy." May 24, 1979, Section C, p. 10.

The twentieth century is in the hands of the historians, and design of the 1950s is dissertation material. A general discussion.

822.   "A Unified New Language of Design." May 27, 1979, Section 2, pp. 25, 37.

New York's Max Protetch Gallery held a show of sketches, renderings, models, and photographs by Michael Graves. Some of his work is discussed.

823.   "A Visionary and a Classicist." June 10, 1979, Section 2, pp. 31, 34.

A review of two projects commissioned by the Museum of Modern Art: Roger Ferri's "Pedestrian City" and Allan Greenberg's "A Proposal for an American Architecture and Urbanism in the Post Petroleum Age."

824.   "Alvar Aalto's Humane Environments." June 17, 1979, Section 2, pp. 35, 38.

Cooper-Hewitt Museum has mounted drawings and photographs for an Alvar Aalto retrospective. "Aalto was clearly a square peg in a round modernist hole."

825.   "The Season of Aquarius." June 19, 1979, p. 20.

An essay on New York fountains, many of which are quite recent.

826.   "A New York Blockbuster of Superior Design." July 1, 1979, Section 2, p. 25.

The Bonwit Teller site on Fifth Avenue at Fifty-eighth Street is to be demolished for a fifty-eight-story structure to be developed by Donald Trump by his architect Der Scutt. "A dramatically handsome structure," but with questions about the size and scale permitted by zoning.

827. "'The Main Event Is the City Itself.'"   July 8, 1979,
      Section 2, pp. 25-26.

      The third "Immovable Objects" show at the Cooper-Hewitt
      Museum, called "Urban Open Spaces," explores how this
      kind of public environment has functioned for a very long
      time. This is one of several exhibitions in New York on
      public open spaces.

828. "Rome and Artistic Fantasy."   July 15, 1979, Section 2,
      pp. 25-26.

      "Roma Interrotta" is an exhibition at the Cooper-
      Hewitt Museum in which seventeen erudite cult figures of
      the architectural profession fantasize a series of urban
      projects based upon Giovanni Battista Nolli's 1748 map
      of Rome.

829. "Model Rooms: Images of Past and Future."   July 19, 1979,
      Section C, pp. 1, 8.

      Mrs. Huxtable's first job was selling Organic Design
      Furniture at Bloomingdale's. Later she became acquainted
      with model rooms at the Museum of Modern Art. A general
      survey of model rooms, which "will always haunt me."

830. "A Radical Change on the City's Skyline."   July 22, 1979,
      Section 2, pp. 27-28.

      Peter Kalikow has commissioned from Eli Attia and Assoc-
      iates a new, elegant skyscraper that contributes to art
      and urbanism, on Park Avenue between Fortieth and Forty-
      first Streets. Attia was working for Philip Johnson when
      Kalikow was seeking an architect!

831. "Architecture: 'Bigger--and Maybe Better.'"   August 26,
      1979, Section 2, pp. 25-26.

      Corporate or speculative building is on the upswing
      again. A brief overview, plus a mention of forthcoming
      exhibitions and new architectural commissions.

832. "'Gritty Cities' of America's Industrial Past."   August
      30, 1979, Section C, p. 10.

      Mary Procter and Bill Matuszeski's book *Gritty Cities*
      analyzed forty small industrial towns hard hit by twentieth-
      century changes. The introduction is good, the writing
      sensitive and understanding, but "no clear image of any
      single one [town] emerges."

833.   "Decorative Objects with Special Magic." September
          16, 1979, Section 2, pp. 31, 34.

          Pioneers of the Modern Movement never intended to out-
       law decoration, even though the decorative arts have
       long been in limbo. Decoration is, however, coming into
       favor again, as seen in "Recent Acquisitions: Architec-
       ture and Design," at the Museum of Modern Art, and "The
       Cooper-Hewitt Collections: Glass," at the Cooper-Hewitt.

834.   "The 'Side Street Spoilers.'" September 23, 1979, Sec-
          tion 2, pp. 31, 36.

          Realtors use the argument that the higher one builds,
       the greater the use of land, but on Manhattan's cross-
       town streets this means the destruction of pleasant
       aspects of the city. Examples given.

835.   "A Radical New Addition for Mid-America." September
          30, 1979, Section 2, pp. 1, 31.

          New Harmony, Indiana, is an historic town. A contro-
       versial building has been added at its north-west edge:
       Richard Meier's Atheneum Center, to open October 10,
       1979.

836.   "Design Notebook: It's a Century Since Edison Lit Up the
          World." October 4, 1979, Section C, p. 10.

          The National Museum of History and Technology in Wash-
       ington, D.C., mounts an exhibition to celebrate the
       centennial of Thomas Alva Edison's invention of the
       lightbulb.

837.   "The Austere World of Rossi." October 7, 1979, Section
          2, pp. 31-32.

          Aldo Rossi won the competition in 1976 for the design
       of Modena Cemetery. Now the Max Protech Gallery has
       "Aldo Rossi; Architectural Projects" and the Institute
       for Architecture and Urban Studies, "Aldo Rossi in Amer-
       ica: 1976-79," both in New York City. A Marxist with
       a preoccupation with death, he is a geometric minimalist.

838.   "Boston's Museum in the Market." October 14, 1979,
          Section 2, pp. 31, 34.

          Part of the Boston Museum of Fine Arts has been relocat-
       ed at Faneuil Hall for a two-year period, five months of
       which has already passed. During this time a record

130,765 visitors have passed through its exhibitions.
A great success on a low budget, it is devoid of expensive gimmicks.

839.   "A Squint at South Street." October 17, 1979, p. 26.

The Rouse Company which successfully developed the
Faneuil Hall Marketplace, Boston, is to attempt the
same at New York's South Street Seaport at a total
cost of $210 million. Old blocks in the vicinity must
also be protected against market pressures.

840.   "The Museum Upstages the Library." October 28, 1979,
        Section 2, pp. 31, 39.

The Kennedy Library, Cambridge, by I.M. Pei, is "by
far the best of the bunch," even though, as in other
similar complexes, the museum, maintained at public
expense, predominates: This was not the original intent.
"The tail totally wags the dog." It is separated from
the Kennedy School of Government and Institute of Politics, now built on the Harvard campus, even though the
whole was to have been a single complex.

841.   "Liberty Park--First of a New Breed." November 4, 1979,
        Section 2, pp. 33, 36.

Geddes Brecher Qualls Cunningham, architects, with
Zion and Breen, landscape architects, have designed
Liberty State Park, New Jersey, and the Museum of Modern
Art has mounted an exhibition on the subject.

842.   "Remnants of an Era: Two Silent Stores." November 8,
        1979, Section C, pp. 1, 10.

F.W. Woolworth stores celebrated their centennial in
1979 at a time when the "five and dime" has become a
thing of the past. Two large Woolworth and Kress stores
stand empty on Fifth Avenue, the latter an example of
1935 Art Deco by Edward F. Sibbert.

843.   "... And Celebrates Its Landmarks." November 18, 1979,
        Section 2, pp. 1, 40.

Surveys "Art of the Twenties" at the Museum of Modern
Art.

844.   "'All New' Vs. Rehabilitation." November 25, 1979, Sec-
        tion 2, pp. 23, 37.

Exchange Court, by Clinton and Russell, and the Woolworth

Building, by Cass Gilbert, are both on Broadway. The
former represents a prime commercial development site;
the latter is being renovated at a sum greater than its
original cost.

845. "The Centenary of a Famous Firm." December 2, 1979,
        Section 2, pp. 31, 37.

        This year is the centenary of the founding of the firm
of McKim, Mead & White, and the Low Library (by McKim)
at Columbia University is housing an exhibition of their
work. Their significance is assessed.

846. "Is This the Last Chance for Battery Park City?" Decem-
        ber 9, 1979, Section 2, pp. 39-40.

        Mixed residential and commercial development was the
idea for Battery Park City on the Hudson River waterfront
of Manhattan. First proposed in 1966, ten schemes later
it seems just as likely that it will never be built.

847. "Redeveloping New York." December 23, 1979, Section 2,
        pp. 31-32.

        I.M. Pei's New York Convention Center will stretch from
Thirty-fourth to Thirty-ninth Streets, Eleventh to Twelfth
Avenues. It will be a handsome space-frame. All aspects
of Midtown renewal are being considered with relation to
the project.

848. "Design Notebook: A Mansion That Deserves More Than Plati-
        tudes." December 27, 1979, Section C, p. 10.

        New York's Jewish Museum is exhibiting photographs and
seven drawings of its home, the Felix M. Warburg house,
1907-1908, by C.P.H. Gilbert. Mrs. Huxtable asks who
was architect Charles Pierrepont H. Gilbert?

849. "The Retreat Continued." December 30, 1979, Section 2,
        pp. 23, 31.

        I.M. Pei is this year's architect, having been awarded
the gold medal of the AIA. His New York Convention Center
design is on display at the Museum of Modern Art. The
year is also surveyed in general terms, and reference is
made to the work of Gordon Bunshaft.

Part II
Articles by Ada Louise Huxtable
in Magazines, Periodicals, and Journals
Other Than *The New York Times*

1953

850. "Geodetic and Plastic Expressions Abroad." *Progressive Architecture*, 34 (June 1953): 111-16.

Developments in reinforced concrete construction since World War II have led to new possibilities in architectural form, exemplified by the works of Nervi in Italy and Niemeyer in Brazil, which are here described and illustrated.

1954

851. "Designed to 'Sell.'" *Art Digest*, 28 (March 1, 1954): 12, 25.

Reviews an exhibition of four American graphic designers at the Museum of Modern Art.

852. "Signs of the Times." *Art Digest*, 28 (April 1, 1954): 6-7, 30.

Reviews the show "Signs in the Streets" at the Museum of Modern Art.

853. "New York Revisited: The Produce Exchange." *Art Digest*, 28 (May 1, 1954): 10-11, 25.

"The Produce Exchange building is the work of George B. Post, one of New York's most important architects of the Brown Decades." Provides an appreciation of the building and a perspective of William Lescaze's proposed $25 million replacement (not executed).

854. "Olivetti's Lavish Shop." *Art Digest*, 28 (July 1, 1954): 15.

Olivetti's "lavish showroom" at 584 Fifth Avenue "is New York's introduction to one of the more important aspects of internationally famous design programs of the Olivetti Corporation." Words used to describe the design include: "extravagant ... expensive opulence ... unconventionality ... ostentatious ... never vulgar."

855.   "Post War Italy; Architecture and Design." *Art Digest*,
       28 (July 1, 1954): 6-8.

       Visitors to Rome can see the best of the old and the
       new in juxtaposition and usually complementing
       each other. Most of the new architecture is functional
       and is constructed of reinforced concrete, but there is
       also color, texture, and pattern. Interior and indus-
       trial design is of the same high quality. "Italian
       architecture and design have emerged as a major contri-
       bution to contemporary art."

856.   "Stainless Comes to Dinner." *Industrial Design*, 1, no.
       4 (August 1954): 30-37.

       This article on tableware begins by explaining the
       properties, use, and manufacture of chrome-nickel steel.
       Recent designers have analyzed afresh the useability of
       the knife, fork, and spoon and have come up with new
       shapes reflective of their particular use.

857.   "Japanese House." *Art Digest*, 28 (September 15, 1954):
       14-15.

       Reviews the "Japanese House," an exhibition at the
       Museum of Modern Art. "The separation of art and life
       is one of the tragedies of the Western World.... Every
       phase and aspect of Oriental existence is deeply rooted
       in esthetics." Analyzes the Japanese house.

858.   "Bankers' Showcase." *Arts Digest*, 28 (December 1, 1954):
       12-13.

       Skidmore, Owings and Merrill's $3 million, five-story
       Manufacturers Trust Building on Fifth Avenue is described
       together with its internal sculpture screen by Harry
       Bertoia. "Take away the sculpture and the design of the
       interior loses its emotional impact."

1955

859.   "How Good Is Good Design?" *Craft Horizons*, 15 (March-
       April 1955): 35-37.

       Reviews the fifth anniversary exhibition of Good Design
       at the Museum of Modern Art. In 1950, when listings of
       Good Designs began, there were 250 products. In 1955
       there were 400. Exhibitions should be staged only when
       there are enough good designs to be presented and not on an
       annual basis with deadlines to meet. Discusses criteria
       of good design.

860. "The Art of Glass." *Arts Digest*, 29 (June 1, 1955):
      16-17, 30-31.

      After the "art glass" of the Victorian period and the
      sterility of the Bauhaus came the modern glass, seen in
      two shows in New York City. "They were a clear indica-
      tion of an international revival of the more freely ex-
      perimental and sensuous phases of the glass maker's art."

                              1956

861. "Table Radio Design." *Consumer Reports*, 21 (August
      1956): 374-75.

      "Frenzied over-styling gives this year's models an
      air of flamboyant desperation. Function and ease of
      use often suffer as a result." Prices, electric shocks
      from exposed metal parts, hum, tuning, and readability
      of dial are all discussed.

862. "Architectural Frontiers. The Commercial Building in
      America." *Arts*, 30 (September 1956): 24-31.

      Paralleling a series in *Progressive Architecture* on
      historic American buildings, this article also illustrates
      some early and more recent structures.

863. "Progressive Architecture in America. The Cleveland
      Arcade--1888-90." *Progressive Architecture*, 37
      (September 1956): 139-40.

      The building still stands and offers "an opportunity
      to study the genre at first hand.... The exposed iron
      framing ... was exploited for its psychological and
      esthetic effect as well as for its structural advantages."

864. "Progressive Architecture in America. Grand Central
      Depot--1869-71." *Progressive Architecture*, 37 (October
      1956): 135-38.

      Constructed by Commodore Vanderbilt at a cost of $3
      million. New York's Grand Central shed was the largest
      single span in the United States at that time and, thus,
      became the precedent for later structures. The archi-
      tect was John B. Snooks and the engineer was R.G. Hadfield.
      It represented two American Victorian qualities: progress
      and pretentious display.

865. "Progressive Architecture in America. Jayne Building,
      1849–50." *Progressive Architecture*, 37 (November
      1956): 133–34.

      The Jayne Building, Philadelphia, by William J. Johnston,
      was a "proto skyscraper," built of Quincy granite at a
      cost of half a million dollars. It was damaged by fire
      in 1872 and still stood in 1956 (but has since been de-
      molished).

866. "Progressive Architecture in America. Allendale Mill––
      1822." *Progressive Architecture*, 37 (December 1956):
      123–24.

      The mill, located in Centerdale, Rhode Island, designed
      and built by Zachariah Allen, was of "slow burning" con-
      struction, wherein large timbers, which char and thereby
      self-protect, were used. Since lower insurance rates
      could not be obtained under the circumstances, in 1835
      Allen founded the profitable Manufacturers Mutual Fire
      Insurance Company.

                              1957

867. "Progressive Architecture in America. Harper and Brothers
      Building––1854." *Progressive Architecture*, 38 (February
      1957): 153–54.

      When this New York City publishing house burned, fire
      prevention for the new building was a major concern.
      Building functions were separated, the structure and the
      planning were carefully organized. I-section wrought-
      iron beams, made by Peter Cooper's Iron Works at Trenton,
      were used on the new Harper and Brothers Building in
      1854, a year prior to their use on the Cooper Union build-
      ing.

868. "Progressive Architecture in America. Larkin Company
      Administrative Building––1904." *Progressive Architecture*,
      38 (March 1957): 141–42.

      An appreciation of an outstanding Buffalo, New York,
      building by Frank Lloyd Wright, which was sold for $5,000
      in 1950 and was demolished for a truck storage garage.

869. "The Patronage of Progress." *Arts*, 31 (April 1957): 24–29.

      Reviews the exhibition "Buildings for Business and Govern-
      ment" at the Museum of Modern Art. Patronage for good de-
      sign was to a large extent present in buildings for busines.

and government in the nineteenth century. The six
examples of buildings represented in this exhibition
show that patronage and good design still go hand in
hand.

870.   "Progressive Architecture in America. Eads Bridge,
       1868-74." *Progressive Architecture*, 38 (April 1957):
       139-42.

       Steel was used in this bridge, constructed from 1869
       to 1871 in St. Louis, Missouri. This was not only an
       early use of steel, but the first in bridge construction.
       It was also the site of the first use of pneumatic cais-
       sons, sunk ninety-five feet deep to bedrock. Numerous
       problems involved in the construction are enumerated.
       (See item 622.)

871.   "Progressive Architecture in America. The Balloon Frame
       --c. 1833." *Progressive Architecture*, 38 (May 1957):
       145-46.

       "This novel and admirably simple system of construction
       [was] ... the American dream ... of efficiency, economy,
       and speed." Its birthplace is known to be Chicago, in
       1833, although its inventor is in dispute.

872.   "Progressive Architecture in America. Home Insurance
       Building, 1883-85." *Progressive Architecture*, 38 (June
       1957): 207-208.

       A major landmark in the development of the skyscraper,
       being completely skeletal and as fireproof as possible.
       The frame was carefully analyzed at its demolition in
       1931. Above the sixth floor were I-section steel beams
       twelve inches deep, which were first being rolled at the
       period of the building's construction. Cast-iron columns
       were utilized throughout, as were some wrought-iron beams.
       This Chicago building was designed by William Le Baron
       Jenny.

873.   "Progressive Architecture in America. New England Mill
       Village." *Progressive Architecture*, 38 (July 1957):
       139-40.

       Harrisville, New Hampshire, began when the first red
       brick mills were built, from 1810 to 1819. Housing, a
       church, and other mill structures, some in stone, were
       added in 1835, 1860, 1923, and 1946.

874. "Progressive Architecture in America. The Washington
      Monument, 1836-84." *Progressive Architecture*, 38
      (August 1957): 141-44.

      Commissions, competition, enquiries, scandals, stops,
      and starts for almost a century: The history of the Wash-
      ington Monument is presented in detail.

875. "Progressive Architecture in America. Reinforced Concrete
      Construction. The Work of Ernest L. Ransome, Engineer--
      1884-1911." *Progressive Architecture*, 38 (September
      1957): 139-42.

      Ransome Americanized the European systems of concrete
      construction, but he was equally an initiator in its
      development. Some of Ransome's well-founded discoveries
      were, at first, ridiculed. His works are listed and il-
      lustrated.

876. "Progressive Architecture in America. Factory for Pack-
      ard Motor Car Company--1905." *Progressive Architecture*,
      38 (October 1957): 121--22.

      Albert Kahn's Packard Factory, Detroit, Michigan, "is
      one of America's most significant contributions to the
      history of building." Simple modular structure and "the
      trussed-bar reinforcement against shearing stresses" were
      innovative.

877. "Progressive Architecture in America. Factory for Ford
      Motor Company--1909-1914." *Progressive Architecture*,
      38 (November 1957): 181-82.

      Ford's "unprecedented ideas made almost incredible
      demands on men and machinery. Consciously (or uncon-
      sciously) he [Albert Kahn] forced technical innovations
      and development in structure, design and plan," in this
      Highland Park, Michigan, plant.

1958

878. "Progressive Architecture in America. Store for E.V.
      Haughwout and Company--1857." *Progressive Architecture*,
      39 (February 1958): 133-36.

      The scene on Broadway a hundred years ago, in the
      shopping district, is recreated as a backdrop to J.P.
      Gaynor's design for this cast-iron structure (still
      standing), with its then new safety elevator.

879. "Progressive Architecture in America. Quincy Market--
      1825-1826, Boston, Mass." *Progressive Architecture*,
      39 (April 1958): 149-52.

      This development cost well over $1 million in the
      1820s when Josiah Quincy was mayor of Boston. Alexander
      Parris was his architect.

880. "Progressive Architecture in America. Granite Wharf,
      Warehouse, Office Buildings--c. 1823-1872." *Progres-
      sive Architecture*, 39 (June 1958): 117-18.

      Boston's Quincy Market, begun in 1825-26, was partially
      destroyed in 1872. Mrs. Huxtable provides street addresses
      of early buildings and mentions architect G.J.F. Bryant's
      edifices of the 1850s and 1860s. Large monolithic slabs,
      rather than individually cut stones, were the order of
      the day in early construction, although Bryant is gener-
      ally associated with ashlar construction.

881. "Progressive Architecture in America. Commercial Build-
      ings--c. 1850-1870." *Progressive Architecture*, 39
      (August 1958): 105-106.

      The Boston fire of 1872 destroyed 152 structures de-
      signed by Gridley James Fox Bryant; thereafter he was
      commissioned to rebuild 111 of them. This short article
      contains interesting details of Bryant's life, and of
      the city in which he lived and worked.

882. "Progressive Architecture in America. Brooklyn Bridge
      --1867-1883." *Progressive Architecture*, 39 (October
      1958): 157-60.

      "The significance of Brooklyn Bridge is hard to measure
      in terms of engineering alone." It "is made up of equal
      parts of science, esthetics, history and myth ... the
      first suspension bridge to use steel." Other innovative
      features are described. John A. Roebling and Washington
      Roebling, engineers.

883. "Progressive Architecture in America. River Rouge Plant
      for Ford Motor Company--1917." *Progressive Architecture*,
      39 (December 1958): 119-22.

      "The Rouge plant grew out of Henry Ford's personal ob-
      session with industrial self-sufficiency ... his idea of
      a manufacturing center that would function autonomously,
      controlling everything from raw materials to the finished
      product." Albert Kahn was the architect, and building
      "B" was begun at Dearborn, Michigan, in 1917.

1959

884. "Art in Architecture 1959." *Craft Horizons*, 19, no. 1
      (January–February 1959): 10–15.

      There are problems with modern art and architecture,
      since the historical integration of decoration and
      building is, with the Modern Movement, no longer accept-
      able. An architect is responsible for the art of archi-
      tecture, but how well has he been trained toward artistic
      collaboration? Provides examples of good integration.

885. "Progress Report: The Work of Dean L. Gustavson Associ-
      ates." *Progressive Architecture*, 40 (August 1959):
      120–31.

      Gustavson began practice in Salt Lake City in 1953,
      and with his partners has built a profitable practice
      of good design potential. He trained under Mies at the
      Illinois Institute of Technology.

886. "Exploring New York." *Art in America*, 47, no. 3 (Fall
      1959): 48–55.

      Tucked among the glass boxes are some historic jewels
      which are easily located by those with an interest. De-
      scribes old New York as a backdrop for architects, clients,
      and their architecture. Discusses some of the city's
      finer landmarks.

887. "Maximum Efficiency/Minimum Cost." *Progressive Archi-
      tecture*, 40 (September 1959): 148–54.

      Accomplished handsomeness with economy is Mrs. Huxtable's
      judgment of this New York City building housing the new
      headquarters for the Girls Scouts of the U.S.A. William
      T. Meyers was the architect, with Skidmore, Owings and
      Merrill as consultants. Gives details of costs.

888. "Art with Architecture: New Terms of an Old Alliance."
      American Institute of Architects Journal, 32 (November
      1959): 108.

      A brief discussion of metal, sand, and glass sculptures
      and abstract tapestries, as they enhance modern architec-
      ture in New York City.

889. "The Four Seasons: Collaboration for Elegance." *Progres-
      sive Architecture*, 40 (December 1959): 142–47.

      "Sumptuous modern architecture requires accessories of

appropriate character ... and uniquely identifiable."
Complete article written by Karl Linn, Richard Lippold,
and A.L. Huxtable in association with L. Garth Huxtable.
The Huxtables' contribution appears on pp. 146-47 and
concerns the design of accessories, place settings, and
equipment for the restaurant.

1960

890. "Concrete Technology in USA: Historical Survey." *Pro-*
     gressive Architecture, 41 (October 1960): 143-49.

     Portland cement was introduced in England in 1824 and
     into the New World by the 1830s. Natural cement rock
     was discovered in New York State in 1818. The discussion
     ranges through early uses and the spread of concrete
     technology to reinforced concrete from the end of the
     nineteenth century to the present--"the Concrete Era, an
     age with the promise of architectural greatness."

891. "The Architect as a Prophet." *American Institute of*
     Architects Journal, 34 (December 1960): 102.

     The "extreme and esoteric proposals for remaking the
     world" have been brought together into the exhibition
     "Visionary Architecture," at the Museum of Modern Art.
     "They present patterns of the future beyond any conven-
     tional contemporary concept."

892. "Twentieth Century Architecture: Old and New Romanticism."
     Art in America, 48, no. 4 (1960): 46-55.

     Great architecture is romantic because it is based upon
     vision. The twentieth century seems to have rejected
     romanticism. By romantic, Mrs. Huxtable does not mean
     anti-classical, but refers to architecture with imagina-
     tion and distinction. The works of the new romantics--
     usually termed the "Form Givers"--are discussed with
     relation to Structural Romanticism, Decorative Romanti-
     cism, and Romantic Classicism. Lists architects who
     combine, or do not fit into, these categories and provides
     examples of their work.

1961

893. "A.L. Huxtable Reply." (To Review by Peter Collins of
     Pier Luigi Nervi. Journal of the Society of Architec-

tural Historians, 19 [December 1960]: 178. See item
981.) *Journal of the Society of Architectural Histor-*
ians, 20 (October 1961): 142-43.

The argument concerns the expression of architecture
versus that of engineering. Mrs. Huxtable writes: "To
me, and to many others (including Aline Saarinen) the
importance of Nervi's revolutionary engineering is that
it is one of the most meaningful architectural break-
throughs of the twentieth century."

1962

894. "Water. The Wine of Architecture." *Horizon*, 4 (May
      1962): 10-33.

      Water has always enhanced architecture. Historically
      this is so, but the years of the 1960s are vintage water
      years. The Renaissance and Baroque gardens of Europe
      and "The Quiet Waters of Asia" have provided royal and
      religious symbolism. The 1960s have borrowed qualities
      from both worlds to create "picturesque exterior settings"
      for residences, and settings of more formal dignity for
      offices and university buildings. Numerous photographs,
      mostly in color.

895. "Holiday Handbook of Dining Rooms." *Holiday*, 31 (June
      1962): 125-30.

      The dining room is no longer economically feasible as
      an individual room within the average modern residence,
      as it has been in the past. Open planned residences
      with screens provide an alternative solution. Remodel-
      ling old houses which have large dining rooms and kitchens
      is another answer. Moral: Good facilities complement
      good food.

896. "Preservation in New York." *Architectural Review*, 132
      (August 1962): 83-85.

      "The preservation score in New York is zero, or close
      to it." Economics and the tax structure are only two
      reasons. Another is attitude. A building has to be
      classical to be old. Discusses casualties, losses,
      replacements, people and societies striving for preserva-
      tion, and some of New York's finer landmarks. "Unless
      we understand and appreciate the nature of this heritage,
      our best efforts are doomed to fail."

897.   "Minoru Yamasaki's Recent Buildings." *Art in America*,
          50, no. 4 (Winter 1962): 48-55.

          "Now one of America's most talented younger architects,
          [he] must also be reckoned as one of the country's most
          important, because of the personal nature of his work
          and the number, variety and prestige of his commissions."
          Yamasaki describes his attitudes toward architecture in
          relation to the way of life in the United States.

1963

898.   "The Attainment of Quality." *American Institute of
          Architects Journal*, 40 (July 1963): 89-94.

          The text of a speech given at the AIA annual conference,
          in 1963, with the theme "Quest for Quality." If we had
          it, "we wouldn't be discussing it.... Bad buildings
          outnumber good buildings on an awe-inspiring scale ...
          pathetic ... to watch today's architects grope.... the
          art of architecture has died.... the architect, himself,
          has buried it.... He has bowed to the gimmick-merchants
          to become one himself." But she is optimistic.

1964

899.   "St. Louis Ironies and Anachronisms." *St. Louis Post
          Dispatch*, July 5, 1964. (Reprinted from *The New York
          Times*, June 18, 1964, item 129.)

          Much of architectural significance in St. Louis was
          razed in the 1930s. More is being lost or scheduled for
          demolition. St. Louisans are reminded of their heritage.

1966

900.   "Building a Third Class City." *Empire State Architect*,
          26, no. 2 (March-April 1966): 6-7.

          The Bard Award for public structures in New York was
          not given in 1966 because of poor design standards, or,
          as Mrs. Huxtable describes the buildings, "Budget Banal
          to Modern Miscarriage ... in this age of exceptional vi-
          tality ... New York is just not with it."

1967

901.   "50 Years Ago This Month: Building the Soviet Society."
       Architectural Forum, 127, no. 4 (November 1967): 32-41.

       Mrs. Huxtable made an extended tour of the U.S.S.R.,
       as architectural critic of *The New York Times*, and this
       article is adapted from her contribution "Building the
       Soviet Society: Housing and Planning," pp. 241-75 in
       The Soviet Union--the Fifty Years, edited by Harrison
       E. Salisbury (a *New York Times* book, published by Har-
       court, Brace and World, 1967). New attitudes are develop-
       ing in Soviet architecture and generally the design is
       good although there are admitted flaws. "The USSR is
       moving faster than any other nation on one of modern
       building's most important frontiers. It has helped re-
       define architecture in the 20th century."

1968

902.   "How to Build a City If You Can." *Forum* (Amsterdam),
       20, no. 5 (1968): 27.

       Subtitled "The Linear City on the Air Rights over the
       Cross-Brooklyn Expressway," the proposed city will be
       5½ miles long and provide space for much-needed schools,
       housing, and community facilities. The total cost could
       be $500 million (in 1968) and the conservatism of the
       Bureau of Public Roads would have to be overcome. Gives
       a brief history of air rights.

1970

903.   "Plan Is Regarded as Break with Tradition." *American
       Institute of Planners Journal*, 36 (November 1970):
       436-37.

       "The *Plan for New York City*, a folksy, plain spoken,
       450,000 word chronicle ... if it ever worked at all, it
       could never work for New York. The world's greatest city
       is also the city of the absurd, and to plan it is a cou-
       rageous and surrealist exercise." The plan contains no
       trend projections because Utopian planning is unacceptable
       today and could never work in New York City. The plan
       is concerned with people, especially minority groups,
       and with solutions to welfare and education needs.

1971

904. "Social Significance Qualms Overcome in Design Award."
Progressive Architecture, 52 (March 1971): 7, 12.

The article is followed by a letter from Ulrich Franzen,
who was on the 1970 awards committee of *Progressive Architecture*. He replies to Mrs. Huxtable's criticisms, stating that architecture with sociological intent, the sort
she advocates, is paternalistic (or does he mean matri-
archal?).

905. "Only You Can Help Yourselves." *Historic Preservation*,
23, no. 2 (April-June 1971): 2-3. (Reprinted from
The New York Times, April 25, 1971, item 478.)

Advice on what to do if you have a building worth saving: Where to look and research; to whom preservation-
conscious buffs should submit material and write. "Every
preservation project is a cliff hanger."

906. "Lyndon Baines Johnson Library. A Success as Architecture and as Monument." *American Libraries*, 2 (July
1971): 669-71. (Reprinted from *The New York Times*,
May 23, 1971, item 482.)

1972

907. "J. Edgar Hoover Builds His Dreamhouse: The New Head-
quarters for the FBI Will Further Shape Pennsylvania
Avenue in the 'Sub-Imperial Style.'" *Architectural
Forum*, 136 (April 1972): 44-45.

This new structure is continually increasing in price,
up to the present $126 million. The building "will not
be one of Washington's pseudoclassical throwbacks."
Presents details of accommodations and other aspects
of the development of Pennsylvania Avenue.

908. "Zoo Builds Rara Avis. The World of Birds Enhances an
Already Splendid Zoo." *Architectural Forum*, 137 (September 1972): 62-65. (Reprint of "New Bronx Zoo Building a Rara Avis," *The New York Times*, June 14, 1972,
item 539.)

909. "You Win Some, You Lose Some." *HUD Challenge*, 3 (December 1972): 22-23. (Reprinted from *The New York Times*,
October 8, 1972, item 549.)

910. "George Gund Hall, Harvard University Graduate School
      of Design." *Canadian Architect*, 18 (January 1973):
      38.

      This $8 million building was designed by John Andrews.
      It is "impossible to say whether the building will work,
      because it is quite unsettled as to what it will have
      to work for." Described in this article, and in greater
      detail by Macy Dubois, pp. 36-45.

911. "All Across America There Are Exciting New Projects
      Underway to Rejuvenate Our Cities. Ada Louise Huxtable
      Talks about New Towns in Town and What They Can Mean
      to You." *House and Garden*, 143 (February 1973): 68-
      69, 91.

      A question-and-answer session on how to prevent cities
      from deteriorating and how to make them live again. The
      city has the "riches of civilization." Mrs. Huxtable
      cites achievements in New York City and states that if
      New York can do it with higher costs in land and con-
      struction and greater political pressure, anyone can do
      it.

912. "Systems: Myth or Reality." *Architectural Plus*, 2 (July/
      August 1974): 70.

      A reprint of "Some Handsome Architectural Mythology,"
      a review of the exhibition "Moshe Safdie: For Everyone
      a Garden." (See item 599.)

913. "Ada Louise, the Mad Bomber." *New York Magazine*, December
      9, 1974, p. 11.

      In replying to Peter Blake's "Who Really Bombed Those
      Buildings" (item 1012), Mrs. Huxtable points out that
      Gordon Bunshaft's "Marine Midland at 140 Broadway is
      not only one of the buildings I admire most in New York,
      but that I admire most anywhere."

1975

914. "Architecture. Destiny Is with You More Often Than Not."
      Vogue, 165 (January 1975): 106.

      Mrs. Huxtable doesn't believe that ignorance, greed,
      stupidity, and sloth are invulnerable.

915. "Wrong But Impeccable." *Progressive Architecture*, 56
      (August 1975): 60-63.

      "Let me make my own feelings clear. I am split right
      down the middle. I believe that the Met has done the
      wrong thing impeccably" at the Lehman Wing of the Metro-
      politan Museum of Art, by Roche and Dinkeloo. Reprint
      of *The New York Times* article, "The New Lehman Wing--
      Does the Met Need It?," May 25, 1975, item 654.

1976

916. "The Battle for the Future." *House and Garden*, 148
      (May 1976): 94-95, 213.

      Excerpt from the introduction to *Kicked a Building
      Lately?* (item 923).

917. "Sprucing-up the Bank of Tokyo--An extract from the *New
      York Times*, December 28, 1975" (item 675). *Space De-
      sign*, 144 (August 1976): 59-73 (text in Japanese).

Part III
Books by Ada Louise Huxtable

While an assistant curator at the Museum of Modern Art, Mrs. Huxtable helped to prepare exhibitions and catalogues. However, none of these catalogue introductions were signed by her, and even when she returned from Italy with research material and photographs, the museum agreed only to a travelling exhibition to be organized by her. No exhibition catalogue was prepared for "The Modern Movement in Italy: Architecture and Design," but there was a seven-page mimeographed listing of eighty-eight panels of text and photographs, enumerated designers, subject matter, and other related material, and including a single-page "Foreword." This is quoted here in full, since it would not normally be found in any library, although parts were quoted in *Interiors*, December 1953 (item 976).

"It is generally acknowledged that Italy is one of the leading post-war forces in the field of architecture and design. Behind this post-war activity is a 25-year tradition of contributions to the development of the contemporary style. Although a small number of the classic examples of Italian architecture have appeared in the Museum's past exhibitions, this quarter-of-a-century development must still be recorded and defined.

"Examples, therefore, include Terragni and Lingeri buildings of the period of the International Style, houses and factories by Figini and Pollini, exhibitions and interiors by BBPR, Nervi's engineering structures, and the integrated architectural program of Olivetti. One section is devoted to exposition design and shops,-- fields in which the Italians have achieved an international reputation for taste and imagination, notably in the work of [Franco] Albini, [Angelo] Bianchetti, and [Ignazio] Gardella--and another to the work of the post-war period by the best of the new young designers. A careful selection of furniture, lamps, and other design objects, of a type not included in previous Italian exhibitions of a handcraft nature, will be circulated with the architectural panels.

"The exhibition is unique in the quality level of the

examples chosen, its historical documentation of an
important and influential movement in contemporary art,
and its presentation of much new and previously unknown
material, gathered first hand in Italy this year." Ada
Louise Huxtable.

1960

918. *Pier Luigi Nervi*. New York: Braziller, 1960, 128p.

Nervi's career is traced from his early competition
successes, his use of skeletal framing and thin shells,
and his development of "ferro-cemento" to, in more recent
years, the growth of his international reputation. (See
items 978 and 981.)

1961

919. *Four Walking Tours of Modern Architecture in New York
      City*. New York: Museum of Modern Art (distributed by
      Doubleday), 1961, 76p.

The Municipal Art Society of New York inaugurated walking tours of New York in 1956. This led to tours of modern
architecture written by Mrs. Huxtable in 1959. This small
publication, the result of earlier mimeographed sheets,
contains four tours of the East Side between Forty-second
and Sixty-sixth Streets.

1964

920. *Classic New York: Georgian Gentility to Greek Elegance*.
      Garden City, New York: Doubleday, 1964, 135p. Pub-
      lished also in paperback by Anchor Books, Garden City,
      New York, 1964.

Relying heavily upon earlier publications on the city
and its architecture, this small book, one of a projected
series of six, lists and describes structures of classical
styles, extant and demolished, in the city. Chapters
and maps systematically cover the old areas of New York.
(See items 931 and 932.)

1967

921. *A System of Architectural Ornament According with a
      Philosophy of Man's Powers.* New York: Eakins Press,
      1967, 75p. 20pl. Introduction only.

      Prelude to a publication which includes drawings for
      the Farmers' and Merchants' Union Bank, Columbus, Wis-
      consin, by Louis Sullivan. The twenty plates, here
      reduced in size, are from an edition of 1924.

1970

922. *Will They Ever Finish Bruckner Boulevard?* New York:
      A *New York Times* Book: The Macmillan Co., 1970, 268p.

      Mrs. Huxtable was around at the beginning of the press's
      interest in the environment and the urban scene. She
      hopes to have changed attitudes, to have influenced the
      public and to have grown and developed, herself--no longer
      an idealist, but a realist. Daniel P. Moynihan wrote the
      preface to this collection of sixty-eight articles re-
      printed from *The New York Times*. Content ranges from a
      description of the despoliation of London to criticism
      of modern architecture. Details of these sixty-eight
      articles have been annotated in Part I. (See also items
      950, 992, 993, 995, 996, 1002, and 1003.)

1976

923. *Kicked a Building Lately?* New York: Quadrangle/The *New
      York Times* Book Co., Inc., 1976, 304p.

      A reprint of seventy-nine of her articles from *The
      New York Times*. Many of the battles which Mrs. Huxtable
      has championed have to a certain extent been won, but
      this does not mean that she has become less diligent.
      New aspects of old problems demand her attention and
      she more than adequately rises to the occasion. (See
      also items 1015, 1018-24, 1026-30, 1032-35, 1037.)

Part IV

Articles and Notations
about Ada Louise Huxtable
in *The New York Times*

924. Goodman, Robert. "Two Designs." June 21, 1959, Magazine Section, pp. 27, 30.

     Goodman, disappointed to discover Wallace Harrison's "fish church" in Connecticut included in Mrs. Huxtable's "The Ten Buildings That Say Today" (see item 8), wants Le Corbusier's chapel at Ronchamp included in the next ten!

1963

925. "City Art Society Honors Architects." May 21, 1963, p. 23.

     Mrs. Huxtable was principal speaker at the Municipal Art Society of New York when awards were presented.

926. "Architecture Critic Appointed by Times." September 9, 1963, p. 23.

     The creation of this new post was announced by the managing editor. Biographical information provided.

927. Reed, Henry Hope, Jr. "Wright Houses." December 8, 1963, Magazine Section, p. 132.

     Wright's houses always had low ceilings and many were built in second-class suburbs. In response to Mrs. Huxtable's article of November 17, 1963 (item 89), "Natural Houses of Frank Lloyd Wright."

1964

928. "Neighborly Spirit Asked by Wagner." May 8, 1964, p. 42.

     At the sixty-seventh annual dinner of the Citizens Union of the City of New York, Mrs. Huxtable was given "the first Albert S. Bard citation for promoting the city's esthetic interests."

929. "Municipal Art Unit to Award Scrolls." May 14, 1964,
      p. 42.

      "The Second Scroll will recognize the *New York Times*
      as the first of the nation's newspapers to appoint a
      full-time critic of architecture" and "for its many
      editorials stressing civic beauty."

930. "Architecture Press Awards." September 12, 1964, p. 22.

      The Long Island Chapter of the American Institute of
      Architects presented its first annual press awards, one
      of which went to Mrs. Huxtable.

931. Ennis, Thomas W. "End Papers." November 11, 1964, p.
      41.

      Classic New York is reviewed here as being the first
      of a six-volume set. "It is her intention to provide
      a richer understanding of the texture and color of the
      city as it grows." (See item 920.)

932. Lynes, Russell. "Where the Wrecker's Ball Hovers."
      November 15, 1964, *The New York Times Book Review*,
      p. 6.

      Classic New York was written by a "conservationist
      uninflicted with sentimentality ... whose enthusiasm
      for the past is balanced by equal enthusiasm for the
      best of the present." (See item 920.)

                            1965

933. Johannesen, Richard Irwin. "Fraunces Tavern Controversy."
      June 6, 1965, Section 2, p. 15.

      Johannesen objects to the description of the Fraunces
      Tavern in "Lively Original vs. Dead Copy" (item 168)
      as being built from scratch. Johannesen puts the record
      straight, although he admits that most of the 1719 struc-
      ture was built in 1907. See Mrs. Huxtable's reply (item
      173).

934. "Newswomen Name Front Page Winners." November 11, 1965,
      p. 12.

      The Newspaper Women's Club of New York presented six
      awards, including one to Mrs. Huxtable for the best fea-
      ture: "Staten Island's Beauty Losing to Builders" (item
      184).

935.   "Honors for Newspaper Work." November 14, 1965, p. 32.

Photograph and caption of Mrs. Huxtable with reference to the award by the Newspaper Women's Club of New York.

936.   "Writers on Design Named for Awards." November 30, 1965, p. 26.

Mrs. Huxtable was one of three writers who won Kaufmann International Design awards. Hers was for articles in *The New York Times*, 1961–65.

1966

937.   "Winners Three" [Advertisement]. January 25, 1966, p. 45.

The Newspaper Women's Club of New York recently named six winners in their annual Front Page Awards for excellence in journalism. Three of them were from *The New York Times*.

938.   "Design Unveiled for National Shrine on Ellis Island." February 25, 1966, pp. 1, 28.

Mrs. Huxtable was named an honorary associate member of the Long Island Chapter of the American Institute of Architects, "for bringing before the public significant issues in architecture and urban design."

939.   "A Poet and a Critic Cited by Skidmore." June 6, 1966, p. 47.

Skidmore College, Saratoga Springs, New York, awarded Mrs. Huxtable a Doctor of Humane Letters degree for her "journalistic recognition of architecture as a public art and social responsibility."

940.   Bracken, John J. "Need for Public Space in Courthouses." August 1, 1966, p. 26.

Bracken, an attorney, supports Mrs. Huxtable's article of July 22, 1966 (item 223) in praise of old courthouses with spacious corridors for conferences and general discussion.

941.   "Governor Makes 13 Arts Awards." May 19, 1967, p. 36.

       The New York State Council of the Arts presented thir-
       teen awards in this second year of its existence. Mrs.
       Huxtable received the only individual award for "her
       consistently incisive and courageous defense of integrity
       in architectural design and urban planning."

942.   Krebs, Albin. "Notes on People." October 8, 1967,
       Section D, p. 15.

       The Pennsylvania Academy of Fine Arts presented its
       Furness Prize to Mrs. Huxtable for "outstanding contri-
       butions to the field of architecture."

943.   "Ada Louise Huxtable Wins Award for Art Criticism."
       February 6, 1968, p. 26.

       "Gets College Art Association $500 Award for Excellence
       in Art Criticism Published Regularly in Newspapers and
       Magazines."

944.   "Architects' Group Announces Awards." February 2, 1969,
       p. 47.

       Mrs. Huxtable was awarded the American Institute of
       Architects' medal for architectural criticism.

945.   "Moynihan Critical of Cities' Designs." June 24, 1969,
       p. 21.

       Daniel Patrick Moynihan was a speaker at the AIA con-
       vention in Chicago where Mrs. Huxtable was awarded the
       medal for architectural criticism. "Devoted to increasing
       the public's visual perception in environmental design,
       she has written conscientious and well informed articles
       on the issues of good design in projects of national im-
       portance. Unswerving in her dedication to focusing the
       attention of an informed public on the environment, she
       has demonstrated the highest form of professionalism."

946. "Arts in the 60's: Coming to Terms with Society and Its
      Woes." December 30, 1969, pp. 20-21.

      Nine critics of *The New York Times* debated the arts.
      When Harrison E. Salisbury asked, "What about the new
      morality or amorality in the arts? What about nudity
      and pornography?" Mrs. Huxtable replied, "There's none
      in architecture."

                              1970

947. Scully, Vincent [Joseph, Jr.]. "Inattention." April
      26, 1970, Section 2, p. 26.

      Scully claims that Mrs. Huxtable's review of his *Amer-
      ican Architecture and Urbanism* (item 399) ignored the
      main point of the book and concentrated on "disheveled
      vagaries" to negatively criticize secondary aspects.
      "It has never been possible to value Mrs. Huxtable's
      writing for critical acumen or command of history. Its
      most positive quality has seemed to be a kind of hectic
      candor, but that too must be called into question now."

948. "Biographical Sketches of Persons Chosen for 54th Annual
      Pulitzer Prizes." May 5, 1970, p. 48.

      Mrs. Huxtable "has not feared to attack the mighty
      cultural institutions in the land." Provides examples
      of her tenacity.

949. "Report of Songmy Incident Wins a Pulitzer for [Seymour
      M.] Hersh." May 5, 1970, pp. 1, 48.

      Mrs. Huxtable also won a Pulitzer, the first for dis-
      tinguished criticism.

950. Jellinek, Roger. [No title]. July 12, 1970, Section 7,
      p. 2.

      "The first Pulitzer Prize given for criticism, the
      occasion for it is conveniently presented in *Will They
      Ever Finish Bruckner Boulevard?*, a selection of her
      articles for The Times. 'What I really want to say in
      assembling these pieces is that, like Kilroy, Huxtable
      was here.'" (See item 922.)

951. Lewis, Michael. "Letters to the Editor: Madison Ave. of
      Vintage Years Recalled." November 22, 1970, Section
      8, p. 8.

Additional reminiscences of the Madison Avenue and
Fifth Avenue of generations past. See Mrs. Huxtable's
article of November 8, 1970, item 450.

1971

952.   "Arts Club to Give Medal to Ada Louise Huxtable." April
       14, 1971, p. 54.

       The National Arts Club gold medal for literature.

953.   "Critic Commended by National Trust." May 13, 1971, p.
       56.

       Max Frankel, Washington's correspondent of *The New York
       Times*, on behalf of Mrs. Huxtable, accepted from Mrs.
       Richard M. Nixon the National Trust Award, for her "'un-
       flagging watchfulness' over America's cultural treasures."

954.   "3 Women on Times Staff among 5 to Get Awards." November
       2, 1971, p. 40.

       An announcement that Mrs. Huxtable is to receive the
       New York Newspaper Women's Front Page Award for her Sep-
       tember 7, 1971, story, "Architecture: A Look at the Ken-
       nedy Center" (item 495).

955.   "Holyoke Art Building Sparks Parley on Museums." Novem-
       ber 8, 1971, p. 50.

       Mt. Holyoke College conferred honorary degrees on five
       women, including Mrs. Huxtable.

956.   Dooley, Arthur D. "We Are Not 'Raping' the Plaza."
       November 21, 1971, Section 2, p. 27.

       The Vice President and Managing Director of the Plaza
       Hotel objects that major changes are not being undertaken
       as suggested in Mrs. Huxtable's article of October 31,
       1971, item 504.

957.   Conrad, Theodore. "For Restoration." December 12, 1971,
       Section 8, p. 2.

       "Bravo to Ada Louise Huxtable. Her recent articles are
       good not only for owners of historic houses but also for
       owners of good modern ones.... We need a new breed of
       architects versed in historic preservation and maintenance."

1972

958.   "Ada Louise Huxtable Wins an Award for Her Criticism."
        April 19, 1972, p. 44.

        The Spirit of Achievement Award of the National Women's
        Division of Albert Einstein College of Medicine was pre-
        sented to Mrs. Huxtable for her "role in making us aware
        of our architectural heritage."

959.   "First Graduation Is Held by Eisenhower College." May
        29, 1972, p. 10.

        "Other commencement exercises yesterday included Trinity
        College in Hartford where ... Ada Louise Huxtable ... re-
        ceived an honorary Doctor of Fine Arts degree."

960.   "Pratt Graduates Hear Call for 'Committed Response.'"
        June 3, 1972, p. 17.

        "Honorary degrees were conferred on ... Ada Louise
        Huxtable."

961.   "Yale Honors Ford, a '40 Dropout, at Calm Graduation."
        June 13, 1972, p. 35.

        Yale confers an honorary doctorate on Mrs. Huxtable.

1973

962.   "Mrs. Huxtable on Editorial Board." September 26, 1973,
        p. 27.

        "Mrs. Huxtable will divide her time between the edi-
        torial board and expanded duties as architectural col-
        umnist for the Sunday paper."

963.   "Mrs. Huxtable Gets City Medal at Fete for Custom House."
        December 4, 1973, p. 52.

        "Mayor Lindsay last night presented the Diamond Jubilee
        Medallion of the City of New York to Ada Louise Huxtable
        in recognition of her appointment to the editorial board
        of the *New York Times*."

1974

964. "Mrs. Huxtable Is Honored as Woman of Achievement." May
     19, 1974, p. 58.

     The American Association of University Women presented
     its 1974 Woman of Achievement Award to Mrs. Huxtable,
     "distinguished critic of architecture."

965. "Architects Will Study Ethical Misconduct." May 21, 1974,
     p. 53.

     The American Institute of Architects conferred honorary
     membership on Mrs. Huxtable.

966. "Cox Warns of Political-Academic Ties." May 31, 1974,
     New Jersey Pages, p. 71.

     Honorary degree of Doctor of Law from Rutgers University
     was presented to Mrs. Huxtable.

1975

967. "Wagner Is 'Shocked' by Attacks on City in Its Fiscal
     Crisis." May 28, 1975, p. 55.

     The New School Center for New York City Affairs honors
     Mrs. Huxtable.

1976

968. "Miss Krupsak Predicts Budget Will Match Austerity of
     1930's." January 18, 1976, Section 1, p. 29.

     Mrs. Huxtable was one of five women awarded the Minneola
     P. Ingersoll Award of the Women's Club of New York.

969. Stein, Carl. "Another View of Modern Architecture."
     July 18, 1976, Section 2, p. 22.

     Stein questions Mrs. Huxtable's arguments in "The
     Gospel According to Giedion and Gropius Is Under Attack"
     (item 695) and states that modern architecture is a
     choice between an architecture of style or an architec-
     ture of reason. All that the counter-revolutionaries
     are doing is exchanging one style for another. Reason
     asks about the time, place, and function of a building.
     Mrs. Huxtable's reply is that the architecture of reason
     is stylistic whether or not the protagonists intended it
     to be.

1977

970. Krebs, Albin. "Notes on People." January 26, 1977,
      Section C, p. 2.

      Nine new members were elected to the American Academy
      and Institute of Arts and Letters, including Ada Louise
      Huxtable. She was one of three women, the most ever
      elected in any one year.

971. Krebs, Albin. "Notes on People." March 23, 1977, Sec-
      tion C, p. 2.

      Recognizing a distinguished person in architecture,
      the University of Virginia has presented Mrs. Huxtable
      with its Thomas Jefferson medal.

972. "Lowell Gets Medal." May 19, 1977, Section C, p. 14.

      Mrs. Huxtable was made a member of the American Academy
      and Institute of Arts and Letters.

973. "Young Seeks to Smooth Relations with Queens." June 3,
      1977, Section B, p. 2.

      Mrs. Huxtable was presented with the degree of Doctor
      of Humanities by the City University of New York.

1978

974. Cummings, Roger. "Vernacular Architecture." March 26,
      1978, Magazine Section, p. 94.

      Criticism of Mrs. Huxtable who "suspends critical judg-
      ment" and accepts the validity of junk architecture.
      (See item 762.)

975. Indelman, Alta. "Vernacular Architecture." March 26,
      1978, Magazine Section, p. 94.

      It is suggested that we take the fast-food megachain
      store architecture more seriously. (See item 762.)

Part V
Articles about Ada Louise Huxtable
in Magazines, Periodicals, and Journals
Other Than *The New York Times*

1953

976. "Modern Movement in Italy, a Museum of Modern Art Travelling Show." *Interiors*, 113 (December 1953): 74-75, 151-
55.

The exhibition consisted of material gathered by Mrs.
Huxtable. The bulk of the article consists of selections
from her essay on the exhibit.

1956

977. "These Are the Men and Women Who Bring *Progressive Architecture* to the World's Largest Architectural Circula-
tion." *Progressive Architecture*, 37 (December 1956):
215.

Portrait with note.

1960

978. Banham, Reyner. [Review of the Braziller Series on
"Masters of World Architecture"]. *Arts*, 34 (June
1960): 12-13, 65.

"The inadmissible titles [in the Series] are Gaudi
and Nervi.... Mrs. Huxtable's *Nervi* is a disappointingly
flat-footed work to have come from her able pen." (See
item 918.)

979. "New York: Offices." *Industrial Design*, 7 (October 1960):
68.

"Garth and Ada Louise Huxtable are the sort of professional husband—wife combination that can develop anywhere, but is much more likely to happen in New York."
Provides background development and names of clients.

980. "Personalities." *Progressive Architecture*, 41 (November
1960): 69.

"Certainly the prettiest architectural critic-industrial
designer to come down the pike in quite a while is...."
List of credits and products.

981. Collins, Peter. "Books: Ada Louise Huxtable, *Pier Luigi
      Nervi*." *Journal of the Society of Architectural Histor-
      ians*, 19, no. 4 (December 1960): 178.

      Collins questions Nervi's role as architect in a series
      on "Masters of World Architecture," since his long-span
      structures can be traced back historically to bridge
      construction. "The confusion between engineering and
      architecture can lead to quite nonsensical judgements."
      (See item 918 and Mrs. Huxtable's reply, item 893.)

982. Van Houten, Lazette. "U.S.A.: Lap of Luxury, Serving
      Pieces for the Four Seasons." *Design* (Britain), 144
      (December 1960): 63.

      "The job of creating a line of extraordinary serving
      pieces for the Seagram Building's plush restaurant 'The
      Four Seasons,' was assigned to a husband and wife in-
      dustrial design team, Garth and Ada Louise Huxtable. It
      was no routine project." One hundred pieces were designed,
      eighteen of which were acquired by the Museum of Modern Art.

1965

983. "Eye on the Environment." *Newsweek*, 66 (August 23, 1965):
      70-71.

      Mrs. Huxtable is "the cultured fortyish ... gadfly to
      public officials, developers and architects ... [who]
      still writes her copy in longhand." Quotes catch phrases,
      mainly of her dislikes.

1968

984. Dunn, Alan. "Ada Louise Huxtable Already Doesn't Like
      It." *New Yorker*, June 15, 1968, p. 33.

      A cartoon caption.

1969

985. "AIA Names '69 Medalists." *Progressive Architecture*,
      50 (March 1969): 45.

Brief mention of Ada Louise Huxtable as recipient of the Architectural Critic's Medal.

986. "Winner of the 1969 Elsie de Wolfe Award: Ada Louise Huxtable, Architecture Critic of the *New York Times*." *Interior Design*, 40, no. 3 (March 1969): 152-53.

"For someone so petite and chic Ada Louise Huxtable packs a surprisingly powerful punch." Elsie de Wolfe was "the woman who is credited with being the first recognized authority in interior design."

987. "AID. Elsie de Wolfe Award to Ada Louise Huxtable." *Interiors*, 128 (April 1969): 8.

"For outstanding contributions in the field of design and related fields." Background information is provided.

988. Hoffman, Marilyn. "Appraisal from a Loftier Peak." *Christian Science Monitor*, April 9, 1969, p. 12.

"Ada Louise Huxtable is ... porcelain pretty." She hates ugliness, agonizes over the city, and explains to Mrs. Hoffman what she's trying to achieve.

1970

989. "Ada Louise Huxtable Adds to Her Critic's Laurels with a New Pulitzer Category." *American Institute of Architects' Journal*, 53 (June 1970): 26.

Announcing her receipt of the first Pulitzer Prize for criticism with brief resumé.

990. "Critics Choice." *Architectural Forum*, 132 (June 1970): 71.

A brief resumé.

991. "1970 Pulitzer Prize Winner." *Interiors*, 129 (June 1970): 12.

Briefly mentioned.

992. Von Eckardt, Wolf. "An Education That Turns Out to Be a Pleasure" [Review of *Will They Ever Finish Bruckner Boulevard?*]. *Book World*, August 16, 1970, p. 3.

Her convictions are erudite and relevant. (See item 922.)

993. Gross, Robert A. "Against Urbicide." *Newsweek*, 76
      (August 17, 1970): 92.

      A review of *Will They Ever Finish Bruckner Boulevard?*--
      "A suspenseful narrative of attempted murder ... of our
      cities." (See item 922.)

994. Nirenberg, S. "Perspectives." *House Beautiful*, 112
      (September 1970): 20-24.

      An interview and a chatty article on her tastes, atti-
      tudes, and professional commitment, with the usual list
      of attributes and awards.

995. Fischman, Jill. "Huxtable, Ada Louise. *Will They Ever
      Finish Bruckner Boulevard?*" *Library Journal*, 95 (Octo-
      ber 15, 1970): 3460.

      Mrs. Huxtable "awakens the reader's political sense,"
      educates the eye, and "calls attention to many topical
      issues." (See item 922.)

996. Jacobs, Jay. "Architectural Blight--And Light. Books:
      Will They Ever Finish Bruckner Boulevard?" *Art in
      America*, 58 (November-December 1970): 59-61.

      "She writes in a sort of controlled rage ... against
      those who out of ignorance, timidity or greed lower the
      quality of the environment" and "demands ... the replace-
      ment of profiteering by planning, and expediency by ex-
      cellence." (See item 922.)

                              1971

997. Ceff, Ursula. "New York's Better Self." *Design and
      Environment*, 2, no. 1 (Spring 1971): 50-51.

      Mrs. Huxtable's rise to eminence is due to her involve-
      ment in and her commitment to the "environmental awaken-
      ing." Her successes are listed.

998. Reilly, Donald. "I'd Give Anything to Be There When
      Ada Louise Huxtable Gets a Load of This." *New Yorker*,
      April 24, 1971, p. 37.

      A cartoon caption.

999. "Ada Louise Huxtable Receives Arts Club Medal." *Interiors*,
      130 (May 1971): 34.

"One of the country's top advocates of good architecture whether it be preserving the past or promoting the present was awarded...."

1000. "The Pleasures of the Plaza: Two New Restaurants." *Interior Design*, 42 (December 1971): 66-69, 94-95.

New York City's Plaza Hotel, designed by Hardenberg, has elegance. To interfere with this, in the cause of atmosphere and excitement, may not have a great deal of meaning to those who frequent the hotel, including Mrs. Huxtable, who wrote two anti-remodelling articles (items 504 and 505) which are here quoted. "Mrs. Huxtable, of course, has never been one to be identified with monotony (unless it is the frequency with which she wins prestigious awards)."

1001. Diamonstein, Barbaralee. "Ada Louise Huxtable." In *Open Secrets; 94 Women in Touch with Our Time.* New York: Viking, 1972, pp. 193-96.

A four-page questionnaire prepared by Diamonstein and answered by Mrs. Huxtable. *Open Secrets* was an expansion of a listing by Diamonstein of "100 Women in Touch with Our Time," *Harper's Bazaar*, 104 (January 1971): 104-10, in which a photograph of each woman was accompanied by a caption. Mrs. Huxtable's read in its entirety (including the ellipses): "Environmental awakener/restorer ... 1st Pulitzer Prize winner for distinguished criticism on architecture and urban design ... urgent voice crying for humane esthetic values in rebuilding the urban scene" (p. 107).

1972

1002. James, Martin. *"Will They Ever Finish Bruckner Boulevard?"* *American Institute of Planners' Journal*, 38 (January 1972): 55-56.

A review which quotes from *Will They Ever Finish Bruckner Boulevard?* Martin states, "Whoever doubts the need for architectural and environmental criticism, vigorous, informed and open to humanistic values, will find his answer in...." (See item 922.)

1003. Thompson, William P. "Books: Ada Louise Huxtable, *Will They Ever Finish Bruckner Boulevard?"* *Journal of the Society of Architectural Historians*, 31, no.

1 (March 1972): 75.

"She is part evangelist, part judge, part historian, part educator, part satirist, part advocate, and part prophet." (See item 922.)

1004. Bailey, M. "GE Journal Talking to...." *Mademoiselle*,
      75 (August 1972): 352.

She's "the gracious, famous and infamous ... architectural critic."

1005. Kriebel, C. "Ada Louise Huxtable, Monumental Critic."
      Harper's Bazaar, 105 (August 1972): 126.

Her likes, dislikes, achievements, and awards; quotations from her writings.

1006. "NSID: New York Products Expo: National Board Meets,
      Gives Award to Ada Louise Huxtable." *Interiors*,
      132 (October 1972): 10.

"None other than the Museum of Modern Art's blazing 'Good Design' pioneer will receive the ... award."

1007. Groves, Stephen. "Heeded Words: Ada Louise Huxtable
      Has Formidable Power as Architectural Critic." *Wall
      Street Journal*, November 7, 1972, pp. 1, 12.

Subtitled "Her *New York Times* Pieces Have Sway with Builders Don't Always Make Friends. Tale of a New England Rat." The article discusses her preservation successes and disappointments, her architectural likes and dislikes. "She questions the role of the architectural profession but has given it uplift."

1008. Marlen, William. "Forum" [Editorial]. *Architectural
      Forum*, 137 (December 1972): 17.

An editorial on architectural criticism, the critic, and, specifically, Mrs. Huxtable. "The critic comes in as a clear, controlled receiver who can take in the well-meant often garbled transmissions, resolve the static, and send the message back out on a beam, and at a frequency, which people can tune in on."

1973

1009.   *Current Biography*, 1973, pp. 196-99.

As complete a coverage of the life, career, and
achievements of Mrs. Huxtable to that date as is to
be found anywhere.

1010.   "Testimonial." *New Yorker*, 49 (December 17, 1973): 43-
45.

Two hundred and eighty people paid $100 each to
attend a dinner in honor of Ada Louise Huxtable when
she was appointed to the editorial board of *The New
York Times*. The reception was held in the Custom House,
Bowling Green, which, appropriately, Mrs. Huxtable had
helped to save.

1974

1011.   *Who's Who of American Women*, 1973-74, p. 457.

The usual information.

1012.   Blake, Peter.   "Who Really Bombed Those Buildings?"
New York, November 18, 1974, p. 102.

According to Blake, Mrs. Huxtable has a vendetta
against Gordon Bunshaft of SOM and to a lesser extent
against Harrison and Abramovitz for some of their
recent designs.   See Mrs. Huxtable's reply (item 913).

1975

1013.   Richardson, Margaret.   "Women Theorists." *Architectural Design*, 45 (August 1975): 466-67.

In searching the shelves of the Library of the Royal
Institute of British Architects for books on architectural theory written by women, only thirteen authors
were discovered.   Ada Luise [sic] Huxtable is "New
York's Better Self."

1976

1014.   [General article on Ada Louise Huxtable].   *Texas Monthly*,
4 (May 1976): 34-40.

1015.   Kay, Jane Holtz. "Ada Kicks Up a Fuss Again." *Build-
        ing Design* (London), November 19, 1976, p. 23.

        Reviewing *Kicked a Building Lately?*, Jane Holtz Kay
        praises Mrs. Huxtable for her diatribe against real
        estate interests and her articles on preservation but
        questions why she dwells on monumental public buildings
        at the expense of those of social amenity. (See item
        923.)

1977

1016.   Stephens, Suzanne. "Women as Critics." *Women in
        American Architecture: A History and Contemporary
        Perspective*, edited by Susana Torre. New York:
        Whitney Library of Design, 1977, pp. 136-43.

        Presents Catherine Bauer, Jane Jacobs, Sibyl Moholy-
        Nagy, and Ada Louise Huxtable. The first three "were
        activists or teachers as well as critics. Huxtable
        has devoted herself to writing, period." Briefly
        touches upon her style. (See item 1025.)

1017.   Wodehouse, Lawrence. "Ada Louise Huxtable and the
        Location of Her Articles." Appendix 1, in *American
        Architects from the First World War to the Present*.
        Detroit: Gale Research Company, 1977, pp. 263-67.

        Brief biographical information and a discussion of
        the difficulty in locating Mrs. Huxtable's articles in
        The New York Times Index.

1018.   [Review of *Kicked a Building Lately?*]. *Viva*, 4 (Janu-
        ary 1977): 40-41. (See item 923.)

1019.   "Huxtable, Ada Louise. *Kicked a Building Lately?*"
        Booklist, 73 (January 1, 1977): 639.

        Although an art, architecture must also cater to
        political and economic pressures. Her "caustic wit
        predominates ... creating confusion unless the reader
        is familiar with the structure under attack." (See
        item 923.)

1020.   Siegel, Lawrence. "Architecture: Huxtable, Ada Louise,
        Kicked a Building Lately?" *Library Journal*, 102
        (January 15, 1977): 190.

        "Rereading the pieces now, it is interesting to assess

their effects over the period.... Huxtable remains a
forceful, articulate, interesting and persuasive advocate of her causes." (See item 923.)

1021. [Review of *Kicked a Building Lately?*]. *Keeping Up*, 4
(January 24, 1977): 21-24. (See item 923.)

1022. Jensen, Robert. "Books: *Kicked a Building Lately?*"
Art Forum, 15 (February 1977): 62.

"Ms. Huxtable identifies what was valuable in our
cities and what was being lost." (See item 923.)

1023. [Review of *Kicked a Building Lately?*]. *Houston Home*,
3 (February 27, 1977): 26-27. (See item 923.)

1024. "Ada Louise Huxtable: You Can Have Your City's Past and
Use It Too." *Vogue*, 167 (March 1977): 222.

A short article among fourteen others under the general
title: "Get Happy. 15 People in the News Tell What Keeps
Them 'Up.'" Mrs. Huxtable talks about a new attitude
towards preservation. "The good news is that the country's architecture, history and culture finally are
seen as economic, esthetic, and environmental necessi-
ties.... The definition of preservation has grown from
a limited preoccupation with the individual landmark to
concern with the nature of the neighborhood and community." At the end of the article Mrs. Huxtable is cited
as the author of *Kicked a Building Lately?* (See item
923.)

1025. "Architectural Criticism: Four Women." *Progressive
Architecture*, 58 (March 1977): 56-57.

A discussion of Suzanne Stephens's essay entitled
"Women as Critics" in *Women in American Architecture*,
edited by Susana Torre (item 1016). Analyzes Mrs. Huxtable's pragmatic methods of exposition, which are based
upon William James.

1026. "Huxtable, Ada Louise. *Kicked a Building Lately?*"
Choice, 14 (March 1977): 51.

"Huxtable is also based on elitist criteria." (See
item 923.)

1027. Murphy, Michael. [Review of *Kicked a Building Lately?*].
Best Sellers, 36 (March 1977): 390. (See item 923.)

1028.   *"Kicked a Building Lately?*, by Ada Louise Huxtable."
        Virginia Quarterly Review, 53 (Spring 1977): 72.
        (See item 923.)

        "Her copy is always readable and often persuasive."

1029.   [Review of *Kicked a Building Lately?*]. *BooksWest*, 1
        (April 1977): 32.   (See item 923.)

1030.   Berenson, Ruth. *"Kicked a Building Lately?" America*,
        136 (April 16, 1977): 361-62.

        "No one writing in America today can beat her at her
        job." (See item 923.)

1031.   Gueft, Olga. "The Villard Houses and Emery Roth and
        Sons' Palace Hotel." *Contract Interiors*, 136 (July
        1977): 66-71, 95.

        Chronicles the plans and the controversy surrounding
        the proposed adaptation of McKim, Mead & White's Villard
        Houses into part of a 1,000-room hotel to be built on
        an adjacent part of the site. Quotes three of Mrs.
        Huxtable's articles (items 637, 657, and 663) which were
        written as the proposal developed.

1032.   Davenport, Guy. "Making It Uglier to the Airport."
        Hudson Review, 30 (Summer 1977): 313-20.

        Essay on the decline of the American urban community
        citing a multitude of studies and books, including
        Kicked a Building Lately? "Her comments are all arrows
        of the chase." (See item 923.)

1033.   Jensen, Jay. "Huxtable, Ada Louise, *Kicked a Building
        Lately?" Journalism Quarterly*, 54 (Summer 1977): 405.

        "Her book ... provides ample demonstration of why she
        is America's leading architectural critic." (See item
        923.)

1034.   Appleyard, Donald. "Huxtable, Ada Louise. *Kicked a
        Building Lately?" Journal of Aesthetics and Art
        Criticism*, 36 (Fall 1977): 119.

        "The most preceptive, readable and fascinating com-
        mentaries that have been written about the state of
        American architecture." (See item 923.)

1035.   Andrews, Wayne. "Books: *Kicked a Building Lately?"
        Commonweal*, 104 (September 16, 1977): 601-602.

Her responsibility is great. "She may repent tomorrow of the judgments she hands down today." (See item
923.)

1978

1036.   "Design Changes in the Past Ten Years." *Interior
Design*, 49 (May 1978): 159.

"A retrospective survey based on interviews with
industry spokesmen" including Mrs. Huxtable, who sees
trends of the 1970s "burst wide open."

1979

1037.   Pevsner, Nikolaus. "Books. The Modern Movement: Theory
and Criticism." *Journal of the Society of Architectural Historians*, 38 (March 1979): 52-53.

In reviewing *Kicked a Building Lately?*, Pevsner asks
what are Mrs. Huxtable's greatest interests, as indicated in the articles presented. His answer is Beaux
Arts and Art Deco! And she doesn't really like the
International Style. (See item 923.)

TITLE INDEX

Numbers 1 to 923 indicate articles and books by Ada
Louise Huxtable. Numbers 924 to 1037 are works about
Ada Louise Huxtable by various authors.

SUBJECT AND AUTHOR INDEX

This index is alphabetized letter by letter ignoring
all punctuation. Buildings are listed geographically
by city, and institutions are listed in direct alphabetical order: For example, exhibitions at a museum
are listed under the museum's name, which appears in
direct alphabetical order, while references to the
museum building appear as sub-headings under the city
in which the museum is located.

Ronchamp, France
  Notre Dame du Haute 924
Roosevelt Commission 243; for Memorial see under Washington,
        D.C.
Roosevelt family 131
Rose and Stone 162
Rossi, Aldo 837
Roth, Emery, and Sons
  Water St., No. 55 351
  Villard Houses 637, 1031
Rouse Company 839
Royal Institute of British Architects
  Heinze Gallery
    Edwardian London exhibition 782
  Library 1013
Rudofsky, Bernard 149, 152
Rudolph, Paul 445
  Endo Labs 140
  Southern Massachusetts Technological Institute 248
  State of Massachusetts Health, Education, and Welfare Build-
        ing 87
  Yale Art and Architecture Building 88, 510
Rumanian architecture 136
Rustin, Bayard 274
Rutgers University 966

Saarinen, Aline 893
Saarinen, Eero 36
  CBS Building 213
  Dulles Airport 44, 753
  Hvitträsk, Finland, house 208
Safdi, Moshe 599, 912
Salem, MA 583
  rape of 661
  Redevelopment Authority 187
  traffic improvements 625
Salisbury, Harrison E. 901, 946
Salt Lake City, UT
  Gustavson's work 885
  State Capitol 385
San Antonio, TX
  "Hemisfair" (World's Fair) 301, 303
San Francisco, CA 19
  City of Paris 628
  Palace of Fine Arts (1916 Fair) 168
Saratoga, NY 296
Savoye, Mme. 224

GARLAND BIBLIOGRAPHIES IN ARCHITECTURE AND PLANNING

General Editor:
Arnold L. Markowitz
Elmer Holmes Bobst Library, New York University